The Last of Us and Theology

THEOLOGY, RELIGION, AND POP CULTURE

Series Editor: Matthew Brake

The *Theology, Religion, and Pop Culture* series examines the intersection of theology, religion, and popular culture, including, but not limited to, television, movies, sequential art, and genre fiction. In a world plagued by rampant polarization of every kind and the decline of religious literacy in the public square, *Theology, Religion, and Pop Culture* is uniquely poised to educate and entertain a diverse audience utilizing one of the few things society at large still holds in common: love for popular culture.

Select Titles in the Series

The Last of Us *and Theology: Violence, Ethics, Redemption?*, edited by Peter Admirand
Theology, Fantasy, and the Imagination, edited by Andrew D. Thrasher and Austin M. Freeman, with Fotini Toso
Theology and Wes Craven, edited by David K. Goodin
Theology and the DC Universe, edited by Gabriel Mckee and Roshan Abraham
Theology and Star Trek, edited by Shaun C. Brown and Amanda MacInnis Hackney
The Spirit and the Screen: Pneumatological Reflections on Contemporary Cinema, edited by Chris E. W. Green and Steven Félix-Jäger
Theology and the Avett Brothers, edited by Alex Sosler
Bob Dylan and the Spheres of Existence, by Christopher B. Barnett
Theology and Protest Music, edited by Jonathan H. Harwell and Heidi M. Altman
Animated Parables: A Pedagogy of Seven Deadly Sins and a Few Virtues, by Terry Lindvall
Theology and Batman: Examining the Religious World of the Dark Knight, edited by Matthew Brake and C. K. Robertson

The Last of Us and Theology

Violence, Ethics, Redemption?

Edited by

Peter Admirand

LEXINGTON BOOKS/FORTRESS ACADEMIC
Lanham • Boulder • New York • London

Published by Lexington Books/Fortress Academic
Lexington Books is an imprint of The Rowman & Littlefield Publishing Group, Inc.
4501 Forbes Boulevard, Suite 200, Lanham, Maryland 20706
www.rowman.com

86-90 Paul Street, London EC2A 4NE, United Kingdom

Copyright © 2024 by The Rowman & Littlefield Publishing Group, Inc.

All rights reserved. No part of this book may be reproduced in any form or by any electronic or mechanical means, including information storage and retrieval systems, without written permission from the publisher, except by a reviewer who may quote passages in a review.

British Library Cataloguing in Publication Information Available

Library of Congress Cataloging-in-Publication Data

Names: Admirand, Peter, editor.
Title: The Last of Us and theology : violence, ethics, redemption? / Edited by Peter Admirand.
Description: Lanham, Maryland : Lexington Books/Fortress Academic, [2024] | Series: Theology, religion, and pop culture | Includes bibliographical references and index. | Summary: "In The Last of Us and Theology, global academics probe theological and moral themes in the acclaimed video game franchise and series. Follow the plight of Joel, Ellie, Tess, and other beloved (and hated) characters while reading chapters examining themes like forgiveness, violence, fatherhood, and God"—Provided by publisher.
Identifiers: LCCN 2024007738 (print) | LCCN 2024007739 (ebook) | ISBN 9781978716353 (cloth) | ISBN 9781978716360 (epub)
Subjects: LCSH: Last of us (Video game)—Social aspects. | Video Games—Religious aspects. | Violence in video games. | Video Games—Moral and ethical aspects.
Classification: LCC GV1469.35.L17 L37 2022 (print) | LCC GV1469.35.L17 (ebook) | DDC 794.8—dc23/eng/20240307
LC record available at https://lccn.loc.gov/2024007738
LC ebook record available at https://lccn.loc.gov/2024007739

∞™ The paper used in this publication meets the minimum requirements of American National Standard for Information Sciences—Permanence of Paper for Printed Library Materials, ANSI/NISO Z39.48-1992.

Contents

List of Figures	vii
Acknowledgments	ix
Introduction: Giraffes and Shamblers *Peter Admirand*	xiii

PART I: VIOLENCE   1

Chapter 1: Separating the "Sci" from the "Fi": The Ominously Real World of Fungal Pathogens and the Possibilities of Asthma, Illness, and Outbreak *David O'Connor and Jerry Hourihane Clancy*	3
Chapter 2: Ellie, Abby, and the Hospital Missions in *The Last of Us Part ll* *Amy M. Green*	17
Chapter 3: The Theologies of Fyodor Dostoevsky and Albert Schweitzer in Dialogue with the Moral Landscape of *The Last of Us* *David K. Goodin*	33
Chapter 4: Everything Happens for a Reason: "Pastor" David, Epistemic Harm, and Religious Trauma Syndrome *Daniel J. Cameron*	49
Chapter 5: Facing the Apocalypse: The Religious Cult of the Seraphites in *The Last of Us Part ll* *Tijana Rupčić*	65

PART II: ETHICS 81

Chapter 6: On Relationality, Human Beings, and Clickers 83
Robert Grant Price

Chapter 7: Genesis in Lincoln, MA: The Creation of Bill and Frank in "Long, Long Time" 97
Ryan Banfi

Chapter 8: Turning Reconsidered: Sam and Henry and the Futility of Nonviolence amidst Racism and Runners 111
Adam B. Banks

Chapter 9: *The Road* and *The Last of Us*: Failed Fathers at the End of the World 131
Peter Admirand

PART III: REDEMPTION? 149

Chapter 10: God's (Non)Presence, Interdependence, and Hope in *The Last of Us*: A Theological Reflection 151
Pavol Bargár

Chapter 11: *The Last of Us* and Eschatology for a Post-Apocalyptic World 165
Flora x. Tang

Chapter 12: Carrying the Fire and Finding the Fireflies: Hope, Despair, and Godtalk in the Dystopian Stories of Naughty Dog and Cormac McCarthy 179
Matthew C. Millsap and Ched Spellman

Chapter 13: "Save Who You Can Save": Soteriology in *The Last of Us* 193
Rebecca Chapman

Chapter 14: Conclusion: "Too Much Faith in Humanity?" 207
Peter Admirand

Index 213

About the Contributors 227

List of Figures

1.1 Military Pamphlet Showing the Stages of Cordyceps Brain Infection   5

1.2 X-Ray of the Skull of Someone Showing the Severity of the Fungal Spread through the Head   6

9.1 Wendy Lower's *The Ravine* Examines This Photo of a Holocaust Massacre Committed by Germans and Locals in Miropol, Ukraine, on October 13, 1941 (USHMM)   133

9.2 *Scene from the Great Flood* (1826), by Joseph-Désiré Court   134

9.3 Giotto's *The Last Judgment* (for the Arena Chapel, painted from 1304–1313)   135

9.4 Hieronymus Bosch's *Hell* (1490)   136

14.1 Ish Notes, Number 5, from *The Last of Us*   210

Acknowledgments

My last book examined ethical and theological themes in two of my favorite comic books (*Y: The Last Man* and *Saga*) and now this edited one is on my favorite video game, *The Last of Us,* and another I deeply respect, *The Last of Us: Part II*. This means hours I spent trying to check every imaginable cupboard and drawer in the post-apocalypse, looking for who knows what, are apparently justified. As an aside, when my wife asks me to find something of hers, and I genuinely try to find it (and almost never do), I think I spend 1/10th of the energy, time, and exertion as I do compared to seeking bags of sugar, random notes, and—while I lean toward pacifism in real life—as many guns as possible for Ellie and Joel. We live in a strange world and strange times. And for those who don't play video games, there are chapters in this book that also examine the HBO series (but it may, finally, be time for you to grab that controller. If you have kids, they'll like you more, even if their screentime might now be shortened—a win-win).

Let's also get this out of the way. Joel and Ellie are not individuals I would like to invite over to my house. This is not because Ellie's language is R-rated; no one would blink an eye in my kitchen at that. But Ellie (or Joel) would steal all my comic books, for one, and when my wife asks where the sugar went, it might get awkward. But despite the very horrible and morally questionable actions these poor souls do (or we make them do), it is a joy and gift to not only think and reflect on their world, but to have others do so, too—because there are a lot of cupboards and drawers to open and we can't do all this ourselves. Such is to say, thank you to all the contributors to this book for your care, deep thoughts, and sound writing on interesting and provocative topics. Whether you like it or not, we are now in this together—bloaters, hunters, typos, and all.

I won't hold grudges against Naughty Dog for not responding to my queries seeking permission to have a copyrighted *The Last of Us* image for the cover. Unlike Ellie and Abby, I forgive rather easily. So thank you, Neil Druckmann, for your gifted narrative vision and all the hundreds (how many are there?) who helped bring the games to life (especially the voice actors, Troy Baker and Ashley Johnson), the soundtrack from Gustavo Santaolalla, not to mention the HBO series, co-written with Craig Mazin, and brilliantly acted by, among others, Pedro Pascal and Bella Ramsey.

How can I not thank Matthew Brake, series editor and founder of this series, Theology, Religion, and Pop Culture. Matt immediately supported this project, and I appreciate his availability throughout the process and his editorial suggestions. At Lexington Books/Fortress Academic Press, Galya Freeman, associate editor, first shepherded this book through the proposal stage, and then her successor, Megan White, brought the book to publication. Thank you. I also express gratitude to Nicole Carty, production editor, and Susan Higgins, proofreader. I would also like to thank Madelon Nanninga-Franssen for her stellar work on the index (and catching many typos). My university also helped me open one of those drawers; in this case, for the index, so here I write: "This book received financial support from the Faculty of Humanities and Social Sciences Book Publication Scheme at Dublin City University." Speaking of the university, while my office is full of books, G.I. Joe Classified figures, comics, and various knickknacks (like drawings from *The Last of Us* or a bobblehead Alana and Marko)—and so a home away from home—it is really my colleagues and students who enrich my life and support the kind of diverse, interdisciplinary, interfaith, and eclectic theological work I do. They also don't ask too many questions if I casually mention bloaters and Rattlers in moral and theological discussions.

I also thank my parents for those Ataris, Segas, Nintendos, and PlayStations that have clearly borne so much fruit from my youth. (But Mom, seriously, you will not like *The Last of Us* [too violent and profane!]. I know you want to support me—a few years shy of my 50th!—but stick with my books on interreligious dialogue.)

And in that same vein of parental love, my five kids are the highest joys any video game could even try to offer—hours of endless discovery and fun (a bit of repetition and sometimes the need to start over), but never needing to be upgraded because they are priceless and so impossible to discount or trade for something else. Just remember, and this is really important (though you do know this), if there is a fungal pandemic or some end-of-the-world scenario, I know I'm a fairly nice guy, sing the odd catchy tune, and talk with you older ones about the intricacies of life and listen to your friend and relationship drama, but do whatever your mother tells you. She'll give you the best chance to make it through the final episode. I'll mean well, but—"Dad, look out for that_____!" It won't be pretty. But really, listen to your mom. She'd be a match for Joel—and clickers would have nothing on her.

I love all of you, but this one is dedicated to Chris, the second oldest. He is my mountain running and *The Last of Us* buddy. We played the second game together at the same time and watched all the shows—and he gave expert advice and opinions. If he didn't hate writing, I'd say he could contribute a chapter to the (hopefully) sequel to this book. But I need to leave now because a chocolate bar went missing and I can't blame the dogs, kids—or Ellie and Joel—for that one.

My Office (boring, I know), Dublin City University
9 Days before Christmas, 2023

Introduction

Giraffes and Shamblers

Peter Admirand

The first I heard of *The Last of Us* was a decade ago after a basketball game in Dublin. I don't remember whether we won or lost, but a teammate driving me home asked if I knew of this game? I hadn't. He began to explain the story. As I listened, a gentle rain swished across the windshield. It was dark. He then spoke about how a giraffe scene—which meant nothing then—had him in tears. He was smiling as he said it, implying, "I couldn't believe it, either." Squeamish about gore, I was hesitant to play, but intrigued by the narrative. Days later, tears from my eyes soon trickled but at a much earlier point in the game, the father in me watching Joel's distraught and horrified face as his "baby girl" is dying in his arms and there is nothing he can do about it. Did they really now kill cute, innocent girls in video games—even ones that you momentarily play as? It seemed like some commandment had been broken, if not theological then game-ological. My eyes burst in shock and sadness—as they also did when Henry later turned the gun on himself.

Emotions and feelings exploded like nail bombs during gameplay. I was petrified at some points (especially from runner grunts and howls, and of course, clicks from clickers) but also intrigued and exhilarated while surviving against dubious odds, or finally succeeding after repeatedly watching Joel's (my?) face ripped apart by a bloater. While not opposed to a well-aimed sniper shot to a hunter's head from (let's say) three klicks away, I loved the scavenging and exploring the most, discovering notes about Ish or Firefly pendants hanging from tree branches. But it was the growing bond between the daughterless father and the fatherless daughter that propelled me through the misery and hopelessness. Sometime around Pittsburgh, I was way past the point of no return with my need to protect Joel's cargo—risking my life and limb if it meant another *Savage Starlight* issue could be found for her. Perhaps the bond was even further cemented when Joel was shot and near death during "Winter," and I first played as Ellie. After the disturbing escape from David's cell and killing his goons in a blinding snowstorm, we were trapped in a flaming restaurant with a sadistic, cannibalistic pedophile, and trying to avoid the scrunch of broken glass as we scurried, amidst his diabolic taunts: "run, little rabbit, run." And my teammate was right about the giraffe scene—an image of it now hangs on my office wall along with my PS3 and PS4 copies of both games.

Because something about the Fireflies made me distrust them, I was fully on Joel's side the first time he (I?) woke up in St. Mary's Hospital and discovered Ellie would die during an experimental and desperate operation. When Joel (I?) killed the doctor (who we now know is Jerry Anderson), it surprised me, but I quickly thought we need to escape, my heart racing, morals and consequences, apparently, be damned. Still feeling the heroic dad, carrying Ellie and avoiding trigger-happy Fireflies, I didn't process Joel's slaying of Marlene. Instead, fully complicit and identified with Joel and Ellie (almost as if the game was a form of trauma), I didn't really think how Joel (me?) had just murdered and lied his way to keep Ellie safe. I was just glad she was alive. Did any of those others really matter? What other choice did we have?

Much of this unprocessed, unthinking, or vengeful state would have severe consequences in the second game, which is more cynical and hopeless than the first—at least if you still sought to protect that once sheltered girl (now young woman) who was engulfed by rage and haunted by revenge. Yet the questions the narrative raises about the consequences of violence and the game's demand both to participate in that violence and to feel empathy and compassion for apparent enemies provide conflicting, frustrating, and deeply illuminating moments. Such is to say, for those of you who have only watched the excellent first season of HBO's *The Last of Us*, I am jealous that you still have a first experience with the games in your future—but also pity you on the bloody path ahead. There is much to like in the second game and some of that material is brilliantly discussed in this book, but the game is more one you admire than necessarily enjoy, though my overall verdict depends on how and whether some deeper redemption occurs in part III; hence the question in this book's subtitle.

RATIONALE, PURPOSE, AND STRUCTURE

In the call for proposals for this book, I did not restrict *TLOU* source material—whether the games, the HBO series, *The Last of Us: American Dreams* comic books, or the excellent art companion books, *The Art of The Last of Us* and *The Art of The Last of Us Part II*. Those visually striking books also served as helpful references (and so did you, contributors to *The Last of Us* Wiki). While both games are now upgraded and enhanced for the PS5, this book can serve as a helpful companion as we wait until the next game and season. There are many ethical and theological undercurrents to wade through in the meantime—even if some of us may have initially avoided them in our bonding with Joel and Ellie. But the pulls are there and they are robust, and reckoning comes one way or another.

Above I sketched the genesis of my falling for *TLOU* and it has been a joy to be involved as the editor of this book. As noted, while my aims were expansive in terms of what *TLOU* material writers could draw from, the focus was on ethical and theological issues and themes. Some of us might rejoice in a God of creation who fashioned artists, writers, game developers, and actors who can bring a world like *TLOU* to life, but the fungal virus, the violence, and the betrayals told within also mirror much of our world, and here the call and journey for meaning and purpose, or for theists, a search for God's presence, can be as tenuous and jarring.

The thirteen chapters are divided into three parts, which echo the book's subtitle—*Violence, Ethics, Redemption?*—with the question mark not referring to violence, for who can deny its ubiquity, or the need (if not the fragility) of ethics, but how, whether, why, what, and who can be spoken of as redeemed or redemptive. Such a claim demands pause and uncertainty, especially amidst the hellish landscape of *TLOU,* where morally vacuous and heinous actions are committed by nearly all its main protagonists (especially Ellie, Abby, and Joel). Redemption is also always linked to a question as a work-in-progress, the possibility for backsliding or cyclical degeneration, and the inevitable taint of sin and suffering. Redemption remains more a hope or goal than a fixed state, especially in this world, where the stories of the living are not complete and moral catharsis and moral failure linger and cusp the possible. Judgments perhaps could be rendered if *TLOU2* was the definitive end, but we anticipate and thirst for still untold or unresolved narratives—and perhaps a firmer, more tangible sign of healing and renewal, whether for Abby and Lev, or that once little joke-book aficionado who is now utterly alone and with much blood upon her.

In this book, I did not separate chapters according to whether it focused on the games or the TV show as many contributors drew freely from the various genres, but signposts are signaled throughout the book to distinguish what is being referenced, as the first game and the HBO series are generally compatible but there are still differences, or shades of nuance.

Part I, "Violence," opens with perhaps the scariest chapter in the book because it is the one most rooted in science and fact. David O'Connor and Jerry Hourihane Clancy first explain the myths and realities of the cordyceps fungi and highlight previous and current outbreaks or illnesses that may be caused from fungi. What is frightening is how little scientists still know about fungi and fungal species and how climate change and rises in global temperature make a fungal outbreak more likely. Examining the scientific veracity or myths behind the game and HBO series, they say one is more realistic than the other when it comes to scientific fact. Before reading their chapter, think about that for a moment! They didn't say it was only fiction.

In chapter 2, Amy M. Green tracks Ellie and Abby in their intertwined but opposing journey during two hospital missions in *TLOU2*, Ellie's showing her further fall into hatred and revenge, and Abby's trying to redeem some part of her after her brutal murder of Joel in the lodge. Green's close reading of both Abby's and Ellie's moral trajectories include a fascinating account of Abby's battle with the Rat King—which transpires because Abby is trying to get medicine for the Seraphite Yara (and so an enemy of her group). Meanwhile, Ellie's parallel boss battle involves her torture and murder of Nora. Ellie returns to Dina shaking and traumatized, whatever news gained not worth the price of her moral dissolution. This focus brilliantly depicts the parallel and converging paths of these two protagonists trying to find some peace and meaning after the murders of their fathers, with Abby providing a warning to Ellie that the price of revenge will be too costly.

As *The Brothers Karamazov* is one of my favorite novels, it was a pleasure to have David K. Goodin investigate the moral landscape of *TLOU* through the theological thought of Fyodor Dostoevsky and the Nobel laureate, Albert Schweitzer. Schweitzer's undying commitment to and reverence for all life is a needful reminder in any age—especially as it raises challenges in times of war, or for our context, the post-apocalypse. For Goodin, one of those clear and arduous questions is how and whether Christianity still makes sense, and more specifically, whether the Christian call for *agape* and Christ's call to embrace enemies are impossible moral imperatives. For Goodin, though, the theologies of Dostoevsky and Schweitzer can provide a possible positive response to those questions.

Can religion, though, and more specifically Christian faith, really provide a meaningful response to such horrors, which may be metaphorical or fun in the game setting, but which are often all too real in life amidst mass poverty, disease, and conflicts? And what about when religion itself, or especially its leaders and practitioners, spread, and don't alleviate suffering and evil? For Christian minister Daniel J. Cameron, who grew up in a Christian fundamentalist context, sadly religion has often caused great epistemic harm in what has become known as Religious Trauma Syndrome. As a Catholic theologian who has previously written about the horrors of the child abuse scandal and cover-up within the Catholic Church, I can recognize how Cameron's focus and warning still need to be more widely addressed. In this regard, he highlights David's depiction in the HBO *TLOU* show, whose creators turned David from a pedophile cannibal into a Christian minister who is a pedophile cannibal. Cameron shows how this change represents the failure and abuse of religious rhetoric within Christianity where moral ideals are sullied to protect the powerful, vengeful, and abusers.

In *TLOU2*, we first encounter the Seraphites as vicious and lethal killers whose whistling can send the heart pounding and whose anti-technology positions can seem cultish. However, as Tijana Rupčić highlights, the initial story of the Seraphites was one of nonviolence and community. While their turn from modern technology may seem extreme, their beliefs also provided a meaningful path for those in the throes of the fungal pandemic. Unfortunately, the torture and murder of their leader, The Prophet, and the encroaching violence of the Washington Liberation Front (WLF), spurred a more totalitarian and merciless response. And yet, such a group also produced Lev and Yara who still believed in the ideals of the Seraphites and were one of the few characters in the game who adhered to a moral code of compassion and goodness. The ethos of The Prophet better reflects a moral way forward, for example, than the family-only approach of Joel or the vengeance-obsessed one of Ellie.

After grappling with the many levels and manifestations of violence depicted in part I, the contributors, in part II, "Ethics," analyze or attempt to find some viable moral response or thread in *TLOU*, which for many of our contributors is linked to theological concerns and searches.

In "On Relationality, Human Beings, and Clickers," Robert Grant Price draws upon the Jewish thinker Martin Buber and the Protestant theologian Dietrich Bonhoeffer to seek what relationality means, not only among humans, but in the world of *TLOU*: clickers and humans. If relationships among humans are situated in seeing oneself in another, as Emmanuel Levinas writes, and if such empathic seeing is a key source for connection and ethics, what hope is there for any positive relation for a human with a clicker? Such a question spurs issues about ontology—what is a human being and what is a clicker, as well as questions about free will and responsibility. While the mere thought or image of a clicker may hinder any possibility for connection let alone understanding or partnership, it is not difficult to transplant this block within our communities or histories where certain groups or people are ostracized or deemed "not like us"—usually with harsh words and actions. While space is needed to form and encourage a healthy level of difference, if too stark, relational links can wither. In this regard, Price ends his chapter with some promising examples from *TLOU*, guided by Buber and Bonhoeffer.

In chapter 7, Ryan Banfi focuses on the curmudgeonly prepper, Bill, and his partner, Frank, first through joining the few details offered in the video game and then providing a close analysis of the celebrated HBO episode, "Long, Long Time." Banfi highlights Bill and Frank's meeting, connection, and love through a comparison with the opening creation stories of the Book of Genesis as well as the theme of fruitfulness, biblical texts, and queer union in the light of thinkers like Michel Foucault. While Bill's and Frank's double suicide will be viewed differently by contributors in this book, their love and commitment to one another provide comfort and hope for meaning beyond scavenging for tools or only seeing another as a potential threat.

In the face of violence, then, what is the best moral response in a fractured world without justice and little hope of mercy? Adam B. Banks provides a challenging and persuasive examination of how and whether Jesus' call to turn the other cheek when struck by a blow from an adversary is either moral or realistic when faced with the bloaters and hunters of *TLOU*, or for many Black people throughout U.S. history, white supremacists and government and police brutality or indifference. In making his case, Banks explores the story of the Black inhabitants of Lowndes County, Alabama, during the 1960s. They were abandoned by the government and a target for white neighbors and their white police protectors. Can Jesus really have expected these vulnerable Black civilians—or other victims of mass violence—to not defend themselves? Such is to say, what role can pacifism play in *TLOU*, let alone sites of conflict and war in our world?

In closing part II, I excavate Cormac McCarthy's celebrated novel *The Road* as a comparison and launch point, but focus on failed and false fathers, adapting Irving Greenberg's contested terminology which describes Jesus as a failed but not a false Messiah—failed only because Jesus did not inaugurate a reign of peace, but not false because he strove to usher in God's reign. He may have failed (like Moses and others before him) but his failure was still in seeking the good and justice. Likewise, in normal and post-apocalyptic times, we fathers will always fail our children in some way—but woe to us who become false fathers, those who harm or neglect their children or show them the wrong path to follow. Examining fathers in both *TLOU* games and *The Road*, we will see who is more of a false or failed father.

As mentioned earlier, while no one can doubt the reality of violence and at least attempts at some ethical response, is there hope for any means of redemption, or in religious terms, salvation, after so much heartbreak and moral failures, some of which might be unforgivable? And yet, as much as the search for the goodness of human beings despite evil is a crucial one, theodicy questions that seek to locate (or exonerate) God despite horrors are timeless. In a word, where is God? Such are some of our concerns in part III, "Redemption?"

In chapter 10, Czech theologian Pavol Bargár cogently depicts how God's (non)presence in *TLOU* is still made manifest, drawing upon feminist, postcolonial, and queer theologies. He contends that even during the terrors of a post-apocalyptic world, traces of hope can be found through loving relationships, whether Bill's and Frank's, as depicted in the HBO version, or the community of Jackson—especially when contrasted to the cannibalistic horrors occurring in Silver Lake. Helpfully, he turns to Korean theologian Wonhee Anne Joh's notions of *han* and *jeong*, the former meaning loss and suffering, while the latter refers to compassion, love, and vulnerability. When taken together, especially in community, Bargár contends there can be growth and interdependence. This communion is especially possible where there is place for connection. Yet, what kind of connection, save parasitic and violent, is possible between humans and clickers? Like Millsap and Spellman below, Bargár seeks echoes and traces of God in seemingly dark and unlikely places.

Then, there is the problem of those who have tried to prove God's presence to justify unjustifiable acts or to argue such was necessary as part of the end times. And as Flora x. Tang asks: "What does it mean to speak about eschatology *after* the end of the world?" For Tang, such a question, in the context of Joel and Ellie's journey out west and amid *TLOU*'s ruins and decay, can challenge previously held notions of American Manifest Destiny that fused ethnonationalism, land conquest, and genocide as a specifically Christian undertaking. Such a pernicious ideology created and concocted narratives that erased or silenced Indigenous people already living on the land (while adulterating Christ's invitation for a discipleship that welcomes the stranger and chooses the path of peace). Rebuking such justifications, Tang also seeks to move discussion of eschatology towards the spatial, and so draws on decolonial thinkers like Vine Deloria Jr. Such inclusion evinces how nature renews and returns in *TLOU*'s post-outbreak context and highlights the importance of the addition of Marlon and Florence, a married Native American elderly couple, in the HBO episode "Kin." Despite the fungal pandemic, the land Ellie and Joel traversed was inhabited, and not just by groups trying to kill and conquer.

In the penultimate chapter, Matthew C. Millsap and Ched Spellman (like Admirand) explore *The Road* in their examination of *TLOU*, assessing theological discourse in each of those works as a search for hope despite pervasive despair. One of the difficulties of such a search is the collapse of language and societal cohesion because of both pandemics. How do you talk of God or the good after not only so much violence but the disintegration of once common norms of decency? And yet, despite these erasures, characters still try to locate and name some kind of meaning. In *The Road*, the father's and son's lives are mostly focused on scavenging and surviving, and yet the father has passed on to his son notions of "carrying the fire" and being one of the good guys. Joel and Ellie are on a somewhat parallel journey of survival, but unlike the father in *The Road*, Joel's moral compass was nearly shattered after Sarah's murder. Any initial values he passes on to Ellie seem less than exemplary. But unlike the boy, as Millsap and Spellman note, Ellie is deeply curious about the former world. In my reflecting on their chapter, perhaps Ellie's badgering of Joel for answers not only helps to form a connection and relationship between them, but could form and renew what had been a lost moral language that seemed to perish with Sarah's murder.

Closing part III, in Rebecca Chapman's examination of soteriology in *TLOU*, she includes the work of Paul Tillich to assess how and for what people are saved, particularly if following Tess's mantra in the HBO series— "save who you can save." Using the model proposed by Clive Marsh, Chapman asks, what characters are "saved from, saved by, and finally saved into"? Key to this ethical evaluation of the kinds and types of saving is the role of love—for one can save for the wrong reasons or save the wrong people or ideology—those that are more likely, for example, to cause destruction for others. Was Joel right to save Ellie in St. Mary's Hospital—and how and in what ways has Ellie saved Joel, or at what cost has David saved the people in his Silver Lake Community? Like all the terms and themes examined in these chapters, no easy answer is forthcoming if we try to see from multiple sides. Saving, like love, forgiveness, and reconciliation, are rarely points reached with no more room to expand and grow—or sadly fall back from and regress.

The book concludes with my attempt to bridge and reflect on both where we are morally and theologically at this point in the *TLOU* franchise and whether it is David or Ish that has the more persuasive and realistic worldview. But first, let's join scientists David O'Connor and Jerry Hourihane Clancy and talk cordyceps.

PART I

Violence

Chapter 1

Separating the "Sci" from the "Fi"

The Ominously Real World of Fungal Pathogens and the Possibilities of Asthma, Illness, and Outbreak

David O'Connor and Jerry Hourihane Clancy

SCIENTIFIC FACT IN A FICTIONAL WORLD

The first impression that *The Last of Us* (*TLOU*) gives us, be it as a player or viewer, is that of a standard-fare zombie apocalypse setting, in which a survival-drama narrative can take place. As we progress further into the story, however, it soon becomes apparent that work has been done to make this zombie outbreak different from those we've seen hundreds of times before. For one, this outbreak has an entirely different source, mechanism of infection, and outcome for the infected (more on that later). For another, it is not unreasonable to say that from a scientific standpoint, this "fictional" outbreak is well researched and thought out to the extent that it appears both plausible and possible that it could happen to us, at any point in time.

Cordyceps Fungi: The Game and The Show

The cordyceps fungi, as it appears in *TLOU's* universe, has mutated one way or another with the ability to infect humans. In the game, the U.S. Food and Drug Administration (FDA) bans the import of all crops from South and Central America, and major companies recall products due to "crops potentially tainted with mould." The lack of information adds to the fear, as the little information we have is that 60 percent of the global population has died or been infected, according to a newspaper clipping seen in the University of Eastern Colorado, written roughly one year after the initial outbreak.[1] We know nothing about the twenty intermediate years after the initial outbreak, and put simply, not enough is known or understood about what just occurred.

The TV show approaches this aspect slightly differently, opening with a televised panel show in the 1960s, in which scientists hypothesize whether a fungal-based outbreak was even possible, and what conditions would be required to facilitate it. Their conclusion is that it would only be possible if the global average temperature rose by a couple of degrees so that a fungus could adapt to the warmer interiors of the human body (37°C). This frightening declaration is, unfortunately, accurate, and in the last few years has been observed in several real and pathogenic fungal species, including *Candida auris*, which has devastated nursing homes in Spain and the eastern United States in recent years.[2] There is a lot more information given in the TV show, and some notable changes, such as the origin of the outbreak being moved to Jakarta, Indonesia, and the change from showing a food recall in the background, to having a series of near comedic close calls between Joel, Sarah, and various grain- and flour-based breads, cakes, cereals, and cookies, whilst completely unaware of the imminent danger they are in.

The infection spreads within the host in the same way for both media, starting with loss of brain function, and an increase in aggression, not unlike those seen in a rabies-infected animal, with visual symptoms being little more than bloodshot eyes and involuntary muscle spasms.[3] In the show, there is the addition of tendrils that emerge from the mouth and appear to act as the mechanism for infection through the biting of another person. As the fungus begins to spread, the skin becomes veiny or bumpy in appearance as hyphae grow and spread throughout the body. Fungus starts to visibly grow on the face of an infected person, and out of the eyes, impairing sight, resulting in the development of rudimentary echolocation senses by the infected people.[4] After about a year, all vision is gone and the person, whose head resembles that of a large collection of mushrooms and their skull broken apart by fungal growth, is left with just the essentials; a jaw and teeth to bite with, and a throat to maintain abilities of echolocation to "see" via the croaking or clicking of their vocal chords. As years pass, the infection can continue to grow and spread, keeping the host alive but enveloped in thick layers of fungal growth that are thick and hardened. Furthermore, the fungus now produces mycotoxins that can be produced and thrown at perceived threats. An in-game FEDRA guide of these stages and an X-ray of an infected individual, can be seen below (see Figure 1.1 and Figure 1.2).

Outside of the host, in order to infect others, the difference between the show and the game could not be more pronounced. While both relying on the fungus spreading via the traditional zombie methods of an infected host biting an uninfected, the game appears to show that the saliva contains the

Separating the "Sci" from the "Fi"

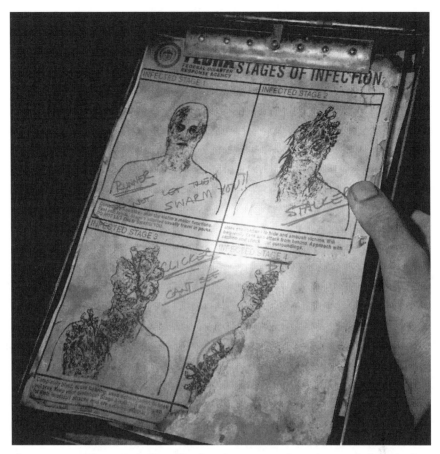

Figure 1.1. Military Pamphlet Showing the Stages of Cordyceps Brain Infection. *In-game screenshot from* The Last of Us, *David O'Connor*

fungus, without explaining it outright, as every in-game bite swells and becomes blistered and infected; even Ellie's own bite shows signs of this. In the *Left Behind DLC*, one set of notes chronicles a group's attempts to cut off a bitten limb before the infection spreads. The show explicitly focuses on a set of tendrils that emerge from the mouth and into an open wound or orifice as seen when Trish is infected in episode 2 of the HBO series. The major difference, however, is that in the game, the primary infection method is that of the release of airborne fungal spores, that when inhaled, infect the lungs of an unsuspecting passer-by. These spores develop if a host dies before the fungus has fully developed. The infection envelops the corpse and produces sprouts that grow and burst, releasing thousands of spores that fill the air with a thick, dusty cloud. The concentrations required to cause airborne infection

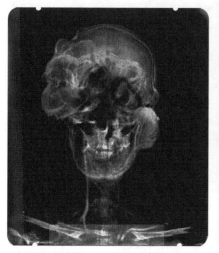 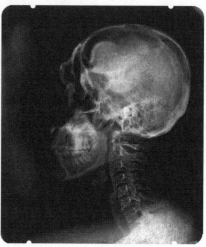

Figure 1.2. X-Ray of the Skull of Someone Showing the Severity of the Fungal Spread through the Head. *In-game screenshot from* The Last of Us, *David O'Connor*

are high, high enough that the spores cannot cause outdoor infection, and concentrations must be enough to be visible to the naked eye, appearing as a yellow-brown cloud lingering in a hallway or damp basement. As a result, all survivors carry gas masks and filtering canisters with them wherever they go, for if they make a wrong turn and take the wrong breath, they're done.

CORDYCEPS: REALITY

The fictionally portrayed cordyceps fungus does have a real-life counterpart. The original creators of the game have in the past described that their inspiration for the game came after watching the "Jungle" episode of David Attenborough's BBC series *Planet Earth*.[5] As they watched the parasitic cordyceps fungus infect and control the mind of a helpless ant, it was then they thought about what kind of impact this pathogen could have on a human brain. What the game and show appear to have done is take properties and characteristics of various real-world fungal species and amalgamated them into one fictional "Frankenstein" spore type. The "mind control" characteristic, for example, does exist in cordyceps, as has been mentioned, but in reality, the ant doesn't go rabid or succumb to the will of its fungal illness. The motor neurons are taken over, allowing the fungus to move and "puppet" the ant around, while the ant is powerless to stop it, still retaining its same level of awareness of what's happening around it.[6] If this is what was occurring in the fictional world, one can only imagine the trauma and pain an infected person feels, as their limbs grab and their mouth bites, trying to eat and kill their own family, while they helplessly watch, unable to stop, as if they are immersed in the world's most sadistic virtual reality movie.

As for the ability of the cordyceps spore to go from infecting insects to infecting humans, that is a lot less likely. There are an estimated 3.8 million species of fungus in the world, but less than 10 percent of those have even been categorized, meaning the vast majority of types are simply unknown. For cordyceps specifically, we have thus far identified roughly 600 species. That may sound like a lot, but the different species are all highly adapted to extremely small habitats, some only a few meters across. You could pick up a cordyceps-infected ant in one part of a forest, and drop it only a couple hundred meters away, and the cordyceps fungus would be completely unequipped to infect the ants in that area, due to slight differences in species or sub-species variation.[7] Cordyceps as we know it is regarded as safe enough that we often consume it. It is an ingredient in the smoothies of Gwyneth Paltrow's goop brand, and many eastern cultures will have a jar of cordyceps within reach as one of their many alternative medicines. Many doctors even recommend injecting cordyceps during an organ transplant, as it has traditionally been believed to help the body to accept the organ. This apparent medical treatment and smoothie ingredient have no beneficial impact that is backed by empirical evidence.[8]

The number of mutations required to allow human infection is so astronomically high that it's not worth seriously discussing. To increase the likelihood, *TLOU* creators have discussed the possibility that it was a strain of mutated cordyceps that was itself infected by a mutated virus. Could there be a chain of infected mutated living things, each themselves infected by something else, also mutated, thus allowing it to jump or hop from species to species? Maybe. That was one of the leading theories for how the Coronavirus pandemic took over the world. That COVID origination theory stated that a person badly handled or prepared a pangolin for consumption. The pangolin in question had possibly gotten sick from the eating of an infected bat.[9] Other illnesses such as malaria, HIV, and Ebola originated in species-to-species exchange. As for fungal spores other than cordyceps specifically, there are many thousands of species that can and do infect many species of mammals, including people, every year. In fact, for every malaria death, four people die from a fungal infection.[10]

The spread of the cordyceps at the beginning of the pandemic in *TLOU* is through infected grain- or flour-based products. In reality, many fungal species have wreaked havoc on our crops and on us throughout history. The most famous example is that of the potato blight, which even the mention of still triggers a generational trauma response in anyone with Irish ancestry, as the fungal-impacted crop resulted in the decimation and scattering of a population so severely that it has yet to recover in the nearly 200 years since.

With regard to grains and cereals, ergot fungi have time and again infected rye and barley crops, resulting in breads, biscuits, or any other product of these cereals, causing whoever consumes the contaminated cereal to suffer a mixture of severe symptoms similar to those experienced by the first stage of the fictional cordyceps infection.[11] If you ate the wrong, ergot-infected sandwich, you may suffer involuntary muscle spasms, convulsions. If you've eaten more than your fair share of baked goods, be prepared for full-on psychosis and manic episodes to accompany your spasms! Just to be clear, ergot isn't the only mind-altering fungus. Most people have heard of magic mushrooms, which are consumed for their psychoactive properties, along with the lab-refined fungal drugs, LSD and psilocybin. Intentionally or accidentally, people have been having their brains controlled and changed by the fungus for millennia. Hopefully, you can see now how much truth and science lie beneath all the entertainment we consume.

Looking back to some historical events with this updated knowledge, some researchers have hypothesized that the events surrounding the Salem witch trials are tarred with all the signs of an ergot poisoning event.[12] The "witchcraft" and the response to it can be explained by a combination of all the aforementioned symptoms, with the "witches" having experienced their share of convulsions and spasms, or the townsfolk sharing in mass hysteria and delusion, all from one bad batch of ham on rye. Ergot poisoning is mostly a relic of the past, at least in Western societies, but as recently as the 1950s a set of no less than fifty villagers in a remote French village had to be interned in mental asylums, so severe was the damage caused by fungus in the flour.

How does cordyceps infect and spread in reality? It's much closer to that of the video game of *TLOU* than the show. As in both media, the fungus controls the body of the host (in this case an ant or similar insect), and just like with humans in the show, once the ant begins its spasm and erratic behavior, it is removed from society by the other ants. In this case, they physically move the ant away from the population as they know exactly what happens in the later stage of infection. The ant, controlled by its fungal foe, is forced to climb to the highest point on a nearby branch or leaf. It then grabs on to the surface in a "death grip" from which its mandibles can never release, thus determining its final resting place.[13] The ant succumbs to the fungus, which grows and sprouts out of the ant's head and face. The growing tendrils and fruiting bodies stretch upwards, before bursting in a cloud of spores, hopeful that in climbing high enough, the spores will fall or be carried by the wind, to be inhaled or consumed in some way by another poor unsuspecting ant. Alas, there is no rabid zombie ant rampage, in which an infected ant bites and infects the others in its colony. That one is for our entertainment only!

CLIMATE CHANGE: NEVER NOT RELEVANT

As with any topic vaguely related to nature and humans, or the relationship between us, the climate change that we've caused is the unstoppable force smashing through the easily movable object that is our society.[14] As mentioned, the TV version of *TLOU* begins with a show of its own, in which a panel of professionals in the 1960s opine that the one major natural barrier to a fungal apocalypse is the difference in temperature between our internal bodies, and the optimal fungal growth temperature. These professionals claim that as long as conditions don't slowly but consistently change on earth, resulting in warmer and wetter weather each year, we should be just fine.

This is the worst thing they could have said, as their greatest fear is exactly what has happened! But truthfully, they are right, and that's because the segment wasn't actually filmed in the 1960s, it's from today. With the benefit of hindsight, we see there are fungal species that have done exactly this. Because of a changing climate, as well as an improved response to "traditional" pandemic- and epidemic-causing organisms, namely coronaviruses, influenzas, and the like, the WHO has had to turn its attention to the new most likely global threat. In 2022, due to increasing concerns, a new list was developed, researched, and published.[15] It is known as the "Critical Priority" fungal pathogen list, and the majority on the list are species of fungal pathogens that either were not known to exist, or simply were not adapted to infecting humans two decades ago. One of the most recently discovered is a fungus known as *Aspergillus fumigatus*, a fungus that is often found living in domestic compost bins.[16] It wasn't an issue when first discovered, as most of those infected could recover quite easily with simple treatments, but the nature of a fungus is that antivirals and antibiotics will never work. It needs an antifungal treatment. Recently it has grown increasingly resistant to known treatments, to the point that if you inhale its spores, some studies say chances of death may have risen to 100 percent. Researchers, meanwhile, are scrambling to catch up to the ever-mutating pathogen.[17]

Another WHO "critical pathogen," *Candida auris*, did exactly what the fictional *TLOU* scientists said may happen. It used to be unable to survive the warm temperatures of the human body, but thanks to climate change, it began infecting humans, with the first case identified in 2007.[18] Ever since this adaptation, it has been the bane of many hospitals and nursing homes, whose already vulnerable patients are not strong enough to withstand this virile pest, which infects the blood with fungus, and uses the bloodstream to get into the organs of the body, before taking root, growing, and eventually killing its host.

Ultimately, the fear of the unknown is what's driving this attention from the WHO, as they refocus their efforts from pandemic management to prevention. We simply don't know enough about fungi, fungal species, and their potential.[19] The TV show illustrates this very well in the second episode, when the leading mycologist in Jakarta analyzes a fungus sample. Every question she asks results in an answer that causes her eyes to widen. She is portrayed as someone who is aware of how much we still have to learn about the fungal kingdom, and not the usual media portrayal of the "doubtful scientists" who deny what is right in front of them because it just cannot be. When she is told the source is a human infection, she doesn't deny the possibility, she simply asks more questions, and once she has enough information, she delivers her verdict without the need for any more evidence. She announces there is no possible cure, and that the government should bomb the city immediately, thus killing everyone including herself and her family. There is no suggestion of closing borders or setting up quarantine zones. This is a fungal pathogen, and this mycologist understands the possible ramifications, and potential scale of damage it could leave in its wake. It turns out in this (fictional) case, that she was right.[20]

FUNGAL SPORES IN OUR LIVES

As the parasitic cordyceps fungus in the show is essentially a mythical virus made of the worst parts of many different fungal variants, you will not be encountering it in your day-to-day life. You do, however, encounter fungal spores all the time. In the game, the fact that they exist in the air is not enough to infect you; a certain concentration threshold must be met before you succumb and turn into a mindless monster. The same is true in our daily lives, as we breathe in potentially thousands of fungal spores every hour. Why don't we notice anything? Well fungal spores are, in some ways, a smaller, less popular cousin of pollen. Everyone knows pollen, and everyone who suffers from hay fever *really* knows pollen.[21] It is possible that sometimes, when you have hay fever, it isn't pollen at all. On occasion, it may be fungal spores that are causing a sneezy nose or an itchy throat. While pollen is seasonal, and people can find out when and where it will appear, fungal spores can be a bit trickier. They do have seasonality, peaking in the summertime much like pollen does, but they can be very weather- and location-specific too. A leak from a bathtub or a damp corner can be a breeding ground for various dangerous and deadly fungi, and warmer weather and increased rainfall will only exacerbate the problems as the years go on.

Many issues not yet known include whether pollution or air quality has an impact on fungal spores. We have seen that with pollen grains, pollutants can damage the outer layer of the grain, resulting in smaller broken particles that can cause much more acute and severe reactions in those who suffer from allergic rhinitis. Fungal spores, being that bit smaller, and that bit harder to source, grow, and experiment on, may have similar properties. We just have not learned enough about them yet. And that is why the creators of *TLOU* saw them as the perfect subject for a zombie series. We know some of what fungal spores can do, and it's scary, but we have only identified a small subset of them, and we know that we don't know so, so much. This can be either a comforting or a frightening admission.

REAL-WORLD MONITORING, RESEARCH, AND PROGRESS: INSIDE A BIOAEROSOL CENTER IN IRELAND

What do we do if a fungal outbreak like cordyceps breaks out? Do we try and stay quarantined at home like during the COVID pandemic, waiting for the inevitable vaccine rollout? Unfortunately, probably no. If the fungus spreads throughout the world through our food supply chains, as it did in *TLOU*, that means two things: one, we are probably in big trouble, and two, something has gone terribly, terribly wrong with our food safety process at every stage. In fact the extent of the initial outbreak was so widespread and so severe that it's hard to believe that this was not spotted earlier. We do sometimes have product recalls and bad batches of foods that make a few people sick, like several lettuce-based *E. coli* outbreaks across the United States in recent years, and the Blue Bell ice cream listeria deaths in 2015, but these are always localized to small regions. While the exact specific origin is never understood, one would have to consider that this could be a case of a government testing gone wrong.

But let's hypothesize that, as often happens, gross negligence does occur, resulting in the second "once-in-a-generation" outbreak of our generation. Realistically a single brand or producer would be affected in one region, so a mitigation process similar to what happened with COVID would occur. As the severity of the illness became apparent, you would see border shutdowns faster than anything previously experienced. Visible symptoms can show up in a matter of minutes, with the longest possible wait before appearance of full symptoms only being twenty-four hours. It's not plausible, though, to say this kind of infection would spread globally, at least by human-to-human contact. In the first game, when Joel and Ellie travel to the University of Eastern Colorado, monkeys are seen to be carriers of the disease, without showing any outward signs of infection. This is learned through collected audio recordings and lab notes, in which we can determine that the monkeys were used for experimentation purposes and may not possess the ability to naturally become infected. This does open the door to the possibility that some other creature could be our ultimate downfall. One could hypothesize that other mammals or types of animals could also be carriers, especially as the fungus has already completed the absolutely insane evolutionary leap of spreading via the rarely analyzed ant-crop-human pathway. But unless we see some concrete evidence based in science or even fantasy science, I'm ruling it out. There may even be arguments against this, as we encounter many different wild animals throughout both the series and games, without ever encountering one that shows outward signs of infection or illness from the cordyceps brain infection.

That, in all likelihood, also rules out the spread of the version of cordyceps as seen in the HBO drama. While we might tragically lose a city or two, even a couple of countries if the outbreak starts somewhere like Central Europe, world ending it is not. The video game strain of the fungus however—now that's scary. It has one major power that could render us defenseless; it is airborne. Now I have mentioned that it would appear people can only get infected from a very high concentration of airborne fungal spores, but this is based solely on the gameplay mechanics. Dark, wet, and warm corners always appear to possess such concentrations, usually pointing to signs of a dead, decomposing infected nearby. Sometimes, though, these large colonies of fungi, with their tendrils dug into the ground and brick, snaking between cracks and crevices, have no obvious source. Is it possible that even though a very large particle concentration is needed to infect a living person, a much, much smaller fraction, possibly only a couple of spores, is required to imbed and grow on a dead animal or plant? Well, yeah, that's kind of the fungus's whole deal! Studies have shown that entire clouds of fungal spores can undergo long range transportation in the air, and the conventional way that we have been monitoring these airborne spores in Ireland is comparatively rudimentary.[22] Even today, the only full-time fungal spore monitors in Ireland, and in many other countries, are composed of what can best be described as a metal case on a rooftop with a small opening to let air in. The case contains a vacuum pump to suck in air, a roll of adhesive tape rotating past the opening via a wind-up clock mechanism, turning around so as to collect anything that is sucked in, and, and that's it! That is the whole setup. Scientists have to open the machine, wind the clock, replace the tape every week, and bring the old sticky tape back to a lab. This tape is cut to fit onto microscope slides because there is only one way those fungal spore species are traditionally identified and the concentrations determined, and that is by counting them, one by one, with an identification key next to the microscope. What does this mean for our newly locked down citizens? Well, it means there is currently no scenario where we could sit out by the cafe, gas mask in our bag, ready to throw it on in the case that a surprise cloud of deadly spores comes rolling across the Irish Sea. In fact, a best-case scenario given the standard tech is where a group of scientists mull over their data and ponder "Ahh, so that's why there was an outbreak in Dalkey last Tuesday. Look at that concentration spike! Must have been the cordyceps."

But even this form of outbreak won't be effective for long. Right now, technologies are, and have been, developed to solve all these problems. In Ireland, real-time, online fluorescence-based laser and light technologies are being rolled out and tested to determine whether they could be our saving grace. These devices can instantly obtain the shape, size, and fluorescence intensity of any particles, and using this data, can be trained and improved using machine learning algorithms to instantly identify species of biological aerosols potentially like the cordyceps spores, among various other potential threats. Live data feeds will be remotely accessible, and in all seriousness, we should have the protection necessary to monitor and follow this hypothetical cordyceps outbreak, before it even lands on our shores. In this near future, tech assisted apocalyptic scenario, as long as it doesn't start in Ireland, and we lock down in time, we will be just fine. Similarly, other small and medium islands like Taiwan and New Zealand have great opportunities to maintain relative safety. Continental populations, on the other hand, may be far more vulnerable and susceptible to widespread fungal dispersion and disease outbreak. Thus it remains imperative that further preventative means are researched. But even back in Ireland, until these research projects and pilot programs run by Dublin City University and Met Éireann are complete, and the system is fully up and running, we will just have to keep our fingers crossed that the "next big outbreak" remains firmly on our screens as part of our PlayStation libraries and our TV watchlists.

NOTES

1. In the game this is during the University chapter.
2. Jeffery-Smith et al., "Candida auris."
3. *Wired*, "Biology Behind 'The Last of Us.'"
4. See Betuel, "The Last of Us 2"; Martin, "The Real Science."
5. See Hess, "Scientists Were All Wrong"; Louis, "Last of Us Showrunner Details The Real Fungus Infection."
6. Gibbens, "Could a Parasitic Fungus Evolve to Control Humans?"
7. See Funnell, "'The Last of Us' Fungus Is Real"; Hart, "'The Last Of Us' Zombie Infection Is Real."
8. Feltman, "Is There Any Science Behind"; Hong, Zhang, and Fan, "Cordyceps Sinensis."

9. Morens et al., "The Origin of COVID-19."
10. Kainz, Bauer, Madeo, and Carmona-Gutierrez, "Fungal Infections in Humans."
11. See Caporael, "Ergotism"; Lienhard, "Rye Ergot and Witches."
12. See Caporael, "Ergotism"; Lohnes, "How Rye Bread May Have Caused the Salem Witch Trials."
13. See Gibbens, "Could a Parasitic Fungus Evolve to Control Humans?"; Jacobs, "'The Last of Us' Creator Says."
14. Gibbens, "Could a Parasitic Fungus Evolve to Control Humans?"
15. World Health Organization, "WHO Fungal Priority Pathogens List."
16. Arastehfar et al., "Aspergillus fumigatus."
17. Arastehfar et al., "Aspergillus fumigatus"; Dhingra and Cramer, "Regulation of Sterol Biosynthesis."
18. Jeffrey-Smith et al., "Candida auris."
19. Dijksterhuis, "Fungal Spores."
20. Funnell, "'The Last of Us' Fungus Is Real."
21. Buters et al., "Pollen and Spore Monitoring in the World"; Kay, Kaplan, Bousquet, and Holt, "Allergy and Allergic Diseases."
22. Mims and Mims III, "Fungal Spores Are Transported."

BIBLIOGRAPHY

Arastehfar, Alireza, et al. "Aspergillus fumigatus and Aspergillosis: From Basics to Clinics." *Studies in Mycology* 100.100115 (2021), doi:10.1016/j.simyco.2021.100115.

Betuel, Emma. "The Last of Us 2: The Real Science That Inspired the Zombie Fungus." *Inverse*, January 23, 2020, https://www.inverse.com/science/last-of-us-cordyceps.

"The Biology Behind 'The Last of Us.'" *Wired*, January 16, 2023, https://www.wired.com/video/watch/wired-news-and-science-the-last-of-us-real-life.

Buters, Jeroen T. M., et al. "Pollen and Spore Monitoring in the World." *Clinical and Transitional Allergy* 8.9 (2018), https://doi.org/10.1186/s13601-018-0197-8.

Caporael, Linnda R. "Ergotism: The Satan Loosed in Salem?" *Science* 192.4234 (1976): 21–26.

Dhingra, Sourabh, and Robert A. Cramer. "Regulation of Sterol Biosynthesis in the Human Fungal Pathogen Aspergillus fumigatus: Opportunities for Therapeutic Development." *Frontiers in Microbiology* 8.92 (2017), doi:10.3389/fmicb.2017.00092.

Dijksterhuis, Jan. "Fungal Spores: Highly Variable and Stress-Resistant Vehicles for Distribution and Spoilage." *Food Microbiology* 81 (2019): 2–11.

Feltman, Rachel. "Is There Any Science behind Gwyneth Paltrow's $200 Smoothie? Either Way, We Drank It." *Washington Post*, October 27, 2021, https://www.washingtonpost.com/news/speaking-of-science/wp/2016/03/21/is-there-any-science-behind-gwyneth-paltrows-200-smoothie-either-way-we-drank-it/.

Funnell, Rachael. "'The Last of Us' Fungus Is Real, Could It Cause a Pandemic?" *IFL Science*, January 27, 2023, https://www.iflscience.com/-the-last-of-us-fungus-is-real-could-it-cause-a-pandemic-67127.

Gibbens, Sarah. "Could a Parasitic Fungus Evolve to Control Humans?" *National Geographic*, January 19, 2023, https://www.nationalgeographic.com/science/article/parasitic-fungus-evolve-to-control-humans.

Hart, Robert. "'The Last of Us' Zombie Infection Is Real—Here's What Scientists Say about the Threat to Humans." *Forbes*, January 16, 2023, https://www.forbes.com/sites/roberthart/2023/01/16/the-last-of-us-zombie-infection-is-real-heres-what-scientists-say-about-the-threat-to-humans/.

Hess, Peter. "Scientists Were All Wrong about that Zombie Ant Fungus on 'Planet Earth.'" *Inverse*, November 9, 2017, https://www.inverse.com/article/38278-zombie-cordyceps-fungus-ant-brains.

Hong, Tao, Minghua Zhang, and Junming Fan. "Cordyceps Sinensis (a Traditional Chinese Medicine) for Kidney Transplant Recipients." *Cochran Database of Systematic Reviews* 2015.10 CD009698. October 12, 2015, doi:10.1002/14651858.CD009698.pub2.

Jacobs, Eammon. "'The Last of Us' Creator Says the Cordyceps Fungus Danger Is 'Real' and 'Has Always Been Here.'" *Insider*, March 21, 2023, https://www.insider.com/the-last-of-us-creator-cordyceps-fungus-danger-real-2023-1.

Jeffery-Smith, Anna, et al. "Candida auris: A Review of the Literature." *Clinical Microbiology Reviews* 31.1 (2017), doi:10.1128/CMR.00029-17.

Kainz, Katharina, Maria A. Bauer, Frank Madeo, and Didac Carmona-Gutierrez. "Fungal Infections in Humans: The Silent Crisis." *Microbial Cell* 7.6 (2020): 143–145, doi:10.15698/mic2020.06.718.

Kay, A. Barry, Allen P. Kaplan, Jean Bousquet, and Patrick G. Holt. "Allergy and Allergic Diseases." *Allerg Dis* 1 (2008): 1–22.

Lienhard, John H. "No. 1037: Rye Ergot and Witches." Podcast, *The Engines of Our Ingenuity*, https://engines.egr.uh.edu/episode/1037.

Lohnes, Kate. "How Rye Bread May Have Caused the Salem Witch Trials." *Britannica*, https://www.britannica.com/story/how-rye-bread-may-have-caused-the-salem-witch-trials.

Louis, Brandon. "'Last of Us' Showrunner Details the Real Fungus Infection Seen on Show." *ScreenRant*, January 16, 2023, https://screenrant.com/last-of-us-real-life-fungus-infection/.

Martin, Laura. "The Real Science behind 'The Last of Us,' According to a Biologist." *Esquire*, January 17, 2023, https://www.esquire.com/uk/culture/a42519847/the-last-of-us-real-science/.

Mims, Sarah A., and Forrest M. Mims, III. "Fungal Spores Are Transported Long Distances in Smoke from Biomass Fires." *Atmospheric Environment* 38.5 (2004): 651–655.

Morens, David M., et al. "The Origin of COVID-19 and Why It Matters." *American Journal of Tropical Medicine and Hygiene* 103.3 (2020): 955–959, doi:10.4269/ajtmh.20-0849.

World Health Organization. "WHO Fungal Priority Pathogens List to Guide Research, Development and Public Health Action." WHO, October 25, 2022, https://www.who.int/publications/i/item/9789240060241.

Chapter 2

Ellie, Abby, and the Hospital Missions in *The Last of Us Part II*

Amy M. Green

INTRODUCTION: ELLIE, ABBY, AND REVENGE

The Last of Us culminates with Joel killing Abby's father toward the end of the game as he rescues Ellie from a Firefly-run hospital where she is to be sacrificed in their vain hope for a cure for the cordyceps pandemic. That death, whether individual players find it justified or not, sets Abby on her path to revenge, tying the first game narratively to *The Last of Us Part II*. The hospital setting also serves as a connecting point between the two games both narratively and symbolically. Abby and Ellie both visit Lakehill Seattle Hospital on the same day, with Abby seeking to retrieve a medical kit for Yara and then Ellie looking for Nora and information about Abby's whereabouts. While they serve different purposes in terms of character development, the two missions follow the same overall pattern. Abby and Ellie begin in a place of relative safety, transverse the ruined city to the hospital, and then descend into its depths to complete their missions. Abby and Ellie both also interact with Nora, who is pivotal to both missions, and then return to their current bases of operation and a semblance of companionship and solace. By sequencing the missions in this way—with players embodying Abby first— the narrative may give pause to players who had initially been only negatively predisposed toward her. Abby, for the first time in the game, does something selfless by trying to get necessary medical supplies. Conversely, Ellie, enraged and out of control, ends up exacting gruesome and bloody revenge on Nora when the latter refuses to divulge Abby's location. A structural analysis of both missions, including examining the narrative, symbolism, and visual language, reveals them as a microcosm of the larger issue of the symbolism of ruins and morality in both games.

Throughout the game, both Ellie and Abby seek revenge and their actions not only lead to the deaths of those close to each of them but also unravel the relationships between them and those who survive. Osgood considers revenge-seekers' mindset, noting a strong belief that they were "doing the right thing" or attempting to "get even," with some participants specifically reporting that they thought they were "doing justice." Moreover, those who chose to give the wrongdoer forgiveness reported viewing this gesture as "noble" or "merciful," which suggests the would-be revenge seeker views revenge as justified.[1]

Once the game flips perspective, as it does in the first of the hospital missions, forcing the player to embody Abby, the issue of revenge gains additional complexity and nuance, as the player witnesses the loss Abby endured when Joel killed her father. Abby could have declined going to the hospital for medical supplies, leaving Yara's amputation surgery far riskier. Instead, she makes the attempt—even without any guarantee she will find the supplies or return in time, as Mel indicates the operation cannot be delayed for long. The two hospital chapters thus play an important role in developing each character and underscoring the personal price of revenge.

Nora is present at Joel's beating and is critical to developing the characters of Abby and Ellie. While Nora does not attack Joel, she attacks his brother, Tommy, and holds him at gunpoint, fully in support of Abby's actions. Nora is also steadfast in not betraying Abby, both to the Washington Liberation Front (WLF) and to Ellie, out of a strong sense of loyalty and friendship. Conversely, some of the other WLF members present at Joel's beating—most notably Mel—begin to question Abby's character. Abby's hospital mission provides a narrative attempt at humanizing her—showing that she is capable of decency. Ellie's decision to perpetrate—and the player's mandatory participation in—Nora's savage beating is crucial because by that point, Nora has been infected and will die in the coming hours.

RUINS AND RUINATION: THE MOVIE THEATER, AQUARIUM, AND HOSPITAL

Abby's and Ellie's missions each begin at a place of relative safety, with Abby at the Seattle Waterfront Aquarium and Ellie at the Pinnacle Theater. Both buildings, while still standing, are otherwise abandoned and symbolize a permanently lost world. The Seattle Waterfront Aquarium would once have been a cornerstone of its community, offering a place for families and people of all ages to enjoy an afternoon marveling at its various exhibits.

The Pinnacle Theatre similarly represents a sense of community and shared spectacle. While there are certainly moviegoers who prefer an empty or near-empty theater, many others still flock to opening weekends. *The Last of Us Part II* makes clear that there is little community left in the world—few people and fewer bonds that are long-lasting and free of betrayal. The spectacles presented to the player consist mostly of horrors. In keeping with the very different character development that occurs in the missions, hospitals also exist as a place of symbolic contradiction. Brenner argues, "Like most people, I dread going into hospitals. I fear infection and the looming sense of decay. Hospitals, we know too well, can be the portal to death but also a place of miracles and cures."[2] There is special emphasis placed on the danger of Abby's mission, as she is reminded this was ground zero, the place where patients were taken in the early days of the cordyceps pandemic before its lethality and spread were fully understood. The hospital serves as hope for Abby if she can find the medical supplies for Yara. For Ellie, the hospital will be what it is from the start: a place of death and ruin.

These three settings—the aquarium, movie theater, and hospital—call to mind Svetlana Boym's analysis of the "angel of history." She writes, "The angel can neither make whole the past nor embrace the future . . . the angel of history freezes in the precarious present, motionless in the crosswinds."[3] The game's world exists in such a state of the immediate present, necessitated by day-to-day survival. Further still, younger survivors, such as Ellie and Abby, have no memory of the world that once was, no sense of what a movie theater might have been like during a premiere weekend, or what it would have felt like to wander through the aquarium exhibits in a pre-apocalyptic world.

Ruins form a vital component of the visual language of both games, even if the building in question is not of particular importance. For example, it might be one the player moves past or moves through to reach a needed location. Whether important to the story or not, however, they cannot be ignored and stand as silent testimony to the reality that human civilization worldwide lies in ruins. Devecka writes, "The observation that ruins (like everything else) are 'socially constructed' is a trivial one; for any given society, the how and the why of that construction are both important research questions."[4] This provides an intriguing frame from which to consider ruins, as they exist narratively within the game and externally, with regard to what they might mean to players picking their way through them—moldering and haunting in terms of how nature has started to reclaim them. Further, a significant number of these missions occur in places with little light and no sunlight, especially as Abby and Ellie descend deeper into the ruined hospital. The larger question that looms after the two hospital missions is whether they can carve out lives that are free of rage, revenge, and alienation. The pervasive presence of ruins indicates a darker answer, one that speaks to permanently ruined lives.

ABBY'S MISSION: ARRIVING AT THE HOSPITAL VIA THE SKY BRIDGE

Abby and Lev travel to the hospital to retrieve a medical kit to increase the chances of Yara surviving her amputation procedure. Narratively, this mission provides Abby's character with more depth than it has had so far, underscoring her ability to act selflessly and compassionately. Abby starts at the aquarium, effectively her mission base for now. While the aquarium currently houses some of her friends, those bonds are tense and fraying, especially regarding Mel. Yara and Lev, neither of whom know Abby particularly well, have nonetheless bonded with her and support her emotionally, though they lack the information needed to fully judge her character. They see an Abby who will risk herself for Yara, while characters such as Mel see the ways in which Abby is an untrustworthy and selfish friend. Johnson writes, "As players witness Abby's relationships with her friends, it becomes clear that they have been worn down by the cost imposed on them by her pursuit of vengeance."[5] Notably, Lev accompanies Abby—although Abby has Lev stay behind once they reach the hospital, fearing for Lev's safety. Abby's concern for Lev, while not perhaps transforming her into a better person, demonstrates who she might have been had her father not been killed. It is also important to note that while Abby is given a companion for the mission, Ellie will make the journey alone, underscoring Ellie's increasing alienation from her loved ones.

Abby and Lev use the Seraphites' "sky bridge," scaffolding built between skyscrapers that allows for quick and undetected movement, a transversal method enabling the player to see Abby in a more vulnerable state. Lev comforts Abby, who is terrified of the height and precarious nature of the scaffolding, and quotes from Seraphite scripture: "Only when weak may I carry my true strength." Given the narrative arc of the game, these words fall tragically short of offering any real advice or truth but, in the moment, underscore both Abby's vulnerability and Lev believing there is decency in her. The symbolism of Abby walking high above the city but being emotionally weighted down and morally compromised is profound. While Abby's life was altered by her father's death, the story is careful not to posit this is the sole reason for her personality, just that it explains her desire for revenge. Importantly, the plan to use the sky bridge fails—Abby becomes dizzy and falls from the scaffolding and into an area unfamiliar to Lev. Abby detours to find Lev a gas mask to protect against spores and ensures it is secured and fitted properly before they continue. The care here belies what the player has witnessed through Ellie's perspective—a violent monster. Abby protects Lev again by going to the hospital alone—the WLF is at war with the Seraphites and will kill Lev on sight. No matter where the player goes, they are either part of, or witness to, violence, factions, and hate. Peace is tenuous and ruined by outside forces who will try to destroy it.

ABBY AND NORA

Whereas Ellie will have to fight her way past the WLF to enter the hospital, Abby at first is their ally. However, it becomes immediately clear that Abby's standing in the WLF is weakening—she is ordered back to see WLF leader Isaac and is cuffed and placed in a cell. The WLF seems to have little internal loyalty or freedom, which makes Nora's steadfast loyalty to Abby even more remarkable. The WLF's ideas of rebellion against federal and state governments considered ineffectual in dealing with the pandemic have given way to petty infighting, power grabs, and totalitarian rule. Nora frees Abby from the cell and allows her to continue farther into the hospital, even suggesting she head to the lowest floors for the best chance to find unpilfered supplies, thus potentially setting Nora in the path of Isaac's anger. While Nora appears to be both loyal and genuine, Abby does not act in kind. Presumably to ensure Nora's help, Abby lies about the use of the medical supplies—she claims they are for a wounded Owen rather than Yara (a Seraphite), given the animosity between the two factions.

Nora, when later confronted by Ellie, never wavers in her loyalty to Abby. Given Abby's inability to be honest, the question lingers if Abby would be loyal in turn. The dysfunctional nature of Abby and Nora's friendship represents both an example of an unhealthy relationship and loyalty as a failed concept. Keller argues,

> Materially and psychologically, a life shared with friends is less precarious. To share your thoughts and interests with a friend, and to take an active interest in hers, is to escape a little from your individuality, to reduce the intensity of being you; that, in part, is why it is good to share.[6]

The story consistently focuses on the ways in which rage and vengeance sunder friendships, even in a world where the type of shared life Keller discusses would be a boon. Abby's interactions with Nora end at this point but set up Nora's confrontation with Ellie.

ABBY AND THE RAT KING

Abby's journey through the hospital's lower levels culminates in her fight against the Rat King in the claustrophobic, dark corridors. While the fight plays out like a typical boss fight, the choice of the Rat King is important. Codirector Kurt Margenau says of the boss fight,

> We wanted Abby to have this really intense thing that she overcomes because she's kind of on this redemption mission to get the supplies for Yara's arm and so it seemed like the perfect place for the Rat King. . . . She's gone through all of these trials: overcoming her fear of heights climbing to the sky bridge, fighting through hordes of infected on the way down, and coming out the other side thinking the worst was over—only to be thrown right into this nightmare boss fight.[7]

What is of interest here is that the Rat King introduces a new type of infected, a horrific amalgamation of infected composed into one massive creature. Rat Kings in folklore and urban legend are large numbers of rats whose tails have tangled such that they form one massive biomass. The symbolism can be considered in four primary and overlapping ways directly related to the narrative: Abby and the WLF are the rats, collapsing under their own infighting; Abby and her friends are the rats whose friendship is fracturing; Abby and Ellie, whose lives are now bound together; or Ellie and her loved ones, trying to remain bound together yet being pushed away by Ellie. On a broader scale, the intertwined rats represent humanity, devolving into violence in the aftermath of the pandemic.

Although the rats in the folkloric Rat King are individuals, not one centrally controlled being, they are unable to escape the tangle of their knotted tails. Reilly notes, "It was believed that senior rats would sit on the tails of younger rats to make their nests and that, if the tails tangled, the elder rat would survive by having its meals delivered by the rodent world's proletariat."[8] While the Rat King calls to mind specific images of a monstrous and tangled group of rats and their symbolism ties to Abby and Ellie, the broader symbolism of rats also bears consideration. For many people, rats likely represent filth and are seen as vermin, the consequences of densely populated urban life. Wundram and Ruback note, "Rats continue to survive primarily because urban citizens provide ample food and habitat for the creatures they abhor, unwittingly creating a population of vermin that is both a symptom and a symbol of urban decay."[9] The intriguing question to consider with such potent symbolism lies in identifying what is being equated with the rats, something that the game's narrative leaves open for interpretation. At the broadest level, given that it is Abby who faces the monster, it is associated with her and her friends, who are now actively hunted by Ellie. However, it also comments on the cycle of vengeance and bloodshed ensnaring Abby's and Ellie's lives. The decay, then, is the rot that festers from the point at which Joel kills Abby's father all the way to the conclusion of this game, and an ending that offers little solace or hope.

Finally, as Abby is pursued by, and must determine how to defeat, the Rat King, the scene is bathed in red lights triggered by the alarm system. The initial context here is clearly that red signals danger. In Ellie's time in the hospital, red is used again but has more complexity there than it does here, but the association between red and Abby is important. Pastoureau notes that modern English frequently associates red with danger, as in "red alert" or "red zone."[10] That Abby is in such great peril at this point gives the player pause. For as strong physically as Abby is, and as competent a fighter, she spends most of this fight running and trying to get a shot or two in, as opposed to her dominating the battle. This is a tense and claustrophobic fight for the player. While Abby ultimately wins the fight, it is not a decisive victory, despite her combat skills, signaling the physical toll vengeance has taken. Afterward, Abby returns to the aquarium with the needed medical supplies.

RETURN TO THE AQUARIUM

While Abby has the supplies to help Yara, this comes at great cost. Abby is now a fugitive from the WLF. The mission concludes with further development of Abby as a more sympathetic figure. Abby and Lev spend time together while waiting for Yara to come out of her amputation surgery, and Abby, again, is kind and caring in a way that does not appear to be staged. However, the player witnessed Abby appear to be Nora's friend and yet be willing to manipulate her to get what she wants. The mission ends with Yara revealing to Abby that Lev is transgendered and that Lev has returned to see his mother at the Seraphites' base, an island just off the western coast of Seattle. It is clear that he will likely be killed because of his gender identity. Therefore, Abby and Yara set out to rescue Lev, and the chapter ends with a further narrative attempt at redeeming Abby's character. Yara even tells Abby, "You're a good person." This line is met with disbelief from Abby and raises a larger narrative question as Ellie's mission plays out. What does it mean to be a good person in this broken world? Is Nora good for her loyalty? Abby for avenging her father? Ellie for avenging Joel? By the game's end, none of these questions are fully answered, leaving individual players to make their own moral judgments.

ELLIE'S MISSION: ARRIVING AT THE HOSPITAL AND REACHING NORA

Ellie's mission to the hospital lacks Abby's humanitarian reasoning. Ellie indicates that her purpose is to find Nora to "get her to tell me where Abby is." The ominous implication is that Ellie will attempt to gain the information by any means. Structurally, Ellie's mission follows the same major beats as Abby's as she heads for the hospital. Ellie's trek to the hospital takes her back into the ruins of Seattle, a reminder of the loss of most of humanity and the world that once was. However, the tone of her mission changes once she reaches the hospital. The exterior of the hospital is well guarded by the WLF. It is possible to use stealth to get past some enemies or kill them quietly, and the decision to try to play in this way is up to the player, who may also choose to leave no one alive. However, the game offers no choice to nonlethally subdue and knock out enemies. They must be killed either by stealth or in open combat, or the player must successfully sneak past undetected. In areas that are densely populated with enemies, like the hospital exterior, sneaking unseen is difficult. The reality is that the game is a commentary about violence and revenge and how violence perpetuates itself. By the time Ellie fights her way inside the hospital, she seethes with rage, as she has consistently since Joel's death. For example, stealth killing a WLF member might end with her derisively saying "motherfucker" or "quiet" as she attacks or as their corpse falls to the floor. These responses are not unique to this sequence of the game but reveal a great deal about her tenuous grasp on her rage, given what she does to Nora.

While crawling through a vent, Ellie overhears an argument between Nora and a couple of unnamed WLF soldiers about Abby. Nora refuses to confess to letting Abby go, a foreshadowing of her initial refusal to give Abby's location to Ellie. Nora as a character does not have a large role overall in the narrative, but she perhaps best represents misplaced loyalty or someone blind to self-destructive behavior, a trait that comes more fully to bear by the end of Ellie's mission. In response to Nora's refusal to take responsibility for Abby's escape, one of the soldiers says: "I'm not going down for her, man," presumably about Nora and not Abby. This focuses the rest of the narrative sequence on the limits and price of loyalty, and at what point it might be reasonably broken.

FIRST CONFRONTATION WITH NORA AND CHASE SEQUENCE

Ellie drops down from the ceiling vents to confront Nora in a small, dingy room lit by an overly bright bare lightbulb. As Ellie says, "Don't scream," the harsh light casts Nora in a spotlight. Nora attempts to buy time by warning Ellie that shooting her will draw in more soldiers, but Ellie is unfazed, remarking, "You'll still be dead." This tense confrontation keeps the player, and Ellie, off-kilter. While Nora looks scared initially, and likely is, she quickly shows she is completely on Abby's side, sadistically so. She asks, "Do you still hear his screams?" and adds, "That little bitch got what he deserved." Regardless of the debate over the rightness of Abby's revenge, Ellie ends up a traumatized witness to her father figure being savagely beaten to death. In the first game, Joel kills Abby's father quickly by comparison—either by using the scalpel Abby's father uses to fend off Joel to stab him in the neck or via one of the other weapons in Joel's arsenal. The player can also choose to kill the other two medics in the operating theater as well, but either way, these are acts that Abby does not directly witness. Nora extends hatred of Joel to Ellie, mirroring Abby's attitude.

Nora begins a taunting chase through the maze-like hospital corridors in the hope that the WLF soldiers will kill Ellie. Ellie shouts, "You can't escape this," a statement with larger implications for everyone involved in or witness to Joel's murder. The taunting bears consideration here—it is unsurprising that Nora flees, but what she gets out of the taunting is unclear, perhaps even unfathomable. Keller considers, "When considering a particular belief, you may be unable to admit to yourself that you hold it partly because you are someone's friend, and that your friendship does not make the belief any more likely to be true, without thereby throwing the belief into question."[11] Nora, more fervently than Abby's remaining friends, never falters in her support of Abby's actions. Fletcher argues, "Loyalties generally lead people to suspend judgment about right and wrong. In a loving relationship or in the loyalty of group action, the loyal person defers to the judgment of the other, the person or group with whom one is bound in a relationship of loyalty."[12] This particularly reflects on Nora's actions here and explains them as more than just Nora having a streak of cruelty in her own right. Nora never seems to interrogate the nature of Abby's brutal murder of Joel, or her own—and the group's—participation. While this may classify Nora as having a loving relationship/loyal friendship with Abby in one sense, in another, the relationship is deeply dysfunctional. As was considered earlier, Abby had no qualms about lying to Nora about why she needed the medical supplies. In turn, Nora never applies a critical eye to all that has happened and blindly holds to the belief that Abby was right. She blindly exonerates both her friend and her own actions.

Ellie's pursuit of Nora farther into the hospital leads to completely dark areas illuminated only by her flashlight and then to an area illuminated by red emergency lighting, paralleling the area where Abby fights the Rat King. This red-lit area seethes with infected and is contaminated by spores, which also cause infection. Nora again flees, leaving other WLF soldiers to eliminate Ellie—for all her bravado, Nora runs at the first opportunity. The use of the color red again here bears consideration. In Abby's section, it more clearly delineated the danger from the boss fight with the Rat King. Here, the color's use takes on more nuance. There is danger, certainly. Yet there is also Ellie's ever-present rage and a foreshadowing of her torturing Nora. Regarding medieval Christian attitudes, Pastoureau argues "red was almost always associated with crimes of blood and the flames of hell" and that in medieval Europe, it was a primary part of an executioner's attire.[13] Ellie is in the role of both punisher and punished.

THE FINAL CONFRONTATION WITH NORA

Ellie finally catches up to a wounded and infected Nora in another red-lit room, a small and claustrophobic space, with Ellie clearly in the role of vengeful punisher. The scene composition is important: Nora is on the ground, prone, and Ellie—armed and agitated, moving from side to side, shifting her body weight, and pacing—looms over her. Nora, injured, infected, and dying, offers little fight beyond a clumsy attempt to attack Ellie with a metal pipe. Ellie takes the pipe, and her counterblow clearly breaks Nora's arm, a swift and brutal action foreshadowing the beating that follows. Ellie asks again for Abby's location, and Nora again refuses, seeming to reason she is dying anyway and unaware of how Ellie might cause her to suffer in the hours before the infection kills her. She reiterates "I'm not giving up my friend," which in turn asks the player to consider if Abby would do the same.

At this point, the camera pans completely away from Nora so only Ellie is visible. Ellie's face begins to contort with rage, and at this point, key (PC) or controller (console) input is required from the player to continue. The first action prompt causes Ellie to swing the metal pipe and the player hears the impact of the blow on flesh and bone as blood sprays toward Ellie and Nora's anguished, pained breathing. The player must input a command three separate times to initiate Ellie's blows before the screen goes black. Since this is not treated as a cutscene, the player must act—the swings must be triggered—for the game to continue. Schubert writes,

In this sense, even though the sequence involves a kind of interaction (players have to press a button), it still offers no practical agency and no meaningful narrative choices at all. Instead, it forces players to use Ellie to torture Nora while at the same time making them more complicit in the violence committed than if the cutscene had progressed without any player input.[14]

The point about the denial of agency is important to consider here, but so is the complex responses players may have to actively participating in the beating, which in turn continues the game's commentary on the nature of violence and its perpetuation. Some players may be so completely on Ellie's side that torturing Nora is considered justified. Others may, by this point, either see Abby as less monstrous or fear the escalation in Ellie's behavior.

The player may also consider the deliberate mirroring of Abby beating Joel to death and the scene composition. However, it is possible to skip the cutscenes where Joel is beaten to death, while the choice is taken away here. Both Ellie and Abby act out of a sense of moral rightness, dispensing justice for their loved ones. Certainly, the postpandemic world lacks any modicum of functional government and a fair or functional justice system. However, even with the option of justice from the system, the narrative indicates that Ellie and Abby would seek out their personal and violent revenge. Christensen notes, "Retributive justice itself demands the punishment of persons convicted of crimes, in proportion to the severity of the offense, because that is *what they deserve*."[15] In this scene, Ellie decides that Nora will get what she deserves for her role in Joel's death and for her refusal to reveal Abby's location. It is important to note that even if Nora had told Ellie how to find Abby right away, it seems doubtful that Ellie would have left her to turn from the infection. However, Ellie might have given her a clean death. The scene cuts to black here, with the player not seeing Nora's death and unaware if Ellie managed to get any information at all about Abby.

RETURN TO THE MOVIE THEATER AND DINA

Rather than ending with the beating, the sequence concludes with Ellie's return to the theater and to Dina, a relative safe haven. Jesse is also there, but the focal point is Dina's obvious love and concern for Ellie. Dina is a source of comfort, but even she will eventually leave Ellie for her own emotional well-being. Ellie shares what she learned about Abby's location, an indication that a tortured Nora eventually did reveal some information, but she is bloodied and clearly shaken. Notably, her eyes are unfocused, and she initially does not look Dina or Jesse in the eyes. She seems elsewhere and gaining the information seems to have been traded at far too high a cost, especially since Ellie cannot ascertain its accuracy. Dina, in the privacy of their room, undresses Ellie as if she were a child, with requests such as "arms up." As Dina lifts off Ellie's filthy T-shirt, the scene is shot to show Ellie's back—a brutal mess of scars and wounds, fresh and old. Ellie says, "I made her talk" and seems horrified—perhaps not exactly remorseful but further traumatized. The scene ends with Dina holding her and with the player left in the position of having, mechanically, been an accomplice in Nora's beating.

ETHICS, MORALITY, AND FINDING THE LIGHT

The hospital missions develop Abby and Ellie in ways that might defy players' dispositions toward them. Players returning to the series after playing the first game are likely predisposed to side with Ellie's quest for revenge—having followed Joel and Ellie and embodied both, as the two formed a father-daughter bond. The forced switch between Ellie and Abby in *Part II* forces the player to see parts of the narrative from Abby's perspective. Erb et al. studied player reactions to the switch, which ran the gamut between enjoying this mechanic and hating it. They note for some players

> that it seemed possible to keep the attachment to Ellie and Joel and still form a new attachment to the Abby character. It was clear that after playing the game the players had an attachment to both main PCs, Ellie and Abby, at the same time, and this conflicting attachment was one of the core meaningful experiences for which the players reported to appreciate the game for.[16]

By the end of the hospital missions, players witness Abby being capable of kindness and selflessness, and Ellie capable of unspeakable violence.

The two missions form a crucial backbone to the narrative's exploration of morality and the cost of revenge. Abby asks fellow WLF member and ex-boyfriend Owen, "What happened to us?"—a question with broad implications. He responds, "Maybe we stopped looking for the light," a play on the Fireflies' motto from the first game urging everyone to "look for the light." On the surface, such a slogan sounds inspirational but struggles to find traction in a world torn asunder by plague and terrorized by warring factions. The light does not just come to someone; it has to be sought—meaning effort has to be made, in the face of horror, to be moral, to be ethical, and to try to be a source of peace and solace rather than the perpetrator of more suffering.

No less important to the narrative events of the two hospital sequences is the central role of ruins. Lamarque writes, "One obvious value is that a ruin can serve as a memorial to the past, notably a memorial to the events that caused it to become a ruin."[17] The ruins of the hospital, the aquarium, and the movie theater represent all that the world, and the two central characters, have lost. Johnson considers that trauma exists everywhere across both of the games, even to the landscape itself:

> While communities such as Jackson have made great strides toward the creation of peaceful and relatively safe havens, the trauma of the world can be seen all around: the zombie-like "infected" are found nearly everywhere, the landscapes are littered with the skeletons of dead vehicles and the shells of destroyed or dilapidated buildings, and unknown others are often viewed with suspicion.[18]

Abby and Ellie both move into increasingly dark and claustrophobic spaces within the hospital ruins and, excepting Abby's location of a medical kit, find only danger, violence, and suffering.

By the end of the game, Ellie's life is in shambles, and Abby is not much better off, although she still has Lev's companionship. Yet the narrative refuses to reduce its complex story down to an uncomplicated moral choice of one of them or both being wrong. Johnson says of the resolution of Ellie's story in *Part II*, "An action cue allows the player to attempt to play the guitar—an act which Ellie has done a few times throughout the game, but which is now inhibited by the loss of a couple fingers from her final fight with Abby."[19] The brutal final fight between Abby and Ellie happens outside, in the water, the latter of which may typically be associated with healing or rebirth rather than inside of a ruin. While Ellie backs down and does not kill Abby, even after instigating their final fight by threatening to kill Lev, the outside setting would seem to symbolize no peace for either of them. Abby and Lev escape, sailing into an unknown future. While Ellie appears to have somewhat made peace with the loss of Joel—she has, after all, spared both Abby and Lev and seems to have abandoned pursuing them—it has come at the cost of a chance at family and community, as Dina, understandably, has decided to leave Ellie. The game ends on a note of ruined lives.

NOTES

1. Osgood, "Revenge," 4.
2. Brenner, *Desperate*, 15.
3. Boym, *The Future*, 29.
4. Devecka, *Broken*, 3.
5. Johnson, "Go," 8.
6. Keller, *The Limits*, 38.
7. Beckwith, "*The Last*."
8. Reilly, "Almost."
9. Wundram and Ruback, "Urban," 212.

10. Pastoureau, *Red*, 182.
11. Keller, *The Limits*, 43.
12. Fletcher, *Loyalty*, 36.
13. Pastoureau, *Red*, 98, 100.
14. Schubert, "Playing," 7.
15. Christensen, *Revenge*, 22.
16. Erb et al., "Player-Character," 7.
17. Lamarque, "Values," 87.
18. Johnson, "Go," 2.
19. Johnson, "Go," 11.

BIBLIOGRAPHY

Beckwith, Michael. "*The Last of Us 2* Explains Origins of the Rat King." Game Rant, October 17, 2020, https://gamerant.com/last-of-us-2-rat-king-origins/.

Boym, Svetlana. *The Future of Nostalgia*. New York: Basic Books, 2001.

Brenner, Marie. *The Desperate Hours: One Hospital's Fight to Save a City on the Pandemic's Front Lines*. New York: Flatiron Books, 2022.

Christensen, Kit R. *Revenge and Social Conflict*. Cambridge, UK: Cambridge University Press, 2016.

Devecka, Martin. *Broken Cities: A Historical Sociology of Ruins*. Baltimore, MD: John Hopkins Press, 2020.

Erb, Valerie, Seyeon Lee, and Yuong Yim Doh. "Player–Character Relationship and Game Satisfaction in Narrative Game: Focus on Player Experience of Character Switch in *The Last of Us Part II*." *Frontiers in Psychology* 12 (2021): 1–11, https://doi.org/10.3389/fpsyg.2021.709926.

Fletcher, George P. *Loyalty: An Essay on the Morality of Relationships*. Oxford, UK: Oxford University Press, 1995.

Johnson, Stephen Michael. "'Go. Just Take Him': PTSD and the Player–Character Relationship in *The Last of Us Part II*." *Games and Culture*, November 14, 2022, https://doi.org/10.1177/15554120221139216.

Keller Simon. *The Limits of Loyalty*. Cambridge, UK: Cambridge University Press, 2007.

Lamarque, Peter. "The Values of Ruins and Depictions of Ruins." In *Philosophical Perspectives on Ruins, Monuments, and Memorials*, edited by Jeanette Bicknell, Jennifer Judkins, and Carolyn Korsmeyer. New York: Routledge, 2019.

The Last of Us. Director Neil Druckmann and Bruce Straley. Narrative Director Neil Druckman. Naughty Dog for Sony Interactive Entertainment, 2013. PlayStation 4.

The Last of Us Part II. Director Neil Druckmann, Anthony Newman, and Kurt Margenau. Narrative Directors Neil Druckmann and Halley Gross. Naughty Dog for Sony Interactive Entertainment, 2020. PlayStation 5.

Osgood, Jeffrey M. "Is Revenge about Retributive Justice, Deterring Harm, or Both?" *Social and Personality Psychology Compass* 11, no. 1 (2017): 1–15.

Pastoureau, Michel. *Red: The History of a Color*. Translated by Jody Gladding. Princeton, NJ: Princeton University Press, 2016.

Reilly, Lucas. "An (Almost) Comprehensive History of Rat Kings." Mental Floss, October 24, 2017, https://www.mentalfloss.com/article/506504/almost-comprehensive-history-rat-kings.

Schubert, Stefan. "Playing as/against Violent Women: Imagining Gender in the Post-apocalyptic Landscape of *The Last of Us Part II*." *Gender Forum* 80 (2021): 1–15, https://www.proquest.com/scholarly-journals/playing-as-against-violent-women-imagining-gender/docview/2765805219/se-2.

Wundram, Jane, and R. Barry Ruback. "Urban Rats: Symbol, Symptom, and Symbiosis." *Human Organization* 45.3 (1986): 212–219.

Chapter 3

The Theologies of Fyodor Dostoevsky and Albert Schweitzer in Dialogue with the Moral Landscape of *The Last of Us*

David K. Goodin

The Last of Us (*TLOU*) franchise confronts us with a dystopian end to civilization in a world ravaged by a cataclysmic pandemic, leaving an even bleaker moral landscape for survivors. Culture has been reduced to familial and tribal loyalties at best, Hobbesian survival at its basest—or so it may seem. Subtle character arcs are still discernible, hinting that certain survivors are capable of moving beyond mere self-interest. When cast in an Aristotelian light, both Joel and Abby grow to embrace στοργή (*storgé*), compassion for the vulnerable, as revealed in Joel's awakening to parental love for Ellie, and Abby in turn for Lev and Yara—all of whom were strangers to one another, and in Abby's situation, actually enemies. This is where the storyline approaches, albeit hesitantly and still quite distantly, the religious ideal of biblical ἀγάπη (*agápē*) demanded by Christ when He commanded His followers to love their enemies (Matthew 5:44). Yet is such a dramatic outcome even imaginable in such a dark and menacing world as the one presented in *TLOU*?

There are several interrelated questions here. This first involves how an ethical awakening could be envisioned for Ellie and Abby. The second is whether it would be in any way believable to the fans, some of whom have come to crave the nihilistic brutality. Then there is a theological question that often goes unasked, concerning whether the altruistic ethics prescribed by Jesus of Nazareth in the New Testament are in any way achievable in the real world. There is the disturbing possibility that they were intended by the Gospel writers as hyperbolic platitudes meant to accentuate the ultimate victimhood of Jesus, demonstrating His innocence and otherworldliness in a brazen defiance (or naiveté) of their manifest incredulity. If so, biblical *agape* remains an impossible standard for fallen humanity as a social ideal: humanity has, and will always, fall short of Christ's commands. His words are then not ethics in a social sense, but are reserved exclusively for the rare saint-martyrs of Church history. With respect to society at large, the life, words, and self-sacrificial example of Christ instead are meant to serve as indictments for those who cannot do the same.

This disturbing possibility was presented by a devastatingly insightful theological writer from the Orthodox East, Fyodor Dostoevsky (1821–1881).[1] More on him in a moment. But first, again, let me reiterate that realism is the issue here, a question for both the possible moral awakenings in *TLOU* franchise, as well as with the very idea of wanting or hoping for anyone, even in fiction, to have such an awakening based on the cultural narratives held by the fan base. Stated another way, being "realistic" is a statement concerning acceptable possibilities based on history and expectations; "subverting expectations" being parody and variations upon those preestablished norms. The truly unique and unexpected is a rare thing indeed. Assuming, then, that this franchise will evolve within these narrative parameters, and that religion has shaped the cultural landscape of both the writers and fan base, Dostoevsky's religious insights, I suggest, may be particularly valuable—especially since, as we shall see, he found a way to transform the cruelties of this fallen world into a radical form of altruistic love inspired by that self-same unreasonable Christ.

This alone, however, fails to fully address the realism question since Dostoevsky, after all, is a fiction writer. This is why this chapter will also turn to the theologian Albert Schweitzer (1875–1965). He sought a way to reaffirm Jesus' ethic of love even in face of world wars. The horrors of World War I awakened him to the urgent need to save civilization itself from complete moral collapse. Schweitzer denounced Hitler and Nazism in a public speech in Frankfurt on March 22, 1932 (less than a year before Hitler would be sworn into power as Chancellor), but failed to prevent his rise to power.[2] Yet Schweitzer's postwar intervention in Einstein's and Oppenheimer's campaign against nuclear proliferation proved decisive for the passage of the worldwide Partial Test Ban Treaty of 1963, a modest but important step towards a higher humanity, and away from barbaric warmongering.[3] His life's work sought nothing less than the realization of Jesus' ethics as a social reality and as the specific remedy for the crises in civilization plaguing our world. And while a final victory remained out of reach, Schweitzer did inspire an ethic of altruism that continues to change lives today, including through the Doctors Without Borders humanitarian organization.[4]

These two figures, Dostoevsky from the Orthodox East and Schweitzer from the Protestant West, will provide the foils between which the theological landscape in *TLOU* will be surveyed. The aim will be twofold. One will be to explore possible narrative developments for the future of the franchise. The second will in turn cast a critical light on theology itself, with the perennial question of whether the ethics of Jesus actually make sense anymore, if they ever did. After all, who actually turns the cheek, volunteering to be struck again, or gives thieves more than they demanded in the first place? No, rather, it is the "eye for an eye" vindictive justice that Jesus specifically forbids in Matthew 5:38–40 that is showcased in *TLOU*. Examining the religious dimensions of this game and miniseries is all the more intriguing when our gaze is directed toward the fan base, and wonder what it is *they* enjoy most.

THE LAST OF US

Let's ponder the franchise title, *The Last of Us*. The "us" is a reference to collective identity as society and our common humanity, as well as our social responsibility to the same; the "last" indicating that this sense of collectiveness is dying out in the world, leaving only Hobbesian self-interest in its wake. The story begins with Joel Miller finding only inhumanity in a soldier ordered to execute him and his daughter, being saved by his brother with a brutal headshot dispatching the would-be executioner. But it was too late to save his daughter, Sarah. In the aftermath, he becomes a shell-of-a-man living first as an opportunistic bandit preying upon the gullibility of strangers before killing them for his own survival. Eventually shreds of humanity return as he partners with Theresa "Tess" Servopoulos, becoming smugglers of contraband in the remnant cities. Joel is then contracted to smuggle Ellie Williams to a Firefly compound. The plan goes awry, and Tess makes Joel promise to get Ellie to another Firefly compound in Wyoming, which he only agrees to because it's her dying wish. A strong familial protectiveness begins to take over, much to his resistance against it. Yet, this parental type of love will lead him to kill the very doctor searching to find a medical treatment that could save countless lives. If anything, the murder represents Joel's rejection of the utilitarian logic in immunizing everyone from the parasitic fungal infection at the cost of only a single life. But that life was not ethical abstraction; she was a little girl important to his own reawakening humanity after the death of Sarah.

Joel's death is likewise ethically opaque. Although he saves Abby Anderson, who unbeknownst to him is the daughter of the surgeon he murdered, and who is out for revenge, she betrays his trust with a shotgun blast to the leg. Joel's last words to Abby, sensing this was some kind of personal revenge quest, are: "Why don't you say whatever speech you got rehearsed and get this over with." His tone is a resigned disgust and contempt, nothing more. Whatever revelations he may have had about himself, the world, or of having lived a life motivated by revenge are unstated, if he had any at all at the end. Abby ignores Ellie's pleas for mercy before killing Joel before her eyes. This then sets off another quest for revenge, this time for Ellie.

In the interim, the game forces us to experience this world from Abby's perspective, a character some fans loathe for killing a beloved protagonist. This radical disruption of the antagonist/protagonist divide is a brilliant narrative device, since it complicates simplistic portrayals of any hero/anti-hero/villain to become an ethical morass of moral relativism on one side, and the tragedy of personal truths providing supposed moral clarity on the other. The narrative intent of upsetting emotional investments in certain characters appears intentional, but with respect to the overall narrative aims of the franchise (if any) are yet uncertain. If there is some final message for this franchise, such as love triumphing over the need for revenge, or something more theological about the human condition and destiny, we will have to wait to see.

That there may be a theological theme in the works is evidenced by certain moral transformations caused by a love in the storyline of Abby. She finds herself in alliance with enemies, Yara and Lev. The unlikely alliance comes about, in part, because of a dream she has about the Firefly hospital the night her father was killed by Joel, but now she sees the dead bodies of Yara and Lev hanging dead: she awakes resolved to save those kids. Presumably, the guilt of not having been there to protect her father has been psychologically transferred to these vulnerable strangers. Later, after fighting to get the medical supplies to save Yara, she has a new dream. She's back at the hospital but there are no alarms blaring; she sees her father, who is smiling. The new alliance will eventually lead to a confrontation with Isaac and the WLF where she defends the children with her life, only being saved by Yara's surprise intervention, distracting the soldiers by killing Isaac so that Lev and Abby can escape. She later reassures Lev, "Hey! You're my people." Abby's loyalties have shifted for unknown reasons, perhaps it is merely shared struggle. Even so, she was prepared to die to protect her former enemies, signaling a subtle change.

Meanwhile, Ellie has been tracking Abby, killing her friends including Owen and the pregnant Mel. Abby in retaliation finds her hideout at the Pinnacle Theater and confronts Ellie, who tells her that she knows why she killed Joel. Abby rebukes her that she had let Tommy and Ellie live, and she "wasted it" to stalk her and kill her friends. Abby dominates the subsequent fight, and is ready to kill an unconscious Dina by coldly cutting her throat while Ellie watches helplessly. But Lev stops her with a word, "Don't."

Moved by the plea, Abby leaves with a warning to Ellie, "Don't ever let me see you again." But she will, in a final confrontation.

Ellie finds and frees Abby from a slow, torturous death, a kind of crucifixion tied to poles and exposed to the elements. It was not altruism, but just to force a final confrontation. Abby refuses to fight until Ellie threatens the unconscious Lev with a knife. It is a brutal fight that will see Ellie's hand maimed—two fingers partially bitten-off by Abby. Yet Ellie dominates, drowning Abby underwater with an unyielding grasp around her throat. She only relents after a memory of Joel playing guitar comes to interrupt her rage. Ellie tells Abby to escape with the unconscious Lev as she grieves alone. Later, we see Ellie trying to play Joel's guitar; her maimed hand now incapable of fully recreating the chords, further isolating those memories of fatherly closeness. She has a flashback to a fight with Joel, where she accused him of preventing her from having a life that mattered. But she expresses a desire to try to forgive him nonetheless. Ellie walks alone into the horizon, leaving the guitar behind. Her fate will not be known until part III. But a foreshadowing is hinted at in the last close-up shot of the moth inlay in the guitar fretboard, a symbol of transformation.

DOSTOEVSKY'S COUNTERNARRATIVE

There is a warning in the novel, *The Brothers Karamazov* (1880), often paraphrased as: "If there is no God then everything is possible."[5] It concerns morality and what, if anything, keeps people from degenerating into a Hobbesian war of all against all. *TLOU* certainly mirrors such a godless world; even tribal loyalties are cast aside in personal vendettas, and survival is assured only through pitiless barbarity. The only humanity that remains is found in immediate social connections, often coming through the practical necessity of cooperative survival. Dostoevsky is well familiar with such a moral landscape, having been subjected to a Tsarist gulag, a mock execution, a Siberian exile, as well as the capricious death of his child to an epidemic (tuberculosis in his case). In the background of his novels are also the senseless deaths of the Crimean War where thousands died in a purported holy war, but in actuality was merely a geopolitical power-grab by the Tsar. Dostoevsky experienced, and presents in his novels, a morally broken world where the existence of God increasingly becomes incredulous. And yet he finds Christ in this forsaken world in those willing to forgive the unforgivable. This makes his theological understandings a well-matched foil through which to consider *TLOU* and its possible character arcs.

Friedrich Nietzsche referred to Dostoevsky as the only psychologist of human nature that he ever admired,[6] evidently for both his bleak "тоска" (existential anguish and despair) as well as overcoming it through personal triumphalism. Something similar seems to motivate Ellie, who rages at Joel for denying her the chance to have a "life of meaning" in being sacrificed for others, since mere existence cannot be seen as a "good unto itself" in such a pointless world of unending pandemic and revenge-inspired brutality.

Just as the cordyceps pandemic spreads through often-dormant spores becoming active again once disturbed afresh, so too the human plague of unending revenge spreads for want of forgiveness. Philanthropic love is the only antidote, yet one refused by all. This is the very concept of hell for Dostoevsky, who crafts an image of embittered soul-destroying hatred that is shockingly prescient with respect to *TLOU* (Alyosha in *The Brothers Karamazov*):

> Oh, there are some who remain proud and fierce even in hell, in spite of their certain knowledge and contemplation of the absolute truth; there are some fearful ones who have given themselves over to Satan and his proud spirit entirely. For such, hell is voluntary and ever consuming; they are tortured by their own choice. For they have cursed themselves, cursing God and life. They live upon their vindictive pride like a starving man in the desert sucking blood out of his own body. But they are never satisfied, and they refuse forgiveness, they curse God Who calls them. They cannot behold the living God without hatred, and they cry out that the God of life should be annihilated, that God should destroy Himself and His own creation. And they will burn in the fire of their own wrath for ever and yearn for death and annihilation. But they will not attain to death.[7]

It is an image of a voluntaristic "living hell" of those surviving through hatred and revenge, and one that fits many in *TLOU* franchise, including Ellie and Abby.

In Dostoevsky's vision of unforgiveness, another must be juxtaposed over it, presented later in the novel. Alyosha tells of a wicked woman named Grushenka who was cast into hell for her evil deeds. It was then her guardian angel rose to her defense before the dread judgment seat of Christ, saying that she once pulled a wild onion (scallion) from her garden and gave it to a beggar at her gate. It was but one small act of charity in an otherwise miserable life of wickedness. But God considered what the simple act meant to the beggar. He told the angel to take the onion and extend it to her on the lake of fire, so that she can be pulled to paradise. The angel rushed to her rescue, holding out the onion stalk like a lifeline. The woman reached out, taking hold of it. She was soon being raised out of the lake of fire by the angel. All the other sinners in the lake saw what was happening; they grabbed hold of her legs as she began the rise, and soon all the forsaken in hell were being rescued, thanks to this one act of charity given to a beggar. But the woman kicked at them with her feet: "I'm to be pulled out, not you. It's my onion, not yours[!]."⁸ When she said this, the onion stalk broke, and all fell back into hell forever.

It is a profound meditation on human wickedness and the potentially world-transforming power of love and forgiveness. In an earlier novel, *The Idiot* (1869), Dostoevsky presents forgiveness as a Christ-like transformative force that erases cynicism in all those who witness it.

> I ought to tell you that I never in my life met a man anything like him for noble simplicity of mind and for boundless trustfulness. I guessed that anyone who liked could deceive him, and that he would immediately forgive anyone who did deceive him; and it was for this that I grew to love him.⁹

Perhaps Ellie's decision to let Abby (and Lev) live will become that moral act that transforms them in time, and thereby saves countless others in the future—or maybe the cruelty of revenge will reassert itself, kicking away any "olive branch" of peace just to cast everyone back into the same hell with them. We will have to wait to see.

The key to any such turn back toward higher humanity may reside, not with Ellie alone, but with her "double" Abby,¹⁰ who now too is orphaned with only hatred (or so it may seem) keeping her alive. Her possible path to redemption is also potentially presaged by Dostoevsky. Notably, we are shown a flashback of her father, Gerald "Jerry" Anderson. He is inexplicably struggling to save a zebra trapped in barbed wire, a nonsensical act of kindness in a dystopian world, and for a dumb animal no less. Yet we witness the freed zebra reuniting with her colt in an idyllic scene of motherly love, freedom, and peace. It gives Abby an image of a possible different future where kindness could become the norm again.

The flashback is an intentional inclusion. Throughout the franchise, animals are seen as a symbol of order and harmony, peace and gentleness—from Ellie's giraffes, to seals at the aquarium, monkeys at the University of Colorado, to the fireflies that are the very symbol of FEDRA resistance. They are obviously more than scenery; they play a narrative element important to the storytelling. Perhaps this will be the opening to a higher spirituality, just as Dostoevsky wrote:

> Brothers, have no fear of men's sin. Love a man even in his sin, for that is the semblance of Divine Love and is the highest love on earth. Love all God's creation, the whole and every grain of sand in it. Love every leaf, every ray of God's light. Love the animals, love the plants, love everything. If you love everything, you will perceive the divine mystery in things. Once you perceive it, you will begin to comprehend it better every day. And you will come at last to love the whole world with an all-embracing love. Love the animals: God has given them the rudiments of thought and joy untroubled. Do not trouble it,

don't harass them, don't deprive them of their happiness, don't work against God's intent.¹¹

Only then, Dostoevsky believed, humanity could find itself again, for "beauty saves the world."¹² It is a message, as we will see, echoed by Schweitzer.

REVERENCE FOR LIFE

One theologian who understood the sermons of Jesus as real-world ethics was the Alsatian polymath, Schweitzer. A medical doctor, pastor, philosopher, musician, and more, Schweitzer presented biblical ἀγάπη as the only possible solution to the crisis in civilization after the outbreak of World War I. Schweitzer witnessed his two native lands, France and Germany, wage a savage conflict spanning the globe, not once, but twice. Against this nihilistic ethos of "kill or be killed," Schweitzer offered a counter-narrative: "The ethic of Reverence for Life is the ethic of love widened into universality; it is the ethic of Jesus, now recognized as a logical consequence of thought."¹³ He sought to personify this biblical ethic through the care of lepers, the sick, and the dying in an African rain forest for over fifty years—a selfless act intended to show war-ravaged humanity where our priorities must lay. His life of selfless devotion would be recognized in the Nobel Peace Prize of 1952. And for a brief time, he did help the world remind itself of its higher humanity.

Abby's father, Jerry, in certain ways is like a Schweitzer; he too had to balance utopian ideals against practical necessity and utilitarian logic. For Jerry, it came down to the sacrifice of one child in order to create a vaccine that could save countless millions, and maybe even civilization itself—an easy utilitarian calculus, yet a difficult moral choice since he had to become a murderer to do so. Curiously, despite his Hippocratic Oath, he was prepared to kill the child. Maybe it was apocalyptic desperation; maybe he lost faith in medical idealism. We are not told why. Regardless, Schweitzer's Reverence for Life ethic stands opposed to such utilitarian logic; he steadfastly clung to Jesus' ethic of love regardless of the circumstance.

Schweitzer recounted the evils of child murder in the name of a supposed "greater good" for society. At this time in history, many European and North American nations promoted eugenics to end the supposed suffering of those deemed as having "lives not worth living" because of congenital birth defects and mental handicaps. Schweitzer tells of a fellow physician in Europe who came to him secretly about a "feebleminded child" who had contracted diphtheria.¹⁴ The physician was tormented with the temptation to withhold treatment in order to allow the disease to kill the child, thus ending her supposedly worthless life. The psychological pressure from the medical community was immense "to do the right thing" in allowing the child to die, and it troubled him greatly. "I fought with myself," he said to Schweitzer, "and in the end, [the] reverence for life [theology] triumphed. The child was saved [by medicine], and I bear the responsibility."[15] The physician, Schweitzer tells us, did the right and moral thing by refusing to obey the perverse utilitarian logic justifying child murder.

Schweitzer's Reverence for Life theology is unapologetically deontological—which is to say, it supports an absolute ethic that refuses to make concessions to mitigating circumstances or to allow for special exceptions. Regardless of the situation, Schweitzer points a finger at us and charges that we are responsible for the lives around us. This is the whole aim of his theology:

> An absolute ethic calls for the creating of perfection [of our moral selves] in this life. It cannot be achieved; but that fact does not really matter. In this sense reverence for life is an absolute ethic. It does not lay down specific rules for each possible situation. It simply tells us that we are responsible for the lives about us.[16]

The ethical responsibility upon humankind extends to any and all sentient life, animals included. Schweitzer even operated a veterinary clinic in the middle of an African rainforest for sick, injured, and orphaned wild animals—an activity that perplexed his patients and critics. One cannot help but to recall here Jerry rescuing the zebra caught in barbed wire.

All that said, it is permissible in Schweitzer's system to perform ethical trade-offs, such as he did in his own practice as a surgeon, such as killing blood parasites to save patients, or killing river fish to feed animals at his veterinary clinic. The only guidance is that he always favored higher sentience over lower in such trade-offs: humans over animals, animals over insects, and so forth. Even so, he admonishes his readers that even dying worms on a sun-baked sidewalk should elicit our pity[17] and that not one flower should be plucked for idle amusement,[18] for "is it not possible that they feel and are sensitive even if we cannot demonstrate it?"[19] Schweitzer demands that people bring a conscious awareness of the effect of their actions on each and every living being—and take that "debt" (*Schuld*) awareness and turn it into a deep and sincere intention to repay those trade-offs through good actions aimed at promoting life in others.[20] Reverence for Life asks for perfection but only expects constant and earnest striving towards this end. This is its power. Falling short of these ideals has great mystical significance because compassion is stronger than love. The truth is love can become brokenhearted. Compassion already is. When a person learns the virtue of sincerity, which includes compassion for the imperfect self, such failures are given an avenue for redemption through the other. Altruism brings the two separate lives together where the true essence of humanity is rediscovered, and healing is found. One's life can then move on with renewed determination and deepened sincerity. Reverence for Life draws its strength from embracing these truths as a lived and very personal experience. Only then, Schweitzer believed, can a real and sustaining hope for civilization be carried forward for a better future.

RIDICULOUS DREAMS

Dreams and nightmares are an important storytelling element in *TLOU*. Particularly for Abby, the dreamworld is a chance to reconnect with her father, apparently finding his smiling approval for saving the lives of Lev and Yara. It appears to be a source of moral guidance for her, encouraging her to grow beyond callousness and cruelty. We find this same message in Dostoevsky.

In his *The Dream of a Ridiculous Man* (1877), we encounter a man who is seen as ridiculous for the absurdity of offering kindness in a cruel, uncaring world after a surprising moral transformation. Early in the story, the weight of Russian "тоска" had become unbearable, and so he makes a decision to end it all, matter-of-factly and without remorse:

> It was a gloomy evening, one of the gloomiest possible evenings. I was going home at about eleven o'clock, and I remember that I thought that the evening could not be gloomier. Even physically. Rain had been falling all day, and it had been a cold, gloomy, almost menacing rain, with, I remember, an unmistakable spite against mankind. . . . The sky was horribly dark, but one could distinctly see tattered clouds, and between them fathomless black patches. Suddenly I noticed in one of these patches a star, and began watching it intently. That was because that star had given me an idea: I decided to kill myself that night.[21]

The bleakness of the world had made even his own existence pointless, and so he resolved to shoot himself with a revolver that night. Then the unexpected happened:

> And just as I was looking at the sky, this little girl took me by the elbow. The street was empty, and there was scarcely anyone to be seen. A cabman was sleeping in the distance in his cab. It was a child of eight with a kerchief on her head, wearing nothing but a wretched little dress all soaked with rain, but I noticed her wet broken shoes and I recall them now. They caught my eye particularly. She suddenly pulled me by the elbow and called me. She was not weeping but was spasmodically crying out some words which she could not

utter properly, because she was shivering and shuddering all over. She was in terror about something, and kept crying, "Mammy, mammy!" I turned facing her, I did not say a word and went on; but she ran, pulling at me, and there was that note in her voice which in frightened children means despair. I know that sound. Though she did not articulate the words, I understood that her mother was dying, or that something of the sort was happening to them, and that she had run out to call someone, to find something to help her mother. I did not go with her; on the contrary, I had an impulse to drive her away.[22]

Ignoring her, he returns to his apartment, resolved to end it all. But he falls asleep in an armchair while contemplating why it was that he had felt nothing for the little girl. As a younger man, he would have, but now he had grown too bitter and cynical. He then begins to dream.

At first, he sees himself dead, buried, yet conscious and tormented by the dripping of water on his eyelids falling inside the coffin. He spitefully prays to God that if this is revenge for his suicide, then "let me tell you that no torture could ever equal the contempt" that he feels for having lived in such a godforsaken world.[23] Apparently, in response, he is broken free from the grave and transported to a new world, an Edenic one of innocence and peace, that is orbiting the same star he had glimpsed through the clouds the night he decided to kill himself.

This other Earth was perfect in every way, and people likewise. "Their faces were radiant with the light of reason and fullness of a serenity that comes of perfect understanding."[24] He is adopted by them, and treated to every kindness. And yet, in the end, he ends up corrupting them all with his cynicism, bitterness, and cruelty—just with his mere presence: it infects them. Worst of all was his isolationism and selfish individualism. "All became so jealous of the rights of their own personality that they did their very utmost to curtail and destroy them in others."[25] Soon wars arose, and with them, death, suicide, and all forms of human-caused suffering. He had become a messiah of тоска, contaminating them with his own wretched cruelty. He awoke, horrified and ashamed that he was the cause of it all. He resolves to become a tireless witness of love and peace in the real world, beginning with finding that little girl he scorned the day before.

FINAL REMARKS

We do not yet know where *TLOU* franchise will go with its Abby and Ellie storylines. Perhaps all that will be attempted is a live-and-let-live détente where both forgo further revenge. Everything else will remain the same in an unchanging world of brutality; respite only coming from emotional exhaustion and unhealed grief stopping the cycle from further escalation. Another consideration is that, for the sake of compelling gameplay, the story-writers might not want to do anything more than that since, after all, it is next generation "mortal combat" for third-person shooters. Can we expect Dostoevsky-level moral awakenings in playable characters? Cut-scenes may be just "flavor text" in a world without meaning other than boss fights. This is not high art after all. It's a game. Perhaps that is all it will try to be. We will have to wait to see.

But now that HBO has produced the show's first season with season 2 on the way, there is a chance that true character arcs will be attempted for the sake of compelling drama. Most of the viewing audience, I expect, will want an end to the brutality and the rebirth of civilization, however meagerly expressed, by the end of the show—otherwise, what was the point of investing one's time in such overwhelming bleakness?[26]

This still leaves the larger theological questions regarding Hobbesian human nature and higher humanity, and what if anything the show's setting says about the outlook of the fans on the state of the real world. The unstated premise of the *TLOU* franchise is that civilization is just a lie hiding animalistic brutality lurking beneath the surface, and needing only an excuse to express itself wantonly upon others. If this accurately describes the fan base, in whole or in part, it says a lot about the *zeitgeist* of our times. Has the dream of higher humanity completely died out already in this new century? The final note from the mysterious character Ish suggests otherwise. In it, Ish[27] declares, "I have too much faith in humanity. I've seen that we're still capable of good. We can make it. I have to stay strong—for her [Susan, a character Ish is protecting]."

Schweitzer was a compelling visionary who helped rescue the twentieth century from a similar ethical morass, and someone who profoundly changed the world for the better with his Christian conviction of the power of biblical *agape*. In the wake of World War I, he denounced Hitler in a brazen public speech, then set out to demonstrate true humanity in the care of those the Nazis considered less than human. For Schweitzer, the altruism of Jesus was the very prescription that the war-ravaged humanity needed to save itself, and he gave hope to the world that humanity still had goodness within itself. He would be awarded a Nobel Peace Prize in 1952 as a result of fifty years of selfless humanitarian service to the sick, suffering, and leprous. But now his life has mostly faded from public memory, and the world is once again spiraling toward nihilism.[28] So too the ethics of Christianity, to love one's enemy and to do good to those who spitefully use and abuse you (Matthew 5:44), are increasingly seen as incredulous by a viewing public who prefer to watch dystopian revenge dramas set in an apocalyptic hellscape as entertainment. Where is our higher humanity now?

This all points back to the question of whether Christianity makes sense anymore in the face of such pervasive cynicism, and in turn whether a Christian-inspired resolution for the characters would even be accepted by the fans for *TLOU* franchise. My chapter has been aimed, in part, at *TLOU* reception among a largely Christian and post-Christian gamer community and audience—what drives their interest, and what that in turns says about our contemporary *zeitgeist*. Our popular culture, it seems to me, is such that audiences only seem to find morally ambiguous characters as believable—a symptom, perhaps, of a spiritual malaise that impacts every aspect of modern life. We turn to apocalyptic zombie shows and video games to relieve the unease with our seemingly godless and futureless lives. Yet this is the same moral morass (that is, in its late nineteenth-century Russian guise) where Dostoevsky brought forth an absurdist Christ-like love for the suffering world as an antidote, a message that has resonated with countless readers since then. Perhaps this is where the franchise needs to go. Before we can personify altruism in reality like Schweitzer once did, we have to be inspired by it first in our popular media.

NOTES

1. I am referring to the parable of the Grand Inquisitor in *The Brothers Karamazov* (1880) as told by the character Ivan Karamazov to his younger brother, Alyosha. He tells him that Jesus Christ once returned to the world during the height of the Spanish Inquisition. The gathered crowds marvel at the sight, and when Jesus begins to heal the sick and raise the dead, it awakens joy and newfound hope in all. This is soon noticed by the Grand Inquisitor, who immediately arrests and imprisons Jesus. Under interrogation, the Inquisitor reveals the reason why. The Inquisitor begins with a ruling on the human condition. "Man is constituted as a mutineer; can mutineers ever be happy?" (289). The Inquisitor then lays out his case against Christ. Humankind, he recounts, rebelled in Eden, and people have not improved over the generations. "Look around you and judge, now that fifteen centuries have passed [since the Incarnation], take a glance at them: which of them have you borne up to yourself? Upon my word, man is created weaker and more base than you supposed! Can he, can he perform the deeds of which you are capable?" (294). He then accuses Jesus of not caring about the commoner, only the exceptional saint that distinguishes him or herself from the multitudes. "Or are the only ones you care about the tens of thousands of the great and the strong, while the remaining millions, numerous as the grains of sand in the sea, weak, but loving you, must serve as mere raw material for the great and the strong?" (291). The Inquisitor lays the blame for all these crimes at the feet of Jesus. He had made humanity both free and mutinous, and then expected them to live up to the impossibly high morality set forth in the New Testament. The Sermon of the Mount, the Beatitudes—only few could ever hope to live up to those impossibly high standards

of moral conduct. Most will fail, and Jesus had to know this. This makes Christ a hypocrite and fraud for not loving all of humanity equally. "You are proud of your chosen ones, but all you have are chosen ones" (297). This then is the true criminality of Christ. He expects people to be holy and righteous. "But, I repeat, are there many such as you?" (294). The verdict that the Inquisitor must give could be none other than death. "For if there ever was one who deserved our bonfire more than anyone else, it is you. Tomorrow I am going to burn you. *Dixi* [as I have decreed]" (299).

2. Goodin, *Agnostic in the Fellowship of Christ*, 198.
3. Goodin, *Agnostic in the Fellowship of Christ*, 241.
4. Goodin, *The New Rationalism*, 35.
5. The actual quote is as follows. Dmitri recounts a discussion he had with another character, Rakitin, to Alyosha: "'But what will become of men then?' I asked him, 'without God and immortal life? All things are lawful then, they can do what they like?'" (*The Brothers Karamazov*, 665).
6. Nietzsche, *Twilight of the Idols*, "Raids of an Untimely Man," §45.
7. Dostoevsky, *The Brothers Karamazov*, Part II.VI.i, 412.
8. Dostoevsky, *The Brothers Karamazov*, Part III, VI.3, 449.
9. Dostoevsky, *The Brothers Karamazov*, Part IV.VIII.
10. Dostoevsky developed the doppelganger genre with his novel, *The Double* (1846) where the protagonist is pursued by a look-alike who conspires against him, and yet *is* him in some supernatural way. The brothers in *The Brothers Karamazov* are likewise doubles, being opposites whose fates are linked—a proxy for the author's own struggles with atheism and faith.
11. Dostoevsky, *The Brothers Karamazov*, Part III.g, 406.
12. Dostoevsky, *The Idiot*, Part III.V.
13. Schweitzer, *Out of My Life and Thought*, 232.
14. Schweitzer, *A Place for Revelation*, 37.
15. Schweitzer, *A Place for Revelation*, 37.
16. Schweitzer, "The Ethics of Reverence for Life," 130.
17. Schweitzer, *Kulturphilosophie*, 403.
18. Schweitzer, *The Philosophy of Civilization*, 318.
19. Schweitzer, *A Place for Revelation*, 25.
20. Goodin, *The New Rationalism*, 186.
21. Dostoevsky, *The Dream of a Ridiculous Man*, chapter 1.
22. Dostoevsky, *The Dream of a Ridiculous Man*, chapter 1.
23. Dostoevsky, *The Dream of a Ridiculous Man*, chapter 3.
24. Dostoevsky, *The Dream of a Ridiculous Man*, chapter 3.
25. Dostoevsky, *The Dream of a Ridiculous Man*, chapter 5.
26. Perhaps it can be assumed that a resolution of some kind must be in the works for the characters since how else could the show have drawn such star-power, each of whom are willing to risk their careers to take on these roles? Of course, it does not always work out that way, with *Game of Thrones* being case-in-point for an unforgivably mishandled resolution to what had been compelling drama. But if the showrunners, producers, and writers have learned anything from such recent disappointments (and that admittedly is a big "if"), then it is not out of the question to

imagine Dostoevsky as the "go-to" literary subtext for creating real narrative depth in escaping dystopian nihilism.

27. Notably, we are given only a few details of his life, only that he had been a fisherman, which coincidentally or not, is a very Christian missiological inclusion (Matthew 4:19).

28. At the time of writing, the war against Ukraine is still raging as the world grows increasingly apathetic toward the plight of the Ukrainians in terms of military support, and a new war has begun in the Middle East between Israel and Hamas—a war that threatens to expand dangerously and unpredictably.

BIBLIOGRAPHY

Dostoevsky, Fyodor. *The Brothers Karamazov*. Translated by David McDuff. New York: Penguin Books, 1993 [1880].

———. *The Double*. Translated by Constance Garnett. New York: Dover Publications, 1997 [1846].

———. *The Idiot*. Translated by David McDuff. New York: Penguin Classics, 2004 [1869].

———. *The Dream of a Ridiculous Man*. Translated by Constance Garnett. Read & Co. Classics, e-book, 2018 [1877].

Goodin, David K. *The New Rationalism: Albert Schweitzer's Philosophy of Reverence for Life*. Montreal, Canada: McGill-Queen's University Press, 2013.

———. *An Agnostic in the Fellowship of Christ: The Ethical Mysticism of Albert Schweitzer*. Lanham, MD: Lexington/Fortress Academic, 2019.

Nietzsche, Friedrich. *Twilight of the Idols*. Translated by Richard Polt. Indianapolis, IN: Hackett, 1997 [1889].

Schweitzer, Albert. *Kulturphilosophie—Erster Teil: Verfall und Wiederaufbau Der Kultur*. München: C. H. Beck'sche Verlagsbuchhandlung, 1923.

———. *Out of My Life and Thought*. Translated by C. T. Campion. New York: Henry Holt and Company, 1931.

———. "The Ethics of Reverence for Life." *Christendom* 1.2 (1936): 225–239.

———. *The Philosophy of Civilization, Vol. 1, The Decay and the Restoration of Civilization, Vol. 2, Civilization and Ethics*. Translated by C. T. Campion. Buffalo, NY: Prometheus, 1987.

———. *A Place for Revelation: Sermons on Reverence for Life*. Translated by David Larrimore Holland. New York: Macmillan, 1998.

Chapter 4

Everything Happens for a Reason
"Pastor" David, Epistemic Harm, and Religious Trauma Syndrome

Daniel J. Cameron

"When can we bury him?"[1] the little crying girl asks David after he finished his reading of Revelation 21:1, 3. Her question, filled with mourning, is quickly dismissed because "the ground is too cold to dig."[2] You did not have to be Sherlock Holmes to know, while watching this episode, that something was amiss. As "Pastor" David was reading from the Book of Revelation, behind him hung a white sign that read "When we are in need, he will provide."[3] However, the question remains who is the "he"? The assumption is that it is God; however, as the story continues, you begin to wonder if David thinks that the "he" may be himself.

Only as the episode progresses do you find out that the girl was crying because her dad had died. However, his death came at the hands of Joel, who was trying to protect himself, which David knew. Rather than tell her the truth, David lies to her to keep her calm. The girl's dad was never going to be buried.

Ellie has an encounter with David shortly after this incident. While sitting around a campfire at the end of the barrel of Ellie's gun, David invites Ellie to join them at Silver Lake. Ellie then begins to question David's position within the community, asking him if this is "some kind of cult thing?"[4] David is quick to respond that he is a preacher but not of a cult. Rather, just "some basic Bible stuff."[5] However, anyone who knows "basic Bible stuff" will be quick to realize that what David is doing is contradictory to core biblical teaching. He is using the Bible to manipulate and control this community of people.

In response to this episode, Rainn Wilson, author of *Soul Boom: Why We Need a Spiritual Revolution*, tweeted that, "There is an anti-Christian bias in Hollywood." Wilson gives the following example, "As soon as [David] started reading from the Bible, I knew that he was going to be a horrific villain. Could there be a Bible-reading preacher on a show who is actually loving and kind?"[6]

While the decision of the showrunners to include this religious element could be dismissed as simply another example of Hollywood's anti-Christian bias,[7] arguably more important is that this episode can serve as a diagnostic of how the Christian religion and, more specifically, Christian religious rhetoric,[8] have and can cause epistemic harm and the resulting religious trauma (RT). In fact, a March 2023 study published by the Socio-Historical Examination of Religion and Ministry, estimated that, conservatively, one-third of U.S. adults have experienced RT at some point in their lives, thereby placing religious trauma syndrome (RTS) in the category of a "chronic" problem.[9]

Christianity emphasizes the preached word, the *kerusso*. The sermon is an important part of the service and in Christian seminaries significant time is spent in preaching classes learning the art of rhetoric. The "best" preachers are the best rhetoricians using their rhetoric to inspire, and to motivate. Though they may have the best of intentions, their rhetoric has also been used to harm, to control, and to manipulate, touting the excuse "the truth hurts." This is what we see with "Pastor" David. The very first line of episode 8 is a direct quote from scripture itself used to supposedly comfort another. However, as the episode progresses, David's Christian rhetoric is exposed as a tactic of manipulation to hold control over his "flock."[10] It is the argument of this chapter that, as a dystopian story, *The Last of Us* (*TLOU*), season 1 episode 8, serves as a diagnostic exposing the failure and misuse of religious rhetoric within Christianity,[11] resulting in significant cases of RTS.

To defend this thesis, I will first examine the character of David in both the TV show and the video game to explicate the intentional decision of the showrunners to make David a "Christian" in the TV show. I will argue that the dystopian genre attempts to strip society bare, thus exposing how current society may be in the future if it continues in its current trajectory. Once this has been established, I will make the case for religious rhetoric as a cause of epistemic harm—including both hermeneutical and testimonial injustice—resulting in RTS. All of this will show how *TLOU*, as fitting in the genre of dystopia, exposes the ways in which religious rhetoric has and can be used for manipulation and harm. I will conclude with steps that we can and must take to prevent epistemic harm and RTS.

DAVID AND DYSTOPIA

In season 1 of *TLOU*, the creators of the show made subtle and distinct changes to some of the major characters throughout. The character of David, played by Scott Shepherd, is no exception. In both the game and the show, David's major actions remain the same:[12] he still kidnaps and makes sexual advances to Ellie and is ultimately killed by her. However, the show explores more deeply the way in which David interacts with his own group and thus, we get an insight into his methods of leadership. David is a pastor—or so it seems.

The episode opens with what appears to be a somber religious service. As mentioned, a little girl is crying while David, their apparent leader, is reading to them from the Book of Revelation and giving an impromptu sermon to lift their spirits. The title of the episode—"When We Are in Need"—even sounds like a sermon title. However, upon further observation, those in the crowd do not seem to be quick to accept David's sermon and it takes some individual prompting to get the little girl to calm down. It can be seen from the outset of this episode that there may be something more than meets the eye here. David seems to be nice and caring and yet at the same time is using religion and the Bible to manipulate the emotions of his "sheep."[13] Yet, the question remains, was the decision of the shows' creators to change David's character from the video game and make him religious Hollywood hating on Christians, as argued by Rainn Wilson? Is it simply just a trope, as argued by Jennifer Graham?[14] Or is it something more? Is there anything else that we can take away from this use of religion and the Bible in *TLOU*? I argue, yes. Before we continue, we must explore more deeply who exactly David is.

In the video game, we are introduced to David for the first time when Ellie is searching for the deer that she just shot. The deer did not immediately die but ended up running away and dying at an abandoned village nearby. Upon finding the deer, David and his friend James come out of hiding. They were also hunting for food. Ellie agrees to make a trade with David for penicillin so that she can help an injured Joel. David makes himself known as the leader by telling an obviously skeptical James to go and get the penicillin while he waits with Ellie. While waiting for James to return, they take "shelter from the cold" inside one of the abandoned buildings where, very quickly, they must fight off a wave of the infected including a giant "bloater." After the fight, David and Ellie sit down together, and David, while not religious, is deeply philosophical. He tells Ellie that he believes that "everything happens for a reason." He then reveals that he knows that Joel killed some of his men and that she is with Joel.

It was an intentional decision of the showrunners to introduce David as a religious figure in this episode in contrast to the video game. However, this was not an attempt to be "anti-Christian" but rather to provide a different angle to examine "the other."[15] They intended to show "the other," at least at first, as "humane and with his [David's] own goals, his own community."[16] David seems like a good leader, comforting others, and leading this community through a difficult time. However, from the opening scene, we get the idea that something else is happening because James (Troy Baker) gives David a look that hints at something bigger taking place.

The town of Silver Lake is set up in contrast to the town of Jackson City. Jackson City serves as a functioning society in which the residents are caring for each other and protecting each other. Silver Lake, however, is a place in which control is gained through "fear and oppression."[17] Jackson City is run by a woman who was involved in law as a prosecutor and thus, Jackson City is run on the foundation of law. In Silver Lake, however, religion becomes the dominant foundation of the community, which the showrunners contend violates the necessity of church-state separation, commenting in one podcast: the church does "a terrible job of running the state."[18]

David is both theocratic and patriarchal. As such, we see a community falling apart. While on the surface this episode can be seen as a commentary on the dangers of a theocracy,[19] it is the argument of this chapter that *TLOU*, as a work of dystopia, can offer a deeper critique of the use of religion for harm. What follows in this next section is an exploration of the genre of dystopia and its purpose in critiquing our current society calling us to change.

The word "dystopia" derives from two Greek words, *du* and *topos*, meaning "a diseased, bad, faulty, or unfavorable place."[20] Dystopia did not take a more prominent place in wide readership until sometime in the twentieth century even though it appeared in the eighteenth century.[21] When thinking about dystopia, what most likely comes to mind is absolute catastrophe: streets lined with dead bodies, stench filling the air, the collapse of government, and the rise of anarchy and ultimately individual survival. However, this approach to dystopian literature is reductionistic and thinks of dystopia as nothing more than simply the opposite of utopia, thus leaving us with an overly simplistic mindset about the "good place" and its opposite, the "bad place." This approach, argues Claeys, is a "modern phenomenon, wedded to secular pessimism."[22] In other words, dystopian literature in its popular sense seems to be disconnected from what it intended to be and has since become influenced and tainted by modern pessimism. While there is debate taking place in the literary world concerning the history and nuanced definitions of dystopia, it is fair and accurate to say that dystopia in its "most common use . . . portrays an extremely negative or evil fictional state usually dominated by fear."[23]

Dystopian literature does not exist just for the nihilists and pessimists in society but rather serves a much more important purpose. Works of dystopia explore current issues in our contemporary society by taking those negative aspects of society and placing them into dystopian society. As Keith Booker argues, dystopian works critically examine "both existing conditions and the potential abuses that might result from the institution of supposedly utopian alternatives."[24] Important in this process is the work of "defamiliarization," meaning that dystopian literature necessarily takes those existing conditions mentioned by Booker and places them into new and unfamiliar settings. Through this process of "defamiliarization" dystopian literature removes readers from their familiar setting so that "social practices that might otherwise be seen as commonplace are presented in a fresh manner" or in our case, religious practices.[25] In other words, dystopian literature through defamiliarization shakes us out of our stupor of familiarity and challenges us to reexamine what we consider to be acceptable.

Charlotte Ladevèze and Gerald Farca, in their article "The Journey to Nature: *The Last of Us* as Critical Dystopia," argue that *TLOU* as a work of dystopia "serves as a powerful warning and reminder that should these tendencies continue, we may face a similar catastrophe as depicted and enacted in its virtualized storyworld."[26] While their article focuses on what the video game can teach us about the balance of city life and life in nature, their comment stands that *TLOU* gives us a powerful warning that we cannot and must not allow the tendencies of religious abuse to continue lest we face the same or similar catastrophe depicted in episode 8 of season 1. As indicated earlier, the genre of dystopia has many various subgenres within, and to deepen our understanding of *TLOU* we must understand the dystopian subgenre of the show.

Ladevèze and Farca argue that *TLOU* fits into the subgenre of critical dystopia. While dystopian literature can be seen as crafting "maps of hell,"[27] what can be problematic is equating all forms of dystopia as anti-utopia. That is, dystopian literature does in fact create a world that is grim; however, that does not mean that all is hopeless. What makes critical dystopia unique is that its stories "linger in the terrors of the present even as they exemplify what is needed to transform it."[28] Thus, there is something of hope offered in critical dystopia—a hope, no matter how slim, that things may change. Episode 8 toys with hope. After the episode introduces David and the Silver Lake community, there is an air of hope in this community. However, as the episode progresses, the hope seems to quickly dissipate, leaving the viewer, yet again, filled with dread and hopelessness, exacerbated by the fact that Joel is on the brink of death and Ellie cannot hold a gun and is then captured and sexually assaulted by David. While hope seems extinguished, Ellie fights back and, in a hellish landscape of fire, fights against David who has been fully exposed for the evil man that he has been. During the fight, David continues to try to convince Ellie that he is good and that he is offering her some sort of redemption. Ellie proves that she does not need to be redeemed by him and ultimately gets some sort of redemption—really vengeance—herself by besting him and killing him in an attack that shows us that maybe Ellie isn't so much different than David herself in that she is willing to cross whatever ethical boundary stands in the way of what is best for her. The outcome of hope in this episode is the ultimate destruction of the religious abuser. But it leaves me wondering, is that the best offer of hope in the face of religious abuse? Or can theology offer something more? Something truly redemptive?

Dystopian literature portrays a society which is seeking utopia but is dominated and controlled through fear and punishment. This form of literature serves as a commentary on current cultural trajectories that are left unchecked. However, important for this argument is the point that dystopian stories do not give the reader any semblance of hope. It leaves us in misery as the characters in the story are existing in misery with no sense of hope. These "nightmarish scenarios occupy an increasingly prominent position in our vocabulary and our mental world, but *without the hopeful outcome promised by theology.*"[29] Now that the nature and purpose of dystopian literature have been established, we can now move to discuss what *TLOU* as a work of dystopia can teach us about RTS and the hopeful outcome theology promises.

EPISTEMIC HARM, RELIGIOUS RHETORIC, AND RELIGIOUS TRAUMA SYNDROME

In episode 8, David asks the question, "Is [cordyceps] evil?" This seemingly unnecessary question is answered in a shocking way. David says no. He continues that "it's fruitful and it multiplies. It feeds and protects its children, and it secures its future with violence if it must."[30] As the audience, we have come to understand cordyceps as evil throughout the show. It is the only experience that we are given as viewers. However, David sees it differently and he begins to compare himself and his motivations and methods to the fungus. It is here that we can confidently rebuke the way David defines the good. David comes across as someone who cares and someone who wants to help but in reality he is simply "using religion as a means to push his own agenda."[31] The image of David we receive in the opening scene begins to unravel a little bit later in the episode when he hits the same girl he had comforted at the beginning of the episode telling her that she will always have a father and she must do what he tells her to do. David sets up his entire community to be subject to RT and epistemic harm.

A recent study completed by Darren M. Slade at the Global Center for Religious Research shows that approximately one-third of U.S. adults suffer from RT.[32] While this number is staggering, RTS is not yet recognized in the major mental health handbooks—such as *Diagnostic and Statistical Manual* or the ICD-10—as an actual mental health disorder. This is the case despite Marlene Winell's plea back in 2011 to have RTS recognized as an actual problem.[33] Though not yet recognized in *DST-5* or ICD-10, research on RTS has been growing in the recent years since Winell coined the term.[34] Though the research is growing, Dr. Alyson M. Stone argues that, "Religious trauma is more prevalent than the research suggests and often is a contributing factor to many of the problems that bring people to therapy, including depression, anxiety, and relationship difficulties. For this reason, religious trauma deserves careful attention."[35] RT and RTS are receiving more of this careful attention recently in the mental health field and yet theologians are surprisingly silent about this issue. As mentioned, this chapter seeks to help fill that gap by examining RT and the resulting RTS from a theological perspective.

RT and RTS can lead to disidentification and/or religious deconstruction of the harmed individual.[36] However, while Winell notes that RT is the result of a power-hungry person "coupled with toxic theology"[37]—specifically the doctrine of original sin and eternal damnation in hell—theology itself is not the problem. It is the twisting of theological reality—reality being that which is true—for the sake of power and control that is the problem. In other words, faithful theology in alignment with the character of God is not the problem. As Alison Downie argues, "Theology has a place in this work to become a hermeneutical resource for new knowing, to counter formation in shame and religious trauma, to listen to witness and name the wounds, to speak against shame's fierce silencing."[38] Thus, theology done well, done faithfully for God, can be part of the solution rather than part of the problem. However, before we begin exploring the details of RT and RTS, it is of the utmost importance that we take time to first define our terms. Once the terms are defined, I will extrapolate RT by examining its effect as epistemic harm. Then I can explore the resulting RTS.

DEFINING OUR TERMS

As noted, the research on RT is still very new and therefore the amount of research on this type of trauma is sparse at best. While RT is not unique to Christianity, as a Christian myself, I focus here on RT in a Christian context. However, this is not to say that we know nothing about RT or that there was no RT before the research began but rather that we simply did not realize or recognize it as a form of trauma. The term "religious trauma" is precise and thus more helpful for our discussion than the vague term *spiritual trauma*. RT indicates that the trauma took place within a structured and formal religious context. Spiritual trauma is vague as it does not indicate what community it took place within or even what the structure of that community is and defining the term *spiritual* is much more subjective. So, what is RT and the resulting RTS?

Marlene Winell, in her book *Leaving the Fold*, defines RTS as "the condition experienced by people who are struggling with leaving an authoritarian, dogmatic religion and coping with the damage of indoctrination."[39] She argues that this condition is caused by "authoritarianism coupled with toxic theology which is received and reinforced at church, school, and home" which ultimately results in damage to child development, emotional immaturity, poor self-worth, and unhealthy sexual identity.[40] She ties this specifically to conservative Christianity and the doctrines of original sin and eternal damnation. While it is true that RT can and does occur because of these things, this definition is unnecessarily narrow. Alyson Stone, while working from Winell's definition, broadens this definition such that RT is "pervasive psychological damage resulting from religious messages, beliefs, and experiences."[41] Thus, RT can occur within any religious institution and results from a variety of religious messages. Simply put, RTS is a "group of symptoms that arise in response to traumatic or stressful religious experiences."[42] Restoration Counseling, a mental health care facility in Seattle, Washington, argues that the symptoms that can result from RTS are as follows:

> Confusing thoughts and reduced ability to think critically; negative beliefs about self, others, and the world; trouble making decisions; feelings of depression, anxiety, grief, anger, lethargy; a sense of feeling lost, directionless, and alone; a lack of pleasure or interest in things you used to enjoy; a loss of community; feeling isolated or a sense that you don't belong; feeling "behind the times" with cultural happenings; and many other symptoms of PTSD including nightmares, flashbacks, dissociation, emotional difficulty, etc.[43]

What has been reported to happen, both in others' experience as well as my own,[44] is that the victim of this abuse is often blamed because the pastor was "well meaning" and therefore should not be held accountable. However, as Samuel Fernández cogently argues, what defines this form of abuse "is the harm suffered by the victim and not the intention of the perpetrator."[45]

This can be seen in *TLOU* for David is not a pastor of any particular church or denomination but is manipulating a message of hope ("there will be no more tears") and belief in the sovereignty of God ("everything happens for a reason"). In reality, David is an archetypal authoritarian leader using bad/toxic theology to control the people of Silver Lake. While religious abuse is taking place in David's community, the show does not reveal the full impact that David is inflicting on his followers. It should be noted that RT takes place "through long-term exposure to messages that undermine mental health."[46] Alison Downie argues that what both Winell and Alyson Stone agree on is that RT occurs in the context of "rigid binaries, absolute judgments, and an atmosphere of fear of condemnation."[47] Such is the exact community that David is creating for the people of Silver Lake.

While RT can occur from one's involvement in any religion, Christian RT is especially distressful for me as a Christian because it adulterates proclaiming the good news concerning The Word, that is Jesus Christ. In Christian RT, individuals and communities use Christian words about The Word to harm and control people. The question to be addressed at this juncture is exactly how it is that our words in a religious context bring about harm to those involved. To accomplish this, two terms will be extrapolated: epistemic harm and hermeneutical injustice.

In Mari Ramler's article "When God Hurts: The Rhetoric of Religious Trauma as Epistemic Pain," she argues that "religious persuasion" can and has inflicted epistemic pain upon those involved in religious institutions. By this she means that "religious rhetoric has the potential to harm religious audience members . . . in their identity construction and knowledge production."[48] For this to take place, the speaker, who is using religious rhetoric to persuade someone, enacts epistemic harm upon their hearer when the ability of the hearer to know is called into question. This is what Miranda Fricker calls "epistemic injustice."[49] Fricker defines epistemic injustice as a "wrong done to someone in their capacity as knower."[50] This means that someone with religious authority takes advantage of someone with fewer epistemological resources to control them. This form of epistemic injustice is known as "hermeneutical injustice." Hermeneutical injustice occurs "when a gap in collective interpretive resources puts someone at an unfair disadvantage when it comes to making sense of their social experiences."[51] This form of injustice uses someone's lack of information to control them into what the abuser wants. As the common colloquialism says, "knowledge is power" and thus, the withholding of knowledge is power in the hands of the abuser. This is ultimately an unethical use of rhetorical power.

Ramler identifies hermeneutical injustice as taking place within the context of youth and children's programs at church in which seemingly well-meaning leaders gathering students during a significantly vulnerable place in their human development and often taking them away from their parents for "special programs" designed just for them are then taught things which can and often do result in RT resulting from this form of epistemic harm. Sadly, the youth and children can become "arrested in their development."[52] Hermeneutical injustice takes place when their testimony is silenced.

As Ramler argues, "Their voice and their experience of the world are silenced, and this causes them to doubt their own sense of reality and their own authority as a knower."[53] This hermeneutical injustice strips them of their own voice and ability to understand what is happening to them and therefore how to process their experience which is ultimately a denial of their own personhood.

At the beginning of episode 8 when the little girl asks David when they can bury her father, David uses religious rhetoric to stop the girl from crying. He uses the words from the Bible to literally gaslight her and the experience that she is having of the loss of her dad. It is not just this one instance either. Throughout the episode the sad reality that the people are being fed through secret cannibalism is being kept from the community through this form of injustice. Sadly, it is not just within the fictional world of *TLOU* where this RT is taking place. Currently there are many who are publishing research about the abuse of purity culture and how books such as *I Kissed Dating Goodbye* created a culture of abuse in which epistemic trauma can take place.[54] This has resulted in a movement of people who are now "deconverting." The APA dictionary of psychology defines deconversion as the "loss of faith in one's religion."[55] It is no wonder that those who have experienced the epistemic abuse and now suffer from RTS are making a move away from the faith which they were brought up with. However, is this the only possible solution? I argue no. It is not theology that is the problem, it is the way in which authoritarian leaders use theology for the sake of control. When theology is done in a way that is faithful to the object of theology, that is God, then what results should be freedom and redemption.[56] As stated earlier, dystopian literature gives us a desire for the utopian ideal without the hope of theology. In the show, the only semblance of hope that we get is in the gratuitous murder of "Pastor" David. The hope that is offered in the show is the partial destruction of evil. David may be gone but the clickers are still a threat. However, God does not offer us a hope of the partial destruction of evil but of a complete and final restoration. That is the entire story of salvation beginning in Genesis 3:15 that God would bring about restoration to humanity even to those who we deem too far gone.

CONCLUSION

In this chapter, I argue that, as a dystopian narrative, *TLOU* season 1 episode 8, serves as a diagnostic exposing the failure and misuse of religious rhetoric within Christianity resulting in significant cases of RTS. To support my claims, I first examined the character of David in both the video game and the TV show to assess the intentional differences the showrunners decided upon in making David a pastor in the show. I continued by showing that as a work of dystopia, *TLOU* serves as a critique of the abuse that is taking place in the church through epistemic and hermeneutical injustice. This results in various forms of RTS through this abuse of power. Ultimately, this trauma is not the result of theology itself—that is, faithful theology in accordance with the image and likeness of God—but the misuse and creation of a toxic theology paired with an authoritarian leadership.

Moving forward, to best combat RT, theological research needs to continue to engage with psychology to both expose more deeply the ways in which the use of theology and religious rhetoric has caused significant epistemic harm to people. We must be careful with theology and our speech about God and be aware of the ways in which we can and have caused harm with those words. It is time that we who are Christians repent of the ways that Christian rhetoric has harmed others, both Christian and non-Christian. The truth of the Word and our words should bring life and freedom and it is time we do things differently.

NOTES

1. *The Last of Us*. 2023. Season 1, episode 8, "When We Are in Need." Directed by Ali Abbasi. Aired March 5, 2023, on HBO.
2. "Episode 8, When We Are in Need."
3. "Episode 8, When We Are in Need."
4. "Episode 8, When We Are in Need."
5. "Episode 8, When We Are in Need."
6. Wilson. "I do think there is an anti-Christian bias in Hollywood. As soon as the David character in 'The Last of Us' started reading from the Bible I knew that he was going to be a horrific villain. Could there be a Bible-reading preacher on a show who is actually loving and kind?" March 11, 2023, 2:50 PM, https://twitter.com/rainnwilson/status/1634657997317361665.
7. The claim made by Wilson is outside the purview of this chapter.
8. By this I am referring to the use of religious language in our speech about and towards one another.
9. Slade, Smell, Wilson, and Drumsta, "Percentage of U.S. Adults Suffering from Religious Trauma," 22. RTS, as a subset of Post Traumatic Stress Syndrome, is a term coined by Dr. Marlene Winell with the publication of her book *Leaving the Fold* in 1993. RTS can be defined as "a group of symptoms that arise in response to traumatic or stressful religious experiences." See Slade, Smell, Wilson, and Drumsta, "Percentage of U.S. Adults Suffering from Religious Trauma," 22.
10. "Episode 8, When We Are in Need." David uses this term to refer to the community at Silver Lake.

11. While religious rhetoric can and has been problematic in many religions, if not all, I am focusing specifically on the Christian context as it is my own and it is the religious context of episode 8.
12. Moore, "The Last of Us Episode 8 Makes Subtle Changes."
13. *TLOU,* s01e08.
14. Graham, "Are You Blond and Religious?"
15. "Episode 8, When We Are in Need." *HBO's The Last of Us Podcast*, March 5, 2023.
16. "Episode 8, When We Are in Need."
17. "Episode 8, When We Are in Need."
18. "Episode 8, When We Are in Need."
19. Though the showrunners in their podcast argue that while one could read this into the episode, it was not the main intention. I disagree with this as immediately after they say this, they discuss the comparison of Jackson City and Silver Lake as a critique of a society founded on law versus a theocratic society run by religion. "Episode 8, When We Are in Need." *HBO's The Last of Us Podcast*, March 5, 2023.
20. Claeys, *Dystopia: A Natural History*, 4.
21. Claeys, *Dystopia*, 4.
22. Claeys, *Dystopia*, 4.
23. Claeys, *Dystopia*, 7.
24. Booker, *Dystopian Literature*, 3.
25. Johnson, "Dystopian Literature and the Novella Form," 4.
26. Farca and Ladevèze, "The Journey to Nature," 1.
27. Amis, *New Maps of Hell*.
28. Moylan, *Scraps of the Untainted Sky*, 198–199.
29. Claeys, *Dystopia,* 4. *Emphasis mine.*
30. "The Last of Us," s01e08.
31. Moore, "The Last of Us Episode 8 Makes Subtle Changes to David Compared to the Game."
32. Slade, "Percentage of U.S. Adults Suffering from Religious Trauma."
33. Winell, "Religious Trauma Syndrome."
34. See the following studies as examples: Downie, "Christian Shame and Religious Trauma," 925; Houser, "Altared Bodies"; Panchuk, "Defining Religious Trauma (Draft)"; Ramler, "When God Hurts"; Slade, Smell, Wilson, and Drumsta, "Percentage of U.S. Adults Suffering from Religious Trauma"; and Stone, "Thou Shalt Not," 323–337.
35. Stone, "Thou Shalt Not," 323–337.
36. See Ramler, "Disidentification"; "Deconstructing After Leaving Your Cult or Religion"; Dille, "Healing Spiritual Wounds"; and Thomas, *Church Hurt*.
37. Winell, "Religious Trauma Syndrome."
38. Downie, "Christian Shame and Religious Trauma," 7.
39. Winell, "Religious Trauma Syndrome."
40. Winell, "Religious Trauma Syndrome."
41. Stone, "Though Shalt Not: Treating Religious Trauma and Spiritual Harm," 324.

42. Restoration Counseling, "Religious Trauma Syndrome and Faith Transitions."
43. Restoration Counseling, "Religious Trauma Syndrome and Faith Transitions."
44. I grew up in a Christian fundamentalist context in which religion and religious morality were used to control the people who were attending the church. The church context in which I grew up was more restricting than liberating. It put more burden on me rather than my burden being lightened in my relationship with Jesus.
45. Fernández, "Victims Are Not Guilty! Spiritual Abuse and Ecclesiastical Responsibility," 7. While Fernández uses the term "spiritual abuse," what he is talking about was already discussed and defined as "religious abuse." That is the term I chose to use in this chapter for it is more specific than "spiritual abuse."
46. Stone, "Though Shalt Not," 325.
47. Downie, "Christian Shame and Religious Trauma," 2.
48. Ramler, "When God Hurts," 2. By rhetoric what is meant is the "use of written, spoken, and visual language" to communicate things about God. See https://rhetoric.sdsu.edu/about/what-is-rhetoric.
49. Fricker, *Epistemic Injustice*.
50. Fricker, *Epistemic Injustice*, 1.
51. Fricker, *Epistemic Injustice*, 1.
52. Ramler, "When God Hurts," 7.
53. Ramler, "When God Hurts," 7.
54. Allison, *#ChurchToo*.
55. APA Dictionary of Psychology, "Deconversion."
56. This is what T. F. Torrance calls "kataphysical inquiry." By this, he means that "we direct our minds to the self-giving of God in Jesus Christ and allow our minds to fall under the power of the divine rationality that becomes revealed to him. It is a rationality inherent in the reality of the incarnate Word before it takes shape in our apprehension of it (*a posteriori*), but as we allow it to become disclosed to us under our questions and find that it is opened out before us in an objective depth that far transcends what we can specify of it in our formulations (disclosure models)." Torrance, *Theological Science*, 10. In other words, we must allow God to be *Lord* of our theology such that we are constantly allowing the living God to correct and form our theology into an accurate reflection of God's true image and not the image that we want God to be.

BIBLIOGRAPHY

Allison, Emily Joy, and Lyz Lenz. *#ChurchToo: How Purity Culture Upholds Abuse and How to Find Healing*. Minneapolis, MN: Broadleaf Books, 2021.

Amis, Kingsley. *New Maps of Hell*. London: Penguin Books, 201.

"APA Dictionary of Psychology." https://dictionary.apa.org.

Berger, Josh. "HBO's 'The Last of Us' Depicts Cannibal Enemies from First Game as Christian Zealots." Bounding into Comics, March 8, 2023, https://boundingintocomics.com/2023/03/07/hbos-the-last-of-us-depicts-cannibal-enemies-from-first-game-as-christian-zealots/.

Booker, M. Keith. *Dystopian Literature: A Theory and Research Guide*. Westport, CT: Greenwood, 1994.

Claeys, Gregory. *Dystopia: A Natural History*. Oxford, UK: Oxford University Press, 2018.

———, ed. *The Cambridge Companion to Utopian Literature*. Cambridge, UK: Cambridge University Press, 2010.

"Deconstructing after Leaving Your Cult or Religion." Traumastery, https://www.traumastery.com/blog/after-leaving-religion.

Dille, Allison M. "Healing Spiritual Wounds: The Experiences of Counselors Working with Religious Trauma Survivors." Master's thesis, Moody Theological Seminary, Chicago, March 2023.

Doll, Katie. "'The Last of Us' Shows the Scary Reality of Religion in the Apocalypse." CBR, March 12, 2023, https://www.cbr.com/the-last-of-us-david-religion-apocalypse/.

Donahue-Martens, Scott, and Brandon Simonson. *Theology, Religion, and Dystopia*. Lanham, MD: Fortress Academic, 2022.

Downie, Alison. "Christian Shame and Religious Trauma." *Religions* 13.10 (October 2022): 925.

Farca, Gerald, and Charlotte Ladevèze. "The Journey to Nature: The Last of Us as Critical Dystopia." *DiGRA/FDG '16 - Proceedings of the First International Joint Conference of DiGRA and FDG* 13.1 (August 2016).

Fernández, Samuel. "Victims Are Not Guilty! Spiritual Abuse and Ecclesiastical Responsibility." *Religions* 13.5 (May 2022): 427.

Fitting, Peter. "Utopia, Dystopia, and Science Fiction." In *The Cambridge Companion to Utopian Literature*, edited by Gregory Claeys (pp. 135–153). Cambridge, UK: Cambridge University Press, 2010.

Fricker, Miranda. *Epistemic Injustice: Power and the Ethics of Knowing*. Oxford, UK: University Press, 2007.

———. *Epistemic Injustice: Power and the Ethics of Knowing*. Oxford, UK: Oxford University Press, 2009.

Graham, Jennifer. "Are You Blond and Religious? In Hollywood, That Makes You a Supervillain." *Deseret News*, March 9, 2023.

Houser, Victoria. "Altared Bodies: Evangelical Purity Rhetorics in the Age of Sexual Politics." *All Dissertations*, August 1, 2021.

Johnson, Bryan W. "Dystopian Literature and the Novella Form as Illustrated through Side Effects, an Original Novella." Dissertation, Utah State University, 2012.

"'The Last of Us' Delivered an All-Time Villain of Biblical Proportions." Nerdist, March 25, 2023, https://nerdist.com/article/the-last-of-us-delivered-all-time-villain-david-bible-false-prophet/.

"'The Last of Us' Episode 8: Desperate People Find (Blind) Faith." *Indiana Daily Student*, March 6, 2023, https://www.idsnews.com/article/2023/03/the-last-of-us-episode-8.

"'The Last of Us' Episode 8 Makes Subtle Changes to David Compared to the Game." Comicbook.com, https://comicbook.com/gaming/news/the-last-of-us-hbo-davidepisode-8/.

Marks, Peter, Jennifer A. Wagner-Lawlor, and Fátima Vieira, eds. *The Palgrave Handbook of Utopian and Dystopian Literatures*. Cham: Palgrave Macmillan, 2022.

Moylan, Thomas. *Scraps of the Untainted Sky: Science Fiction, Utopia, Dystopia*. Boulder, CO: Perseus, 2000.

Panchuk, Michelle. "Defining Religious Trauma (Draft)." Academia, https://www.academia.edu/30018951/Defining_Religious_Trauma_Draft.

Ramler, Mari E. "Disidentification (as a Survival Strategy for Religious Trauma)." In *The Routledge Handbook of Queer Rhetoric*, edited by Jacqueline Rhodes and Jonathan Alexander. London: Routledge, 2022.

———. "When God Hurts: The Rhetoric of Religious Trauma as Epistemic Pain." *Rhetoric Society Quarterly* 53.2 (March 15, 2023): 202–216.

Slade, Darren, Adrianna Smell, Elizabeth Wilson, and Rebekah Drumsta. "Percentage of U.S. Adults Suffering from Religious Trauma: A Sociological Study." *Socio-Historical Examination of Religion and Ministry* 5 (March 17, 2023): 1–28.

Stone, Alyson M. "Thou Shalt Not: Treating Religious Trauma and Spiritual Harm with Combined Therapy." *Group* 37.4 (2013): 323–337.

Streib, Heinz. "Leaving Religion: Deconversion." *Current Opinion in Psychology, Religion* 40 (August 1, 2021): 139–144, https://doi.org/10.1016/j.copsyc.2020.09.007.

Thomas, Megan. "Church Hurt: A Therapeutic Approach for Treating Religious Trauma and Spiritual Bypass," 2023, https://encompass.eku.edu/psych_doctorals/25.

Torrance, Thomas F. *Theological Science*. London: Oxford University Press, 1969.

Winell, Marlene. *Leaving the Fold: A Guide for Former Fundamentalists and Others Leaving Their Religion*. Berkeley: Apocryphile Press, 2006.

———. "Religious Trauma Syndrome" (series of 3 articles). *Cognitive Behavioural Therapy Today* 39.2 (May 2011), https://www.journeyfree.org/rts/.

Chapter 5

Facing the Apocalypse
The Religious Cult of the Seraphites in The Last of Us Part ll

Tijana Rupčić

Apocalyptic imagery and narratives seem to occupy most of the popular culture of today. The time when science fiction and imaginaries of the future were more positively inspired by humanity advancing its knowledge, exploring the cosmos, or achieving peaceful coexistence is long gone. In the same manner as other popular media, video games do not exist in a vacuum and are a reflection of the fears humanity is facing today. The majority of popular science fiction books and media tend to describe the future world as one where government structures collapse and human beings turn to violence to survive this new post-apocalyptic reality.[1]

The Last of Us[2] (*TLOU*) and *The Last of Us Part II*[3] (*TLOU2*) are two of the most successful video games in the last ten years and one of the most distinctive in the genre of survival-horror zombie-like games.[4] Conjointly, *TLOU2*, on which this chapter will focus, induced controversy among the gaming community by introducing two female protagonists, Ellie and Abby, both of whom did not conform to general expectations of femininity. Moreover, Ellie and the supporting character, Lev, represent the LGBTQ+ community.[5] These characters were the harbingers of the narrative change in *TLOU2*, and part of the gaming community loudly protested their introductions.

Furthermore, *TLOU2* depicts a more brutal and violent world than its predecessor. In many respects, *TLOU2* is a story of violence and its consequences, or, in other words, how inflicting violence will only produce more violence. By introducing the character of Abby, the creators enabled the players to understand the different points of view as well as the consequences of the violence inflicted by Joel at the end of *TLOU*. This chapter will focus on the Seraphites, a small group of antagonists that the player meets as both Ellie and Abby. However, the storyline tied to the Seraphites is more important when the player takes on the role of Abby, with the introduction of characters Yara and her transgender brother, Lev.

This chapter aims to explore in what ways the creators and writers of *TLOU2* depicted the post-apocalyptic group, deeply entrenched in certain spirituality, with cultic order and defined rituals and sets of rules for its members.[6] The Seraphites start as a peaceful community, trying to make sense of the new reality in the words of their Prophet, who preaches a return to nature and abandonment of the "old ways." However, as the new social order of post-apocalyptic Seattle changes, so does the dynamic in which Seraphites position themselves and interact with other groups. Moreover, the chapter will closely focus on the ways in which a peaceful group that opened its doors to new members became a closed-up and extremely violent cult by drawing some parallels with modern radical environmentalist organizations and cults.

I will use the theoretical framework Bron Taylor provided in his study of religious and violent radical environmentalist groups to study the phenomenon of violent religious cults in video games.[7] Furthermore, I will rely on the studies of William Bainbridge and Rodney Stark for providing a theoretical framework for the study of cult formations.[8] Moreover, as the exploration of this phenomenon is tied to the video game, I will use a game-immanent approach by focusing on game texts as the main source material.[9]

POST-APOCALYPTIC IMAGINARIES AND FEARS

The ideas and imaginaries of the apocalypse have existed since the dawn of time and the first recorded histories. Stemming from the Greek word "apokaluptein" (to uncover), the apocalypse is perceived as a description of a catastrophe that will precede the new reality or truth. Historically, the apocalypse has been the cornerstone of many religious and secular beliefs.[10] However, in contemporary literature and media, the apocalypse is altered into narratives about the post-apocalypse. The themes of the post-apocalyptic genre are tied to representations of disaster, ruin, and decay. Unlike the apocalypse, where the focus lies on salvation from ruin and decay, the post-apocalypse explores the possibilities that could emerge in such conditions. While the apocalypse is tied to the complete destruction of everything, the post-apocalypse is what remains after the catastrophic event that took place. The post-apocalyptic imagination mainly focuses on the possibilities of human life after catastrophe. In many ways, the genre of post-apocalypse is an important ground for examining and enacting sometimes grim, dangerous, and violent possibilities for what remains of humanity.[11]

The post-apocalyptic genre is a very popular format for video games.[12] In many respects, the gaming jargon confuses notions of apocalyptic and post-apocalyptic, which are usually used as synonyms. In terms of the cause of the apocalypse, the narrative offers four possibilities: divine intervention; the human factor; natural disasters; or a combination of the human factor and a natural disaster (in most cases, a natural disaster results from human negligence or arrogance).[13]

In many ways, as Heather Hicks puts it, the pressures of modern society feed the imaginaries of post-apocalyptic scenarios as catalysators of the breakdown of modernity.[14] Moreover, in the aftermath of the COVID-19 pandemic, interest in post-apocalyptic fictions of pandemic disasters significantly spiked. The theme of the pandemic as an instigator of the apocalypse is not uncommon in literature and popular media. The trope of a deadly pandemic nearly destroying humankind can be found as early as 1826 in Mary Shelley's *The Last Man* or Jack London's *The Scarlet Fever*. Furthermore, to name a few more, one should mention Richard Matheson's *I Am Legend* and Margaret Atwood's *Oryx and Crake*. To examine the post-pandemic imaginaries, it is essential to focus on what led to the outbreak and what scenarios are explored "after the end."

In the cases of *TLOU* and *TLOU2*, the instigator of the pandemic was a cordyceps fungus infection that used its victims as hosts. Thus, the victims of the cordyceps fungus become zombified entities that have several stages of existence, and as in the classic zombie portrayal, their only instinct is to hunt down and infect potential new hosts. The cultural fixation on zombies is hardly new. The trope of the zombie apocalypse is very much present in movies, novels, comics, and other popular media.[15] Very early on, the popular cultural discourse of zombies and the zombie apocalypse found its way into video games. Furthermore, the myth about zombies has roots in old legends of enslaved Haitians, but the image of zombies as we know them today only emerged recently in American popular culture.[16] Regardless of their origins in voodoo, zombie imaginaries are almost always tied to the collapse of civilization and the disintegration of societal structures. Following this disaster, a new reality is formed, one in which the survivors must find new ways to overcome new problems and avoid zombies.[17] The creators of *TLOU* and *TLOU2* take us on a journey to the post-apocalyptic United States of America, plagued by zombies mutated by the cordyceps fungus. The zombies of the *TLOU* world are not supernatural beings but rather people infected by mutated fungi.

POST-APOCALYPSE AND VIOLENCE

The world of *TLOU* and *TLOU2* is full of violence. After the societal collapse in the post-apocalyptic United States and the spread of the cordyceps virus, human survivors fight both against the infected and other people for scant resources. In this post-apocalyptic scenario, there are no possibilities to rebuild the old society, and what endures are only small groups trying their best to survive. However, as we have seen in the game, these factions are more concerned about fighting each other than fighting the infected, which make *TLOU* and *TLOU2* less zombie-focused games.

The brutality and violence of the post-apocalyptic United States did not go unnoticed in the first installment of *TLOU*; however, in *TLOU2*, the violence is taken to the next level and is omnipresent, both psychologically and physically.[18]

Even today, much of the study of video games centers on the violence they depict or—despite widespread debunking—the violence they cause. The post-apocalypse of *TLOU* builds around the assumption that a future challenged by disasters such as a deadly pandemic would inevitably lead to fragmentation of law and order and violent conflict for survival. These ideas draw upon the ideas already present in political thought, from Machiavelli to Hobbes. In this instance, the creators of *TLOU* relied on the philosophy of Thomas Hobbes, who saw violence as a "state of nature," humanity's original form.[19] In such a post-apocalyptic future, many surviving individuals embrace violence as an acceptable means of individual struggle for survival. This is especially depicted in *TLOU2*, where the creators focused on the experiences of individual characters, the violence they enact, and the psychological consequences it brings to them.

SERAPHITES: POST-APOCALYPTIC ANARCHO-PRIMITIVISM?

The Seraphites represent the smallest fraction a player encounters while playing *TLOU2*. As previously mentioned, the Seraphites appear in both instances: during the first half of the game, where we play as Ellie, as well as during the other half of the game, where the story switches to the point of view of the main antagonist, Abby. For the purpose of the analysis of the Seraphites in this chapter, their encounters with Abby are far more relevant for several reasons. First, while we meet Seraphites only as common enemies who are hostile towards us, while playing as Abby, we engage deeper with this cult and its members, mainly Yara and Lev, siblings whom Abby helps and takes on the role of their protector. Second, the introduction of Yara and Lev belongs to the redemption ark of Abby. Finally, the apostasies of Yara and Lev paint a peculiar picture of how a peaceful movement of spiritual people transformed into a zealous, violent cult.

So, who are the Seraphites? The Seraphites, also called Scars because of their distinctive face scars that symbolize human imperfection, are a primitivist cult and antagonistic party in *TLOU2*. The history of their beginnings goes back to 2013, the year of the outbreak. In some period between September 2013 and March 2014, an unnamed woman allegedly had a vision of the incoming collapse of society and started preaching that the only way to be saved from certain catastrophes is to turn to an egalitarian way of life and abandon all technology and "the old ways." This antitechnology attitude of the Seraphites is reminiscent of the anarcho-primitivism that arose in the 1970s. The radicalized anarcho-primitivists believed that civilization was the main reason for humanity's downfall. Only within civilization was it possible to create concepts such as state, private property, patriarchy, and technology. Civilization separated humans from nature, and only with civilization's breakdown can humanity achieve reconnection with nature.[20] The Seraphites depict possible human reaction in case of catastrophe where the future goes back to the primitive. The Seraphites' belief that the pandemic was a punishment is mirrored by the primitivist belief that capitalist modernity will inevitably lead to environmental collapse.

The Seraphites' entire belief system stems from the preaching of the Prophet. By the time the player is introduced to the Seraphites, their Prophet is no longer alive, and only representations of her are found in murals painted around the Seattle suburbs. Even her name is unknown to us. The Seraphites refer to her exclusively as the Prophet, and her name recurs in scattered notes that can be found. Judging by the murals dedicated to her, she was Caucasian, in her mid-fifties, had black, grayish hair that she put in a braid, and brown eyes. She inspired others not only with her preaching but also with her example of fighting the infected. The Prophet fiercely fought to keep safe her newly formed community in the Lower Queen Anne suburb of Seattle.

According to sources, her sermons proclaimed that the cordyceps infection was a punishment for humanity because it abused nature. However, these claims did not support the notion that the Divine being was responsible for this punishment. She proclaimed that those who managed to survive the outbreak had been given a second chance and had an obligation to atone for humanity by leaving technology behind and living in accordance with nature. After her death, the Prophet achieved the status of Messiah, and her murals and shrines appear all across the Seattle territory. In many of these shrines, wooden statues of her are placed there by her followers. Subsequently, her teachings were transferred into a book to serve as a foundation for the

Seraphites. The importance of her teachings is attested to by her followers who often quote from them, even during combat.

In the conversations Abby has with Lev, it is revealed that the texts containing the Prophet's teaching also give a set of instructions for the members to live in line with nature and conceal themselves from the rest of the world. There is a strong distrust in technology and civilization, and the Prophet marked them as the main reason for humanity's downfall. Therefore, the members of the Seraphites returned to their agrarian roots, do not use cars for transport but horses, and any resources that are deemed to belong to the "old world" are put under taboo. Furthermore, their homes are basic and simple, and the only embellishments allowed are ones of a religious nature. Moreover, all members dress identically.

The traditions and rules of the Seraphites are very strict. They avoid coveting material wealth and possessions, and their culture is highly communal and collectivist. After the Prophet died and the Seraphites were left without a leader, the council of Elders was formed to serve as the new leader of the group. With the formation of the institution of Elders, we can trace the first changes in the rules and norms of the group. Furthermore, the Elders represent the highest strata inside the group and exercise the right to make and enforce rules, as well as the special privilege of getting the first share of food rations.

Like other groups, the Seraphites also inflict violence on others. However, their violence is centered around ritualistic practices. If the members of the group break any of the rules, the consequences for such actions are brutal and, in many cases, punishable by death. Furthermore, their ritualistic killings of enemies are far more elaborate. The first encounter with the Seraphites is when Ellie runs into them in the wilderness while they are executing one of the WLF (Washington Liberation Front) soldiers. The soldier is treated as a sacrifice in a very brutal ritual. The Seraphites hang their sacrifices by the neck and disembowel them by chanting, "Now they are free." The ritual is conducted in the belief that sacrifices are "nested with sin," and the ritual is the only way for them to atone for their crimes and wrongdoings.

FROM PEACEFUL MOVEMENT TO RADICAL MILITANT CULT

The process of cult formation involves two distinct steps. First, new religious concepts and meanings must be invented. Second, there has to be a minimal acceptance of these ideas, at least among a smaller group of dedicated followers. In their study of cult formation, Bainbridge and Stark defined cults as social enterprises that are mainly employed in the creation and exchange of novel ideas. They present three types of cult formations: the psychopathology model, the entrepreneur model, and the subculture-evolution model. For the purposes of this study, I will rely on the psychopathology model.

The Seraphites formed in a specific moment of crisis; however, we can speculate that their leader was already tapped into a spiritual state of mind that had its roots before the outbreak. The psychopathological model of a cult is most likely to form during a societal crisis when we have a large number of people facing the same problems and challenges. The Seraphites are in many ways similar to groups described in the theory of revitalization movements proposed by Anthony Wallace. He suggests that the perils that society faces in instances such as pandemics can cause large amounts of stress on people and thus trigger the creation of such individuals as the Prophet.[21] The frightening reality of a fungus disease outbreak and the collapse of society led the Prophet and people in her proximity to find solace in her ideas that nature punished humanity because of their arrogance. It is not clear from the information provided in game notes and conversations whether the Prophet had any kind of mental illness prior to the outbreak, nor are we provided with information about whether the Prophet received visions during psychotic episodes. According to the account that came from Sally, in her letter to Cam, she did not believe the Prophet was mentally unstable and that such claims were only part of the WLF propaganda. However, there are testimonies that the Prophet claimed that she had a vision of the outbreak and that it was revealed to her that the only way for humanity to redeem itself is to leave the old ways of living and to embrace nature. In this stage of existence, the Seraphites were a peaceful group of individuals who decided to lead an egalitarian and isolated life away from the decay, conflicts, and violence of post-apocalyptic Seattle. Within the options of the dystopian world, the Seraphites fall under the "back to nature type."[22]

In the beginning, her teachings did not find the ears of many people, but as the situation deteriorated in the Seattle Quarantine Zone and the attacks of the infected became more frequent, the Prophet gained more followers, mostly because of her fierce fighting against the attackers. Step by step, the Lower Queen Anne community became completely dedicated to the Prophet's teachings that they must return to nature. Furthermore, the Seraphites detached themselves from physical pleasure and the commodities of technology and isolated themselves from the rest of the world. The community became completely self-sufficient by growing their own food and arranging a communal way of life for its members. In many ways, the early Seraphites remind us of contemporary spiritual movements that celebrate earth and nature. Ecological concerns are a very common part of the contemporary world.[23] The growing fears of natural disasters caused by global warming and violent changes in climate are omnipresent in many video games published in the last few years.[24] In response to catastrophe, the Seraphites turned to a spiritual way of life and respect for nature. The spiritual ecology is not a product of contemporary times; it goes back to biblical passages, ideas of Francis of Assisi, and nature spirituality in the East. In more recent times, Rudolf Steiner and Pierre Teilhard de Chardin, for example, propagated the divinity of nature and the awareness of its sacredness.

In the aftermath of the apocalyptic catastrophe, Seraphites organized into a collective in an attempt to overcome conflicts and isolate themselves in an effort to be protected from the violence of other groups in a fight for resources. The notion of survivalism is one of the main discourses of zombie culture.[25] In the world of *TLOU*, every fraction or character practices a different type of survivalism. In this instance, the Seraphites are a peaceful group entrenched in a spirituality and respect of nature as they fear a new pandemic that will destroy all of humanity.

The Seraphites were very successful in their self-sustainability. Therefore, by March 2014, when FEDRA (Federal Disaster Response Agency) encountered the group, it was impressed with how they managed to organize themselves and that they survived as the only community that was without military support in a fight against the infected. Moreover, the military reported that many group members were starving as their food and other supplies were short and not split equally. For this reason, FEDRA suggested the group join them and integrate into FEDRA-controlled quarantine zones, but the Seraphites refused and insisted on remaining self-governed and isolated. However, FEDRA's commander, Torres, did not consider this a threatening situation. He considered the Prophet and her followers a group of fanatics, but as they were not violent and minded their own business, FEDRA found them less troublesome in comparison to the WLF militia.

TURNING RADICAL

In the conflict between FEDRA, the military, and the WLF, the WLF turned out to be victorious. The Seraphites and their Prophet used this change in fractional interactions to occupy some suburbs that were previously controlled by FEDRA. However, this brought on strife as some of the residents of these suburbs did not look favorably upon the ideas that the Prophet preached. This led some of the residents to flee and join the WLF cause. On the other hand, those who stayed were convinced by the Prophet's ideas and quickly joined the Seraphites.

Around this time, the first conflicts between the WLF and the Seraphites took place. In the beginning, the Seraphites did not want to engage in hostilities and tried to avoid fights. In efforts to escape the attacks of the WLF, the

Seraphites retreated to the central parts of Queen Anne. When the flood cut the Queen Anne suburb from the main city, the Seraphite settlement, Haven, became an island and even more isolated than before. In efforts to expand her influence and preach her words and way of life, the Prophet established a group of Elders to promote this lifestyle.

Nonetheless, the conflict with the WLF became inevitable. The WLF fostered hatred towards the Prophet and her group, and the leader of the WLF, Isaac Dixon, dealt harshly with suspected followers of the Seraphites. For example, the WLF executed the teenager Jimmy when they found out he had the Seraphites prayer book. Afterwards, the attacks of the WLF on Seraphites became more frequent. To counter the growing WLF threat, the Prophet formed an army among the Seraphites and made an exemption for them to carry guns and rifles, even though they represented the remnants of the "old ways." According to Abby, the conflicts between the Seraphites and the WLF were not considerable until the Prophet and her group of soldiers attacked the supply convoy of the WLF and killed the soldiers accompanying it. On the other hand, Lev claimed that the Prophet did not do this to evoke more violence but only because she was forced to get more supplies for her people. Whatever the cause, this sparked the bloody guerilla war between the Seraphites and the WLF.

Thomas Robbins differentiates few factors when it comes to enhancing the probability of extreme violence by religious groups. In the first place, there is a tension between social and cultural factors, where social factors concern the structural order of leadership and cultural factors concern the beliefs of the religious group.[26] Another important factor in the radicalization of the Seraphites is the figure of the Prophet herself. As already mentioned, her influence on group members was powerful, and her persona attracted new members. The Prophet is an archetype of charismatic authority. The concept of charismatic authority, as famously formulated by Max Weber, relates "to a certain quality of an individual personality by virtue of which he is set apart from ordinary men and treated as endowed with supernatural, superhuman, or at least specifically exceptional powers or qualities."[27] Charismatic authority is rooted in the array of exceptional possibilities of an individual. The Prophet demonstrated many of the characteristics that Weber attributes to charismatic authority. She possessed charisma, exercised a strong relationship of emotions and thrust between the leader and the followers. Moreover, the trust of the Seraphites in her leading position was near-absolute. The Prophet was a visionary and an emotional leader, very much involved in the lives of her followers, and an exemplary model of group expectations. The charismatic leader is also one of the prerequisites of a world-rejecting sect that strives for absolute detachment from broader society.[28]

However, the violence of the Seraphites did not emerge from the group itself but was provoked by social conflicts that emerged in the light of the formation of the WLF. At some point during this conflict, the Prophet got captured by the WLF. While in captivity, the Prophet continued preaching her worldview and started to influence the soldiers that were guarding her. This prompted Isaac Dixon to deem her too dangerous to be left alive, and he arranged for her execution.

The death of the Prophet radicalized the Seraphites even more. After the Prophet was executed, the council of Elders assumed control and declared war on the WLF by attacking the outpost where the Prophet was killed. Even before her death, the Prophet held an extraordinary place among the Seraphites, but after her death, she became a messianic figure. The place of her execution became the Martyr's Gate, and the Seraphites made it a sacred site where they would gather to pray. Furthermore, they drew murals with her face and messages around Seattle and made shrines for her with wooden figures in her likeness.

The spirituality of the Seraphites, in the beginning, was held up as a peaceful vessel. However, when the circumstances changed and they were not only targets of hordes of infected but also of other fractions, violence became justified, and the members of the cult got caught up in this process. In the contemporary world, the violence exercised by modern religious or spiritual movements is often targeted by the state. In the case of Seraphites, their radicalization and exertion towards violence were provoked by another fraction that posed itself as the main one. Mark Juergensmeyer argued that religious violence can be inspired by the suggestive pursuit of a war that cannot be won.[29] In the case of the Seraphites, after the Prophet's death, this cause for war broadened from only infected people to other survivors who did not share the same worldview as them.

In many ways, the Seraphites resemble what Hall and Schuyler identify as a group with "apocalyptic expectations," or, in other words, a group with a vision of definitive transformations of the world, which is a main characteristic of spiritual movements that engage in extreme violence.[30] Many apocalyptic sectarian groups share the conviction that they are the elect ones in a society that is doomed and are predestined to survive the turmoil caused by the incoming apocalypse. In light of their radicalization, the Seraphites embraced a dualistic way of thinking, the mentality of "us" versus "them." This kind of attitude leads to the belief and expectation that the "Other" must be destroyed as it is demonized, filthy, and parasitic.[31]

One of the most central expressions of violence practiced by the Seraphites is undoubtedly the ritual killing of their captives. The ritual is closely connected with their belief that the cordyceps fungus was punishment for humanity, which became greatly reliant on technology and alienated from nature.³² In this way, humanity would be cleansed and put back on track to live in balance with nature. In a post-apocalyptic world where contagion is a real threat, anxiety is rooted in a deep abhorrence of disease and bodily frailty. The ritualistic sacrifice is reserved for the "Others" as a part of the repugnance and fears of contagion.³³ This practice is rooted in the emotion of disgust towards a body infested with pathogens and parasites. The "Others" are in Seraphites' beliefs "nested with sin" and their exposure to pathogens invokes "moral disgust at violations of social norms."³⁴ The ritual serves as both a way of achieving the prophesized utopia in which humanity lives in balance with nature and a burst of violence as an expression of fears of infestation and losing control over oneself.³⁵

Finally, the brutal violence of the Seraphites is not reserved only for those they consider enemies but also for the members who challenged the rules. While playing as Abby, gamers first meet the siblings Yara and Lev, now Seraphite apostates. The Seraphites are about to ritually sacrifice a captured Abby when they are interrupted by Yara, who helped her rebellious brother Lev escape the cult. Lev, a transgender male, refused to be married to one of the Elders and cut his hair as an act of defiance. This placed Lev in mortal danger, as the Seraphites would never recognize him as male or allow him to live his life as a man. His older sister Yara helped him escape, and for this she was punished by crushing her arm with a hammer, or as the Seraphites referred to this punishment, "clipping her wings." With precise and deadly arrows, Lev prevents the Seraphites from breaking Yara's other arm. The siblings free Abby, and the three of them fight and flee the infected and the pursuing Seraphites. Yara and Lev then become important parts of Abby's redemption arcs as she focuses her efforts on protecting them. Her dedication to them runs so deep that she follows Lev as he returns to Haven in an effort to save his mother. However, Yara and Lev's mother is an example of what Maxim Podvalny calls a fanatic follower, "a sincere believer of a certain religion."³⁶ Their mother's devotion to the Seraphites' cause was greater than her love for her children. In the final confrontation with his mother, Lev was faced with a woman who would rather kill him than abandon the rules and beliefs of the Seraphites. Lev ends up killing his mother and escapes Haven just before the WLF army burns the island. Unlike other characters in *TLOU2*, Yara and Lev avoid conflict at all costs. Lev's path is different than Ellie's and Abby's. Even though he goes through immense suffering, Lev has no interest in revenge or violence in and of itself. Even though he is rejected by his community, Lev is still deeply religious and believes that the Prophet never intended her words to be used as a vessel for the cruelty and violence that the Seraphites exercised. Lev is a positive character, a reminder that even in a world full of violence, revenge, and decay, it is possible to stay true to yourself and not be part of ever-present violence.

CONCLUSION

The post-apocalyptic America of *TLOU* depicts the collapse of society after the deadly pandemic, infested with zombies and smaller fractions of "savage" groups led by different types of charismatic leaders, some of them cruel and calculated, others engaged in peaceful coexistence. The creators of *TLOU*, with the example of the Seraphites, painted an example of a fraction inspired by a charismatic religious leader propagating the idea that pandemics were the "revenge of nature."

In the beginning, the Seraphites were a peaceful group seeking an egalitarian and self-sustainable way of life. However, after further interactions with other fractions of post-apocalyptic Seattle, such as FEDRA and WLF, the Seraphites were forced to radicalize and embraced violence. Their radicalization took an ominous turn with the martyrdom of their Prophet. By the time the player is introduced to the Seraphites, they are already radicalized and engaged in ritualized brutality and violence. This violence is directed at both outsiders and their own members. As I previously pointed out, the inspiration for Seraphites could be found in contemporary radical environmentalist movements and apocalyptic cults. Their progression in radicalization gives an example of how a peaceful movement could be easily radicalized.

In the background of *TLOU*, there are omnipresent fears and anxieties about the perils and consequences of a pandemic. Even though *TLOU2* is mostly focused on the revenge, violence, and redemption of two main protagonists, the world in which they exist is still infested with infected, and the society that crumbled in the face of the violent disease is not in sight of being restored.

Yara and Lev are in contrast to other characters in *TLOU2*. The siblings were raised by the Seraphites and expressed deep devotion to the Prophet's words and teachings. However, when confronted with the rejection and brutality of the Seraphites, Yara and especially Lev stood their ground, firmly believing that violence was never a part of the Prophet's teachings. Lev remains calm despite the immense suffering inflicted on him by his fellow cult members as well as by his own mother. He is not in search of revenge, nor does his faith in the words of the Prophet fall into doubt.

In the face of the apocalypse, many people react differently. The existence of the Seraphites portrays a possible reaction in front of a force stronger than an individual, a group, or even a society. Furthermore, in the character of the Prophet and the blind devotion of the Seraphites are warnings of an inherent risk of adhering to a charismatic leader and the proclivity of followers to exhibit unquestioning loyalty. This can result in a state of internal corruption, in which an individual's own moral guidance system gets corrupted. Even though these narratives are fictitious, they reflect the possibilities of such developments in real life and the human need to justify traumatic events by believing that human disrespect of nature leads to their demise.

NOTES

1. Veale, "Making Science Fiction Personal," 41–48.
2. *The Last of Us*, 2014.
3. *The Last of Us Part II*, 2020.
4. Mago, "The Last of Us Part II," 87–88.
5. Muncy, "Perspective: The Trans Narrative in 'The Last of Us Part II' Is Compelling. There's So Much More to Be Done."
6. In the context of this discussion, the term *cult* is used for convenience and should be understood with caution due to its potential pejorative connotations. It is acknowledged that the term has been historically employed to stigmatize certain New Religious Movements (NRMs), many of which are nonviolent in nature. Scholars and researchers have debated the appropriateness of using this term, and its usage here is not intended to pass judgment on the legitimacy or practices of any particular group.
7. Taylor, "Radical Environmentalism's Print History," 54–54.
8. Bainbridge and Stark, "Cult Formation: Three Compatible Models," 283–295.
9. Heidbrink, Knoll, and Wysocki, "Theorizing Religion in Digital Games."
10. Bendle, "The Apocalyptic Imagination and Popular Culture," 1–11.
11. Pitetti, "Uses of the End of the World," 437–454.
12. Pérez-Latorre, "Post-Apocalyptic Games, Heroism and the Great Recession."
13. Bosman and van Wieringen, "Video Games."
14. Hicks, *The Post-Apocalyptic Novel in the Twenty-First Century*.
15. Luckhurst, *The Public Sphere*.
16. Mariani, "From Haitian Slavery to *The Walking Dead*."
17. Hunt, "A Utilitarian Antagonist," 107–123.
18. Schubert, "Playing as/against Violent Women," 30–54.
19. Malešević, "Violence and the Apocalypse," 135.
20. el-Ojeili and Taylor, "The Future in the Past," 168–186.
21. Wallace, "Revitalization Movements," 264–281.
22. Pérez-Latorre, "Post-Apocalyptic Games, Heroism and the Great Recession."
23. King, "One Planet, One Spirit," 74–95.
24. For example, the Anthropocene, global warming consequences, and extinction are main par to the narrative of *Death Stranding* (Kojima Productions).
25. Murphy, "Lessons from the Zombie Apocalypse in Global Popular Culture," 44–57.
26. Robbins, "Sources of Volatility in Religious Movements," 57–79.
27. Weber, *The Theory of Social and Economic Organization*.
28. Taylor, "Religion, Violence, and Radical Environmentalism," 418.
29. Juergensmeyer, "Religious Violence."
30. Hall, Schuyler, and Trinh, *Apocalypse Observed*.

31. Robbins and Anthony, "Sects and Violence," 343–363.
32. Farca and Ladevèze, "The Journey to Nature."
33. Booth, "Organisms and Human Bodies as Contagions in the Post-Apocalyptic State," 17–30.
34. Curtis and Biran, "Dirt, Disgust, and Disease: Is Hygiene in our Genes?" 17–31.
35. Green, "The Reconstruction of Morality and the Evolution of Naturalism in *The Last of Us*," 745–763.
36. Podvalnyi, "Religious Cults in the Fictional Universe of the RPG *The Witcher*," 91–104.

BIBLIOGRAPHY

Bainbridge, William S., and Rodney Stark. "Cult Formation: Three Compatible Models." *Sociological Analysis* 40.4 (1979): 283–295.

Bendle, Mervyn F. "The Apocalyptic Imagination and Popular Culture." *Journal of Religion and Popular Culture* 11.1 (2005): 1–11.

Booth, Robert A. "Organisms and Human Bodies as Contagions in the Post-Apocalyptic State." *Race, Gender, and Sexuality in Post-Apocalyptic TV and Film* (2015): 17–30.

Bosman, Frank, and Archibald van Wieringen. "Video Games." In *Critical Dictionary of Apocalyptic and Millenarian Movements*, edited by James Crossley and Alastair Lockhart, Centre for the Critical Study of Apocalyptic and Millenarian Movements, 2021, https://www.cdam-m.org/.

Curtis, Valerie, and Adam Biran. "Dirt, Disgust, and Disease: Is Hygiene in Our Genes?" *Perspectives in Biology and Medicine* 44.1 (2001): 17–31.

el-Ojeili, Chamsy, and Dylan Taylor. "The Future in the Past: Anarcho-Primitivism and the Critique of Civilization Today." *Rethinking Marxism* 32.2 (2020): 168–186.

Farca, Gerald, and Charlotte Ladevèze. "The Journey to Nature: The Last of Us as Critical Dystopia." *DiGRA/FDG* First Joint International Conference, Dundee, 2016.

Green, Amy M. "The Reconstruction of Morality and the Evolution of Naturalism in *The Last of Us*." *Games and Culture* 11.7–8 (2016): 745–763.

Hall, John R., Philip Daniel Schuyler, and Sylvaine Trinh. *Apocalypse Observed: Religious Movements and Violence in North America, Europe, and Japan*. New York: Psychology Press, 2000.

Heidbrink, Simone, Tobias Knoll, and Jan Wysocki. "Theorizing Religion in Digital Games. Perspectives and Approaches." *Online-Heidelberg Journal of Religions on the Internet* 5 (2014), https://doi.org/10.11588/rel.2014.0.12156.

Hicks, Heather J. *The Post-Apocalyptic Novel in the Twenty-First Century: Modernity Beyond Salvage*. New York: Palgrave Macmillan, 2016.

Hunt, Nathan. "A Utilitarian Antagonist: The Zombie in Popular Video Games." *The Zombie Renaissance in Popular Culture* (2015): 107–123.

Juergensmeyer, Mark. "Religious Violence." In *The Oxford Handbook of the Sociology of Religion*, edited by Peter B. Clarke (pp. 890–908). Oxford, UK: Oxford University Press, 2011.

King, Ursula. "One Planet, One Spirit: Searching for an Ecologically Balanced Spirituality." In *Pierre Teilhard de Chardin on People and Planet*, edited by Celia Deane-Drummond (pp. 74–95). Abingdon: Routledge, 2017.

Lachman, Gary. *Rudolf Steiner: An Introduction to His Life and Work*. New York: Penguin Publishing, 2007.

Luckhurst, Roger. *The Public Sphere, Popular Culture, and the True Meaning of the Zombie Apocalypse*. Cambridge, UK: Cambridge University Press, 2012.

Mago, Zdenko. "The Last of Us Part II." *Acta Ludologica* 3.2 (2020): 87–88.

Malešević, Siniša. "Violence and the Apocalypse." In *Violence and Reflexivity: The Place of Critique in the Reality of Domination*, edited by Marjan Ivković et al. Lanham, MD: Lexington Books, 2022.

Mariani, Mike. "From Haitian Slavery to *The Walking Dead*: The Tragic, Forgotten History of Zombies." *Atlantic*, October 28, 2015, https://www.theatlantic.com/entertainment/archive/2015/10/how-america-erased-the-tragic-history-of-the-zombie/412264/.

Muncy, Julie. "Perspective: The Trans Narrative in 'The Last of Us Part II' Is Compelling. There's So Much More to Be Done." *Washington Post*, July 23, 2020, https://www.washingtonpost.com/video-games/2020/07/21/trans-narrative-last-us-part-ii-is-compelling-theres-so-much-more-be-done/.

Murphy, Patrick D. "Lessons from the Zombie Apocalypse in Global Popular Culture: An Environmental Discourse Approach to *The Walking Dead*." *Environmental Communication* 12.1 (2018): 44–57.

Naughty Dog. *The Last of Us*. Sony Computer Entertainment, 2014.

———. *The Last of Us Part II*. Sony Computer Entertainment, 2020.

Pérez-Latorre, Óliver. "Post-Apocalyptic Games, Heroism, and the Great Recession." *Game Studies* 19.3 (2019), https://gamestudies.org/1903/articles/perezlatorre.

Pitetti, Connor. "Uses of the End of the World: Apocalypse and Post-Apocalypse as Narrative Modes." *Science Fiction Studies* 44.3 (2017): 437–454.

Podvalnyi, Maksim. "Religious Cults in the Fictional Universe of the RPG *The Witcher*." *State, Religion, and Church* 7.1 (2020): 91–104.

Robbins, Thomas. "Sources of Volatility in Religious Movements." *Cults, Religion, and Violence* (2002): 57–79.

Robbins, Thomas, and Dick Anthony. "Sects and Violence: Factors Enchasing the Volatility of Marginal Religious Movements." In *Armageddon in Waco: Critical Perspectives on the Branch Davidian Conflict*, edited by Stuart Wright (pp. 236–257). Chicago: University of Chicago Press, 1995.

Schubert, Stefan. "Playing as/against Violent Women: Imagining Gender in the Post-apocalyptic Landscape of *The Last of Us Part II*." *Gender Forum* 80 (2021): 30–54.

Taylor, Bron. "Religion, Violence, and Radical Environmentalism." *Pomegranate* 10 (1999): 4–18.

———. "Radical Environmentalism's Print History: From Earth First! To Wild Earth." *Environment and Society Portal, Virtual Exhibitions* 1 (2018), doi.org/10.5282/rcc/7988.

Veale, Kevin. "Making Science Fiction Personal: Videogames and Inter-affective Storytelling." In *The Projected and Prophetic: Humanity in Cyberculture, Cyberspace, and Science Fiction*, edited by Jordan J. Copeland (pp. 41–48). Leiden: Brill, 2011.

Wallace, Anthony. "Revitalization Movements." *American Anthropologist* (1956): 264–281.

Weber, Max. *The Theory of Social and Economic Organization*. Edited with an introduction by Talcott Parsons. New York: Simon and Schuster, 2009.

PART II
Ethics

Chapter 6

On Relationality, Human Beings, and Clickers

Robert Grant Price

One of the strangest moments in the TV version of *The Last of Us* (*TLOU*) is a kiss. In crossing the hellscape that is Boston, Tess is bitten by a clicker (what *TLOU* call zombies).[1] She orders her partner Joel and Ellie, the girl she wants to help, to flee the horde of the undead, then spills gasoline and grenades across the floor of the Massachusetts State House. Before she can set off the explosion—her lighter will not light—one of the clickers breaks from the throng, approaches her, and opens its mouth. Strands of fungus reach out to Tess from the clicker's mouth. The two kiss. In this moment, Tess transitions from a sovereign person into a node in the clicker hive mind. It is only through force of will that Tess is able to drop the lighter and blow up herself and the army of walking corpses.

This moment illustrates the conflicting natures of the human and the clicker. As this chapter hopes to explain, the human being's nature is relational: Humans exhibit a "*towards-others*"[2] orientation, or to put it another way, an affinity for difference. The nature of the infected, by contrast, is non-relational. The infected are animated by cordyceps, a mind-controlling fungus that slowly colonizes the individual mind. The franchise's storytellers never really explain the biology of the infected, but on the television version of *TLOU*, people captured by the fungus tend to pass through various stages of infection and eventually are incorporated into a clicker hive mind. This collective intelligence cannot relate to what is not itself, and so to find relation, the clicker must assimilate the other, a process that consumes and eliminates the one it touches.

The oppositional relational natures of humans and clickers—with human relation, there is difference; with infected, there is sameness—cannot be reconciled, and the irreconcilable conflict fuels the narrative of the franchise. The never-ending conflict between the humans and the clickers also provides a warning of what becomes of human-to-human relations when differences cannot be reconciled, and it is a horror.

DEFINING RELATIONS

"In the beginning is the relation," writes Martin Buber (1878–1965), a Jewish philosopher best remembered for his dialogical theory of relations that he outlined in *I and Thou*.[3] This phrasing echoes the opening lines of the Book of Genesis[4] to show the pre-existent nature of relation to existence itself. In Genesis, God creates each element of the universe and judges each pairing—land and sea, day and night—as "good as a relationship."[5]

The relational basis of reality, Buber argues, presents itself in language. "Basic words are not single words but word pairs."[6] Basic words invoke their opposites. When a man says "I," he also says "You." The "I" contains the "You." "Basic words do not state something that might exist outside them; by being spoken they establish a mode of existence."[7] Ethics emerge from this condition, word pairs that establish a moral framework. To speak to "You" is to address you as another subject, a free person unto herself, since the "I" and "You" linguistically and relationally exist in both. To speak the word pair "I" and "It" recognizes the other as an object, not as a subject. When a person is reduced to an object, evil becomes permissible. The act of degrading another to a thing harms the speaker since the eradication of the other's freedom and subjecthood transforms the speaker's capacity to relate and to know another.

Emmanuel Levinas (1906–1995), a famously difficult philosopher and ethicist, wrestled with the concepts of Self and Other in ways that parallel Buber. For Levinas, relations can be best defined as responsibility.[8] Relationships are not based on what a person can give to another, or on how they might relate (as family relations, for example), but on the responsibility to care for the other's well-being that exists simply by virtue of the encounter between the two. This responsibility is prelinguistic and rooted in the face, the place where Levinas sees the starting point for all relations and the location of "first philosophy."[9] When he speaks about the face, he does not necessarily mean the nose, the eyes, and the mouth; he means that ineffable quality found in the face-to-face encounter. The experience at the heart of this encounter is the first-person singular, the transcendence behind the other and from which relational ethics find their grounding. The face-to-face encounter is a "primordial ethical event"[10] that registers a "'moral summons,' the content of which is to share, to be generous, and most fundamentally to acknowledge and accept the other person."[11]

The face holds a quality that exists beyond classification,[12] what Levinas calls the infinite. Every time one person looks into the eyes of another, they glimpse the infinite. Yet by articulating what the person sees, using imprecise language to capture what cannot be captured, the relationship and the other degrades into a category, some "thing." Case in point: When Joel looks at Ellie, he can classify her (see her) as a burden, as a young woman, as an annoyance, as a friend, or something else. However he chooses to classify her, the act of classification reduces the transcendent potential in her, in the uniqueness in her being, and in the relationship they can form.

But relation demands some sort of category. The categories are bound up in word pairs. "I" speaks of "You." "The living" speaks of "the dead"—or "the undead." This is the dilemma: If you look at another and see a category, then you are not seeing all there is to see. But, of course, we must categorize people if we are to make sense of the one who we encounter. Imagine walking through a forest at the end of the world and seeing a body shuffling towards you. It makes eminent sense to look with the intent to classify that other. Is it a friend, a foe, or a fungus-ravaged bloater? Yet in the vein in which Levinas spoke, the face-to-face encounter cannot help but demand an ethical response. Ethics—the demand for generosity—exists in that point of contact, leaving each person with the choice of how to respond to that ethical demand. To kill that person shuffling in the forest is one response. Murder may, in fact, be the wisest response and the most ethical, if that creature is a clicker. But to kill another human being, even a threatening human being, requires the person to ignore the vulnerability and demand for reciprocation inherent in the other. To put it crassly: It is always wise to kill a zombie. Killing humans . . . well, it's complicated.

This dilemma that both Buber and Levinas articulate finds a shadow logic from the clicker's point of view. The human can look at another, recognize the responsibility owed to the other, and give the other what's needed to thrive. The human is beholden to ethics; evil is a choice. The clicker, on the other hand, is unable to conduct reciprocal relations. The clicker is a parasite. For the clicker, the human is a raw commodity, something to consume, and to use as hosts for its own consciousness. Whether clickers know the evil in what they do does not matter. The point is that humans do. When humans treat others as raw commodities, they become like the clickers. This is the horror of the show: The transformation of the infinite into a singularity, whether that happens when a clicker infects another or when one of the desperate humans erases the infinite potential of another human by turning them into canon fodder, sex object, or nutrients.

TLOU provides a running series of case studies in relational ethics—so much so that the parallels between mowing down an acre of tottering zombies and murdering a group of humans hardly need to be said. The way that characters in zombie films work up the nerve to kill other people is the same way they kill zombies: they turn the human being into a thing and blow their (its) brains out. This denaturing of the human happens in some of the most awful scenes in *TLOU*. In the first episode, a soldier receives orders to kill Joel and his daughter Sarah.[13] The orders make practical sense. Joel and Sarah could be infected, and they must contain the infection no matter the cost. Yet, the soldier hesitates. He hears Joel's pleas. He sees Joel's humanity, his subjectivity, and for a moment the soldier appears to work through the process of transforming Joel and Sarah into objects. He closes off the potential for relation with Joel by eliminating in his own mind the possibility of exchange, and the best way to do that is to shoot Joel in the head. The soldier doesn't get the chance. Joel's brother Tommy shoots him before he can aim. The soldier fires a wild shot that kills Sarah but misses Joel.

JOEL AND RESPONSIBILITY TO THE OTHER

As a character, Joel only develops when he allows himself to see the other as a subject. Before the outbreak, Joel was an ordinary man who juggled parenting with his construction business. He was a good man who could see the need in others. When the next-door neighbors asked Sarah to visit them after school, Joel assured them that she would be there. He saw his neighbors as people worthy of attention, and he wanted his daughter to see others in the same way.

Sarah's death and years of life in a traumatized world transform Joel into a man who will not allow himself to see the personhood in almost any other he encounters. On the television show, he makes a living smuggling contraband and hauling corpses onto pyres; in the video game, he eeks out a barebones existence, killing innocent people as he tries to survive.[14] When, on the HBO show, Marlene begs him to escort Ellie across the country, Joel agrees but reluctantly. He treats Ellie as an obligation. As they journey across the wasteland, he permits Ellie no personal questions. He wants no relationship with her. She is, as he tells her in a moment of anger, "cargo."[15]

Ellie, who grew up during the time of infection, has a different view of others. She wants to know about the times before the infection, and she sees Joel as a source of information and interest. She likes him and tries to relate to him. She demands answers to her questions. She will not let him treat her like a thing.

In the end, Joel recovers the ability to see the other. He appears to see Ellie as a person unto herself, not as a replacement for Sarah—he makes that clear—but as a person he can love. His conversion comes in "When We Are in Need," when he calls Ellie "baby girl," a pet name he had given

Sarah.[16] His commitment to Ellie is total. He is willing to die for her, and he's willing to kill for her. When he learns that Ellie will be sacrificed to find a cure to the plague, Joel rampages through the Firefly hospital and murders everyone, including Marlene, somebody he had once known well.[17] Joe's willingness to commit mass murder undermines the budding character he has developed as a man who had learned again how to see the face of the other. In the game, players have the choice to spare some of the Fireflies, but in the show, Joel kills them all, treating these people as obstacles that he must move so that he can have what he wants: Ellie.

Before Joel had gone on his murder spree, Ellie had told him that she would follow him wherever he went. Originally, Joel had been cold to Ellie's daughterly love but at the end of the first season he reciprocates, going so far as to lie to Ellie about what he had done to save her life. This lie is an act of hope. He has become a person who, after years of trauma and self-imposed solitude, wants relations. Part of the drama of the ongoing serial hinges on whether Joel is capable of ethical relations, given how much he has warped himself through murder and deception. Ellie may be a daughter-like figure who he can love, but if that relation requires that he lie to Ellie, the audience can reasonably wonder if such a relationship is truly relational and reciprocal. Ellie has not entered into the relationship as a free and informed person. While he is far more nuanced than in his other relations, Joel is, again, treating another as an "It" and not a "You" who deserves the truth.

COMMUNICATING WITH THE OTHER

The corruption of "I-You" relations powers the conflict behind *TLOU*. The humans can recognize the subjectivity in others, and by doing so create the potential for relation and reciprocity.[18] But when faced with clickers, the human being cannot act reciprocally. Their only relation seems to be between subject and object, between I and It.

But what can the humans on the show do about it? If they do not objectify these mushroom-infested cadavers and treat them as beings unworthy of relation, the clickers will kill them. And, it should be said, the zombies featured in *TLOU* are like objects. Despite clickers appearing to be subjects—they have eyes that can hold the gaze of another; they can respond to stimuli, make decisions, and act—they cannot speak as an "I" since they appear to be collected into a single distributed consciousness. Is individual clicker personhood even possible if, as Roger Scruton argues, "freewill enters our world through the 'I'"?[19] This image of the zombie as an automaton incapable of first-person subjectivity runs through the genre, notably in *Dawn of the Dead*, which portrays the undead as mindless consumers trying to get inside a mall to shop.[20] The zombie is the person who loses the self, whether to a mob or to a corporate body.

The relational problem between clickers and humans seems at first to be a linguistic challenge. If clickers and humans could communicate using a shared language, they could find a way to relate. But shared language between the human and the zombie proves not to be the barrier to relations. Even though language reveals relation, relation can exist without language. Doctors can care for comatose patients with time, attention, and love even if the patients cannot actively reciprocate. The relationship belongs to both groups (even though one is passive), and both can benefit from the relationship. But such a relationship can only exist when caregivers see the other as a person—as a subject, not as an object—and, as Margaret Sommerville explains, when they see themselves in the other.[21]

In *TLOU*, noncommunicative relations with the clicker seem equally impossible since the zombie is inherently violent and unable to see the potential for relation with humanity. Communication with the zombie is impossible, unless the clicker colonizes and destroys the human's mind. The encounter between humans and clickers highlights the need for relational encounters that acknowledge the inherent worth of the other. But considering that clickers want to dominate humans and humans want to exterminate clickers, community between these species is a fantasy, even in a work of fiction.

DIFFERENCE AND SAMENESS

Levinas saw differences, not similarities, as the foundation for relations. This is how metaphor works, for example. A metaphor must compare two different realms of experience for a metaphor to have any power. "The ocean is like a huge body of water" makes no sense as a metaphor, even though it has a structure of a simile. For Levinas, sameness has an assimilative power; it destroys relations. In an encounter with the other, the move to categorize removes difference and collapses the other into some other thing. The elimination of difference diminishes relations, since sameness cannot relate to itself. A sea meets sea and is sea. But when the sea meets land, a shoreline and the two relate. By this logic, and given the massive differences in relational modes between humans and zombies, the two creatures ought to be able to develop deep and meaningful relations. And they do. Relations between the two species are deep, meaningful, and catastrophic.

Reciprocal relations are impossible because zombie existence is predicated on sameness. Cordyceps, the fungus controlling the minds of clickers, communicates all at once through every node in the network. The effect of immediate communication, for example, sits at the center of *The Expulsion of the Other* by the Korean-German philosopher Byung Chul Han. For Han, instantaneous interaction creates a permanent now and a permanent oneness. "Hypercommunication," he says, "destroys the *you* and *closeness*. Relationships are replaced by *connections*."[22] What Han calls "gaplessness" captures the undead nature of *TLOU*'s infected. There is no distance in the zombie's networked mind, and because there is no distance, there is no closeness and no opposite. If, as Han argues, "things are given life precisely by their opposite,"[23] then the clickers in *TLOU* are certainly dead. As a networked consciousness, they are all the same thing. It cannot see the opposite of what it is. This takes literal form in *TLOU*: In stage 3 of the infection, all the infected lose their eyesight.

The sameness of the infected influences the human survivors in a notable way. As a species, the humans drift towards sameness in their relations. Relationships that harmonize differences become especially fraught in the Quarantine Zones (QZs), the dismal urban centers where totalitarian governments impose a standard rule to secure human life against the fungal menace and demolish individual freedom. The QZ in *TLOU* represents the last and most forceful corporate enterprise in human history. While not nodes in a network, the people are all reduced to the same level. They are objects under the control of a police force characterized by a dreaded sameness of attire and attitude.

COMMUNAL RELATIONS IN THE END TIMES

To the Christian, relation is the irreducible dimension in the human being, a foundation that originates in the triune God, who is Himself pure Relation. "Life is radically a relationship that embraces the dimension of the person and that of the cosmos," writes Maspero. "The deepest and truest identity of the human being is relational."[24] By remaining orientated towards the other, the human comes into being as a person.[25] "Good" relations reproduce the goodness found in God's perfect relation—in their love for the other. Humans can relate to what is other than themselves and, by loving the other, come into full being. "Man finds his center of gravity, not inside, but outside himself."[26]

Community, a vivid expression of humanity's relational nature, is a foundational element in Christian life. *TLOU* asks an important question in regard to Christian understanding of community: How can humans live with something so alien and violent that we cannot even begin to establish relations?

Dietrich Bonhoeffer offers an answer in *Life Together*, a work he wrote during World War II. A Lutheran minister who publicly denounced Nazism and was eventually murdered for his Christian protest against Hitler's tyranny,

Bonhoeffer shows the polarities that can pull a community apart. One of these polarities relates to how the community has formed. Spiritual communities (communities that form to be with Christ) differ markedly from emotional communities (communities that form to satisfy the desire that people have to be with one another). Bonhoeffer warns against conflating sincere spiritual devotion with an overly romanticized or idealized notion of what a Christian community should be. This romantic notion, what he calls "emotional love," rather than "spiritual love," "breeds artificial hothouse flowers."[27] On shallow roots emotional communities bloom and quickly die. And this threat of "confusing Christian community with some wishful image of a pious community, the danger of blending the devout heart's natural desire for community with the spiritual reality of Christian community,"[28] can destroy a community from the outset.

This denunciation of emotional views of Christian life arrives most shockingly in "When We Are in Need."[29] The first glimpse of the Christian community at Silver Lake shows a surface-level of commitment to Christianity. The people read Scripture. They pray together and eat together. To an outsider, they appear to live a communal, Christian life. Life is hard, but at least they have each other and David, a leader who looks out for them. The place seems like the Christian ideal.

Now imagine a sentimental Christian seeking a place to hide from the clickers. She discovers the Silver Lake resort and assumes that because Christians run the resort, it must be safe for Christians. But she would eventually see what the audiences sees: a Satanic horror. David uses Christ to manipulate his scared followers. He insists they call him "father." He commits rape. And he is the one who rationalizes cannibalism. "Christian community is a spiritual and not an emotional reality," Bonhoeffer writes.[30] If the desire to be with other Christians overrides the moral imperative, the Chrisitan community will have no community worth calling Christian. It would be a place like Silver Lake, where the good Christians let their leader terrorize and eat other people.

BILL AND FRANK

In *Life Together*, Bonhoeffer meditates on how to build lasting communities. One maxim identifies the sort of people who will not do well in a community: "Whoever cannot be alone should be aware of community. Whoever cannot stand being in community should be aware of being alone."[31] These two personalities appear in the characters of Frank and Bill.[32]

Frank is the "one who cannot be alone." Gregarious, handsome, forward, Frank seeks community. When he first appears on the screen, Frank says he had been with a group and that everybody else had died. After he's rescued by Bill, Frank works to break the silence—he cannot stand silence—by talking and by playing the piano stationed in the front room of Bill's quiet house. Bonhoeffer warns about the trouble that can erupt from the person who cannot be alone. They will "plunge into the void of words and feelings"[33] to fill the silence. "Such people," Bonhoeffer warns, "will only do harm to themselves and to the community."[34] Frank's desire to be with others goes beyond the natural desire that people have to be among others. Frank is the kind of person who needs community all of the time to keep him from being alone with himself. The worst thing that can happen for a man like Frank is to find himself alone in a lonely world. That is where he finds himself. He seeks out somebody else. The somebody he finds is Bill.

Bill embodies the person who "cannot stand being in community." He's an exemplary doomer, an anti-social, anti-government, gun-toting libertarian who spent his best years in the normal world building a fortress for the End Times under his mother's house. He embodies the lie that a man can isolate himself from the world and be happy. While Bill probably could live alone forever, he shows himself to be a "bottomless pit of vanity, self-infatuation, and despair."[35] He's the one person in the show who seems happy that the world has ended, but that's only because he feels vindicated in his misanthropy. He does not yet have the self-awareness to see what a hell the world has become and how lonely he is.

The episode places these diametrically opposed characters in immediate tension: Bill holds a gun to Frank's face. The two men sense the relation inherent in the polarities they occupy and within hours of meeting each other they end up in bed. The episode travels forward in time to show that Frank and Bill have become the odd couple. They squabble. Frank remakes the house, an outward sign of care for a community that no longer exists, and he hosts a garden party with Joel and Tess to create the illusion of society. Bill, once a violent recluse, accepts these concessions.

By the end of the episode, the two men who were desperately in need of balance show themselves to have been converted into their other through the decades-long relationship they nurtured through the apocalypse. When Frank wakes and announces that this will be his last day—he will commit suicide to spare himself the pain of dying of cancer—Bill admits how he himself has changed. "I was never afraid before you showed up," he tells Frank. When Bonhoeffer speaks about life together, he talks about the challenges of living with the knowledge that in time the people who are most precious to us will leave us. Frank is the person Bill had always feared losing. He had lived with the fantasy of solitude, thinking he was enough to fill himself, and becomes one who cannot be alone.

A similar transformation happens with Frank. At first, Frank abhors solitude but over the course of years develops into a talented painter. Painting is a solitary pursuit, one that demands that the painter engage with himself in silence. Frank gets good at silence.

If we understand what Bonhoeffer has to say, we see that in a world empty of empathy and people, Bill and Frank have managed to create a community between themselves and been transformed through that community. This is the intent of the episode: to show a love story set at the end of time. But since *TLOU* is a horror story, all happy endings must turn bad. That is what happens to Bill and Frank. At the end of the episode, the audience learns that neither man has learned the lesson offered by the other, and neither has learned how to live within community, as Bonhoeffer understood it. When faced again with solitude, Bill, who prior to the outbreak avoided other people, does not return to the silence as a reformed man who can accept being alone with himself. By the final sequence, he is no longer the solitary figure who can speak for himself. He wears the clothes Frank tells him to wear and crushes the pills that Frank will use to kill himself. Bill dissolves in the other so completely that he despairs of being alone. He kills himself rather than face the solitude he once longed for.

And Frank appears to never have fully understood what it means to live in community. He becomes comfortable with solitude, but at the climax of the story (and his relationship to Bill) his discomfort with the Other shows through. Bonhoeffer reminds readers that we all die alone.[36] This is a solitude we must each endure for ourselves. But not Frank. On his last night, he drinks a poisoned glass of wine to spare himself from a natural death. Bill poisons himself, too, and assures Frank that his (Bill's) decision to kill himself "isn't the tragic suicide at the end of the play" because he is "old" and "satisfied." When Frank realizes that Bill will die with him in a joint suicide on their wedding night, Frank remarks in a grimly narcissistic fashion that, while he does not "approve" of Bill's suicide, his decision to die with him is "incredibly romantic" from "an objective point of view."

The delight Frank shows at the realization that he will not die alone is a ghoulish instance of Frank's Bonhoefferian defect surfacing, his not wanting to be without community. Rather than appealing for his lover to live on, Frank glows with satisfaction at the idea that he will die in a community. This final act does not undo their years together, but it shows a misguided understanding of how community should operate. For Bonhoeffer, "the goal of the Christian community is to encounter one another as bringers of the message of salvation."[37] There is no indication that Bill and Frank want a Christian community, but surely the goal of their community was more than just a way to survive the loneliness. And they did more than survive. They built a place of salvation—an oasis of civilization—in the wilderness of the End Times. Yet, as Bonhoeffer predicts, Frank's inability to be alone and to die alone, along with Bill's inability to be alone with himself, leads to a tragic demise of their community and the outpost they had created. Bill could have gone on. He might have found a way to gift his little town to another group. He could have led them. Instead, Bill killed himself and Frank celebrated his suicide. Despite Bill's assertion that his poisoning himself "isn't the tragic suicide at the end of the play," it is tragic.

BASIC STATES

Generally, it is a mistake to reduce fiction to a morality play, yet it is hard not to see the moral dynamics running through *TLOU*. The show defines ethical relations in ways that, while complex, conform to a morality most Westerners know. They know that it is wrong to "other" another. They understand intuitively, as do the characters on the show, that I-Thou relations are the foundation of all reciprocal relationships, and ethics become unavoidable in a face-to-face encounter.

The show illustrates the extremities of human relations. Without distance in relations, sameness reigns. The hyperconnectivity of the marauding zombies on the TV show are not a threat that the viewers face. But the dangers of sameness borne from hyper-connected lives do threaten relations in the real world. The digital mob can turn otherwise "normal" people into nodes in a network that aims to destroy the lives of other people.

The show reveals the reverse, as well. When differences become irreconcilable, and when the gap between two parties becomes too wide to cross, violence erupts. The human and the zombie cannot relate. They have no shared language, and humans have no way to communicate with clickers outside of assimilating into the zombie mind. As the show demonstrates in episode after episode, the zombie cannot see the human as a subject worthy of independent existence. It is a cognitive impossibility for the clicker. Nor can humans risk bestowing personhood on the clickers. The monsters will eat them if they do. There will be war until one erases the other.

If Relation is God, then the show presents us with a world where God is denied, repressed, and hidden. Reciprocity appears as rarely as the sun. When meaningful interchange between people rises as a possibility, a threat always follows. In most cases of the show, the best that the humans can achieve with one another is a temporary moment of togetherness, or in the case of Bill and Frank, a much longer but no less mortal engagement. This is one of the difficulties that makes life together so hard, as Bonhoeffer explains, and as the show illustrates. Bill and Frank, who share one of the show's only workable relationships, ignore the imperative to preserve life and instead kill themselves. Joel finds relation with Ellie, but their relationship is blemished by the many people they have killed and the lie he tells Ellie at the end of the first season—a lie that will surely be a rupture in their relationship when she inevitably finds out. The show presents the horror facing all humans. For zombies, relations are impossible, and they can become impossible for humans, too, if they see the other as a thing, a totality, and not as an infinity. If humans cannot harmonize differences, they must face the fact that the relationship will eventually end in violence.

Thankfully, the show provides a counterpoint to the horror. Despite the monsters, the murders, and the transient nature of the relations on the show, almost every person on the show wants reciprocal relations with others. The characters hurt from having lost the freedom to relate to one another. They want to know others. They want love. Joel communicates this desire most clearly. On the first episode, Joel relishes his role as a father. "Father" is a basic word, a word that contains another inside it. In Joel's case, that word is "daughter." Even though he lost his daughter Sarah, he did not stop seeking his complement. Joel develops as a character when he can find one who can address him as Father. Ellie, an orphan, fits the role of daughter. Their relationship grows only when Joel sees Ellie as more than "cargo" and accepts what she offers him.

Similarly, Frank and Bill find balance in the other. The one who cannot stand being alone and the one who cannot stand the community find, for many years, a way to reconcile their differences. And even if they revert to type at the end of their lives, they do manage a relationship for as long as they can, and live better lives than anybody else on the show because they learn to relate to one another. Their effort shows that love relations can exist in a world that abhors relations. Strawberries *can* grow, if given a bit of love and attention.

NOTES

1. *The Last of Us,* 2023. Season 1, episode 1, "When You're Lost in the Darkness."
2. Clarke, *Person and Being*, 5.
3. Buber, *I and Thou*, 69.
4. Genesis 1:1. All Bible references use the NRSV translation.
5. Maspero, *After Pandemic, After Modernity: The Relational Revolution*, 28.
6. Buber, *I and Thou*, 53.
7. *I and Thou*, 53.
8. Levinas, *Otherwise Than Being*.
9. Hand, *Emmanuel Levinas*, 37.
10. Morgan, *The Cambridge Introduction to Emmanuel Levinas*, 70.
11. Morgan, *The Cambridge Introduction to Emmanuel Levinas*, 71.
12. Morgan, *The Cambridge Introduction to Emmanuel Levinas*, 63.
13. *The Last of Us*, "When You're Lost in the Darkness."

14. In the video game, he at least doesn't deny this possibility to Ellie.
15. "Kin."
16. *The Last of Us*, 2023. Season 1, episode 8, "When We Are in Need."
17. *The Last of Us*, 2023. Season 1, episode 9, "Look for the Light."
18. *The Last of Us*, "Look for the Light," 58.
19. Scruton, *The Face of God*, 39.
20. Snyder, *Dawn of the Dead*, DVD.
21. Somerville, *Death Talk*, 264.
22. Han, *The Expulsion of the Other*, 37. Italics in original.
23. Han, *The Expulsion of the Other*, 6.
24. Han, *The Expulsion of the Other*, 14–15, 89.
25. Bailie, *The Apocalypse of the Sovereign Self*.
26. Clarke, *Person and Being*, 75.
27. Bonhoeffer, *Life Together*, 19.
28. Bonhoeffer, *Life Together*, 9.
29. *The Last of Us*, "When We Are in Need."
30. Bonhoeffer, *Life Together*, 9.
31. Bonhoeffer, *Life Together*,, 57.
32. *The Last of Us*, 2023. Season 1, episode 3, "Long, Long Time."
33. Bonhoeffer, *Life Together*, 56.
34. Bonhoeffer, *Life Together*, 55.
35. Bonhoeffer, *Life Together*, 57.
36. Bonhoeffer, *Life Together*, 56.
37. Bonhoeffer, *Life Together*, 6.

BIBLIOGRAPHY

Bailie, Gil. *The Apocalypse of the Sovereign Self: Recovering the Christian Mystery of Personhood*. Brooklyn, NY: Angelico Press, 2023.

Bonhoeffer, Dietrich. *Life Together*. Translated by Daniel W. Bloesch. Minneapolis, MN: Fortress Press, 2015.

Buber, Martin. *I and Thou*. Translated by Walter Kaufmann. New York: Touchstone, 1996.

Clarke, W. Norris. *Person and Being*. Milwaukee, WI: Marquette University Press, 2004.

Druckmann, Neil, writer. *The Last of Us*. Season 1, episode 7, "Left Behind." Directed by Liza Johnson, featuring Pedro Pascal and Bella Ramsey. Aired February 26, 2023, on HBOMax.

Han, Byung-Chul. *The Expulsion of the Other*. Cambridge, UK: Polity Press, 2018.

Hand, Sean. *Emmanuel Levinas*. New York: Routledge, 2009.

Levinas, Emmanuel. *Otherwise Than Being*. Pittsburgh, PA: Duquesne University Press, 1998.

Maspero, Giulio. *After Pandemic, after Modernity: The Relational Revolution*. South Bend, IN: St. Augustine's Press, 2022.

Mazin, Craig, writer. *The Last of Us*. Season 1, episode 2, "Infected." Directed by Neil Druckman, featuring Pedro Pascal and Bella Ramsey. Aired January 22, 2023, on HBOMax.

———, writer. *The Last of Us*. Season 1, episode 3, "Long, Long Time." Directed by Peter Hoar, featuring Pedro Pascal and Bella Ramsey. Aired January 29, 2023, on HBOMax.

———, writer. *The Last of Us*. Season 1, episode 5, "Endure and Survive." Directed by Jeremy Webb, featuring Pedro Pascal and Bella Ramsey. Aired February 12, 2023, on HBOMax.

———, writer. *The Last of Us*. Season 1, episode 6, "Kin." Directed by Jasmila Žbanić, featuring Pedro Pascal and Bella Ramsey. Aired February 19, 2023, on HBOMax.

———, writer. *The Last of Us*. Season 1, episode 8, "When We Are in Need." Directed by Ali Abbasi, featuring Pedro Pascal and Bella Ramsey. Aired March 5, 2023, on HBOMax.

———, and Neil Druckmann, writers. *The Last of Us*. Season 1, episode 1, "When You're Lost in the Darkness." Directed by Craig Mazin, featuring Pedro Pascal and Bella Ramsey. Aired January 15, 2023, on HBOMax.

———, and Neil Druckman, writers. *The Last of Us*. Season 1, episode 9, "Look for the Light." Directed by Ali Abbasi, featuring Pedro Pascal and Bella Ramsey. Aired March 12, 2023, on HBOMax.

Morgan, Michael L. *The Cambridge Introduction to Emmanuel Levinas*. Cambridge, UK: Cambridge University Press, 2011.

Pieper, Josef. *The Concept of Sin*. Translated by Edward T. Oakes. South Bend, IN: St. Augustine's Press, 2001.

Scruton, Roger. *The Face of God*. London: Bloomsbury, 2012.

Snyder, Zack, dir. *Dawn of the Dead*. Universal City, CA: Universal Pictures, 2004, DVD.

Somerville, Margaret. *Death Talk: The Case against Euthanasia and Physician-Assisted Suicide*. Second edition. Montreal: McGill-Queen's University Press, 2014.

Chapter 7

Genesis in Lincoln, MA

The Creation of Bill and Frank in "Long, Long Time"

Ryan Banfi

This chapter examines how Bill and Frank, two non-playable characters from *The Last of Us Part I*, are adapted for *The Last of Us* (*TLOU*) TV series. In analyzing the third episode of the show, "Long, Long Time," the only segment that centers on Bill and Frank, I use formal narrative analysis to explain how their character arcs embody Adam and Eve's journey in Genesis. By pinpointing the various reference points from the series and explaining how the show matches some key elements of the second creation story involving Adam and Eve in the book of Genesis, I also engage in a discussion about queer theology, namely how the Torah accepts gay relationships (as some of the books showcase gender neutral unions) whereas many of the Christian mainline churches use the Bible to claim that gay unions are against the teachings of scripture.[1] I argue that Bill and Frank's relationship generates a fruitful relationship that stands in contrast to not only societal norms that existed pre-apocalypse, but also the *TLOU*'s world, which is predominantly hell.

To begin, I will explain how *TLOU* video game frames Bill and Frank's affair. I then move to analyze how and why Craig Mazin, the screenwriter for the third episode, expands upon this connection. In the latter part of this chapter, I use Foucauldian and queer theological readings of the Bible to contend that Bill and Frank's union can be deemed as adhering to God's depiction of a productive coupling.

BILL AND FRANK IN *TLOU* VIDEO GAME

"Long, Long Time" is primarily adapted from a single letter and short cut scene from the chapter, "Bill's Town" in *TLOU Part I*. In the cut scene, Bill and Joel argue about how best to travel out of Lincoln, Massachusetts, the city that Bill inhabits. Bill notices that Frank has hanged himself (he identifies him from his shirt) due to being bitten by an infected. The only indication that the two are gay is from Bill telling Joel that he was his "partner." This gay relationship is further confirmed if the player finds the artifact "Note from Frank." Frank's note reads as follows:

> Well, Bill, I doubt you'd ever find this note 'cause you were too scared to ever make it to this part of town. But if for some reason you did, I want you to know I hated your guts. I grew tired of this shitty town and your set-in-your-ways attitude. I wanted more from life than this and you could never get that.
>
> And that stupid battery you kept moaning about–I got it. But I guess you were right. Trying to leave this town will kill me. Still better than spending another day with you. Good luck, Frank.

Joel can find this letter and the player can decide to deliver the note to Bill. This will trigger an optional conversation where Bill will read the note and state, "That's how you feel. Well, fuck you too, Frank. Fuckin' idiot." Another note that mentions Frank in the game is "Smuggler note" in the chapter "The Outskirts" (the prior level to "Bill's Town"). This missive informs the player that a smuggler was scheduled to meet with Frank to sneak him into the Boston quarantine zone. It reads, "Your contact is a dude named Frank—he's the guy on the outside I've been trading with. He wants into the Boston QZ. Meet him in the Park Street exit of the subway station (right by the capitol building)." However, Frank was unable to meet with the smuggler which the smuggler notes by writing, "Where the hell is this guy? I've been waiting here for over two hours sweating bullets. I keep thinking I'm seeing something move in the shadows—feels like a Stalker is going to jump out at me any second now. I'm giving him another 15 minutes and then I'm heading back." Evidently, Frank was bitten and committed suicide to stop himself from turning into an infected, and thus could not rendezvous with the smuggler.

Much of *TLOU*'s narrative exists on the periphery, namely via the artifacts that the player can find which is not essential to completing the narrative, but it is for comprehending all that the game has to offer in terms of narrative content.[2] Both notes are integral to understand Frank and Bill's relationship in the game, and how Mazin adapts Frank's character arc for the TV series. For example, Frank contacts Tess and Joel to trade which is like his actions in the game (more on this later).

Frank's letter to Bill indicates the fall of communication in the current world (in a literal sense and on a human level), and the impact that the artifacts can have on the game's story. By the player finding and delivering the letter, they can gain context of the in-game narrative. In this case, the player can learn about an LGBTQ+ relationship. Although this representation of queerness is minimal, Bill's homosexuality has been celebrated online.[3] The representations of LGBTQ+ characters were further acknowledged in *Part II*.[4] These reactions to the first game likely inspired more representations of queerness in *Part II*, which contains an openly gay playable character, Ellie. Although there are numerous queer video game characters[5] according to Adrienne Shaw and Elizaveta Friesem's research, "Explicitly LGBTQ PCs (playable characters) are rare."[6] Thus, a small detail like delivering a letter can impact a character's story (e.g., Bill and Ellie). Mazin promised fans that Ellie would remain queer for the TV show and that the program would explore sexualities beyond heterosexuality.[7] For this reason, he dedicated the majority of "Long, Long Time" to Bill's relationship with Frank.

HBO's *TLOU*, Adam and Eve's Creation Story in Genesis, and Queer Theology

Craig Mazin developed Bill and Frank's relationship by

> disconnect[ing] Bill from Joel and Ellie, in terms of gameplay, we could expand on this hint of a partnership with Bill and Frank, and maybe give it . . . a radically different, ending. . . . Maybe [their relationship is] not a negative or dark omen, but actually a sign of hope. There is a chance that, in this world, as dangerous and terrible as it is, there can be positive love and a successful long-term relationship. . . . There's the kind of love that is outward and giving and nurturing. As Frank says, "Paying attention to things is how we show love." And then, there's the other part of love, which is the protective, violent, if necessary, vengeful conserving of the people that you care about and love. . . . Bill and Frank's relationship became a codex for me, of how the theme of this storyline was going to play out. . . . The question is, will it always play out as successfully as it does for Bill and Frank, or is there a different kind of version, where it's explosive and actually very dangerous?[8]

I will address Mazin's question later in this chapter as I will compare Joel to Bill; for now, it is evident from this quote that Mazin decided to reform Bill and Frank's relationship within the realm of the apocalypse to produce a relationship that contrasts with the hell of *TLOU*'s world. The downfall of humanity and the desolation of society allow Bill and Frank to start anew. They become the only people in their Eden, thus mirroring the second creation narrative in Genesis. While Adam and Eve's creation story does not directly match up with *TLOU* because the show lacks a clear Satan figure (namely in the Christian interpretation—a serpent who is evil), I will use Adam and Eve's tale in Genesis as the primary text to compare "Long, Long Time" to as the episode clearly draws upon Adam and Eve's storyline.

Genesis opens: "In the beginning when God created the heavens and the earth, the earth was a formless void" (Genesis 1:1).[9] While earth was obviously created (ostensibly via God) in *TLOU*, the "formless void" could describe the world's standing after the spread of the infection as the earth becomes desolate. In creating the world, God said, "Let there be light" (Genesis 1:3). Regardless of God's existence or role in *TLOU*, within the diegesis of "Long, Long Time," light/energy cease to exist because the electric grids no longer function. Bill, moreover, is a representation of Adam as he is the last standing man in his area, and he creates a moral brightness via his generator. Light in Genesis signifies the "good" (Genesis 1:4) and "God separated the light from the darkness" (Genesis 1:5). Bill's ability to generate light illustrates that he is the hero, not a God, but a character who intends to do good. Like Adam, he has control over his territory, for which God planned for Adam as "The Lord God took the man and put him in the garden of Eden to till it and keep it" (Genesis 2:15). Bill chops wood, grows carrots, and cares for chickens. For four years, Bill's only encounters with "people" are the infected which are killed by his traps.

Frank appears almost miraculously as he falls into Bill's hidden hole. This reflects God's creation of Eve who was created from Adam's rib (Genesis 2:22). God noticed that man was alone and to keep him company in the first creation story, "God created humankind in his image . . . male and female he created them. God blessed them, and he said to them, Be fruitful and multiply, and fill the earth and subdue it" (Genesis 1:27–28). Unlike Adam and Eve, Bill and Frank cannot procreate. In Michael Carden's queer reading of Genesis/Bereshit, he argues that "reproductive sexuality was understood in agricultural terms of seed and soil."[10] The protagonists in this episode, however, love one another, and thus their relationship goes beyond solely an agrarian partnership. Frank and Bill's relationship, albeit queer, does adhere to God's demands for a productive union. Brettler describes the liaison between Adam and Eve as necessary because of the "primal human need for companionship and the human destiny, even in the garden, to work"[11] and Bill and Frank's relationship is no different in this regard. Moreover, Qohelet in Ecclesiastes writes "Two are better than one, and because they have a good reward for their toil. For if they fall, one will lift up the other; but woe to one who is alone and falls and does not have another to help" (Ecclesiastes 4:9–10). Qohelet does not specify the gender here, only that companionship is necessary for labor (I will discuss marriage later).

Bill and Frank live in a paradise that reflects Eden which God created (Genesis 2:8). In this utopia, the two men make their own rules which is partly a reaction to a world that othered them. It is obvious from Bill's demeanor and his confession[12] that he had never slept with a man before meeting Frank (he had slept with a woman once) and that he was deeply closeted and insecure about his sexuality. But his fear of coming out is more of a societal problem than his own. Once the U.S. military seizes and murders the people of Lincoln, Bill rejoices that he can live the life that he always desired, or at least the life he thought he wanted as he discovers that he was incomplete without Frank. Frank recognizes that Bill is gay from his wine choices and the Linda Ronstadt sheet music that was stored in his piano bench's seat compartment. According to queer studies professor James Morrison, "Ronstadt is considered a gay icon, and her song 'Different Drum' was a gay anthem in the 1970s–1990s."[13] "Long, Long Time" plays at numerous times in the episode thus celebrating gay love. The titular lyrics denote that the characters will love each other for a long time, possibly into the afterlife.

Of course, Genesis's opening also depicts the fall of humanity. If "Long, Long Time" is an adaptation of Genesis, how do we see the equivalent of Eve and Adam from the Tree of Knowledge? If Bill is Adam, then Frank is Eve. Frank, like Eve, is curious about the outside world. If Frank is Eve, then Joel is the serpent (namely the Jewish interpretation of the snake rather than the Christian reading as Joel is shrewd and offers wisdom). In the video game, Frank reaches out to other survivors while in the show, he contacts Tess and Joel. Frank trades Bill's gun, a symbol of violence, for Joel's strawberry seeds, a representation of life. In effect, Joel provides Bill and Frank with not only a representation of the Tree of Knowledge but the ability to eat from it. Joel can also save humanity, yet he refuses to do so, his actions further confirming his commitment to the Fall (more on that later). Both Frank and Bill eat the fruit together; thus, they are symbolically eating from the Tree of Knowledge (Genesis 3:6–13). In doing so they have disobeyed Bill's cardinal rule of never interacting with the outside world, and therefore obtaining knowledge from beyond their paradise. The next scene shows bandits arriving to pillage Lincoln, a symbolic eviction from their self-made Eden.

Once the raiders attack, Bill's fire traps engulf the enemies. This could reflect God's fortification of Eden to restrict Adam and Eve from later entering paradise as "He drove out the man; and at the east of the garden of Eden he placed the cherubim,[14] and a sword *flaming* and turning to guard the way to the tree of life" (Genesis 3:22–24, my emphasis). While Bill is the one who is keeping others out of his utopia, he must actively do so (whereas before it was a few infected) to maintain his land. For this reason, Lincoln is no longer a haven but one that must constantly be protected. While safeguarding it, Bill is shot, and he commands that Frank contact Joel so that he can support Frank.

While Joel represents the serpent in the second creation story, his name is also a reference to the prophet Joel in the Book of Joel. In the Torah, Joel warns of a disaster, one where locusts have devoured crops (Joel 1:4) and "The grain offering and the drink offering are cut off from the house of the Lord" (Joel 1:9) . . . "the fields are devastated, the ground mourns; for the grain is destroyed, the wine dries up, the oil fails" (Joel 1:10).[15] Namely, he is referencing the past plagues in Exodus which have now happened in Israel. Later in the prophetic poems, Joel announces that "the day of the Lord is coming, it is near—a day of darkness and gloom (Joel 2:1) . . . a great and powerful army comes" (Joel 2:2). Here he is referring to a battalion that will overtake Jerusalem. In the Bible, Joel references the garden of Eden by claiming that it will be left in ruin (Joel 2:3). In the TV show, Joel, like the prophet, notifies Bill that marauders will come in the night to destroy his utopia. The biblical Joel proclaims to unite the nations under the word of God (Joel 3:11) by repenting. He finishes his prophecy by claiming that he will "avenge [the people of Judah's] blood, and I will not clear the guilty" (Joel 3:21). Joel will vindicate the wrongdoers and create a safe location to worship in doing so.

Like the biblical Joel, Joel in *TLOU* is one of the most knowledgeable characters about the pandemic. He is the most capable survivor and knowledgeable about the origins of the plague and humanity's fall (which he educates Ellie about in "Long, Long Time"). Bill dislikes Joel but he trusts him because (unlike Joel in the Bible) he is willing to protect those closest to him at the cost of humanity. Ellie is the only person who matters to Joel, like Frank does to Bill. Bill understands this and thus entrusts Frank to Joel if Bill no longer can shield his partner. Bill's correct comprehension of Joel's priorities becomes evident at the end of the first season when Joel turns his back on the wellbeing of humankind to save Ellie. He could have salvaged the world by allowing the Firefly doctors the opportunity to create a panacea to the cordyceps infection, even if at the expense of Ellie's life. Instead, Joel defends Ellie. His actions are indicative of his desire to replace Ellie as his surrogate daughter for his late child Sarah—another biblical name. Sarah in the Bible is blessed by God "and she shall give rise to nations; kings of peoples shall come from her" (Genesis 17:16). Ellie can later have this opportunity to lead in the town of Jackson.

Bill does not succumb to his wounds, and thus, does not need Joel to protect Frank. He can live out his days with his lover, but their Eden is over thus exposing their mortality, as God states in Genesis, humans "shall die" (Genesis 2:17). Frank's health declines. It is not evident exactly why. Mazin stated in an interview that "We didn't necessarily want to specify [the illness] for the audience."[16] Due to his pain, Frank decides to commit suicide, and Bill follows his decision by not only assisting him but by killing himself as well which does violate the sixth commandment (Exodus 20:13; Deuteronomy

5:17). While Bill joins Frank out of love, their joint decision further paints them as sinners who reflect Adam and Eve after the Fall.[17]

Before committing suicide, though, the two decide to marry. Their marriage is an act of love, and in turn it is also a representation of rebellion towards both church, and state. Since the outbreak occurred in 2003 (in *TLOU*'s alternative timeline), Bill and Frank never received the constitutional rights of LGBTQ+ people, such as the right to marry. Outside the diegesis of the show, same-sex marriage was first legalized at the state level in Massachusetts in 2004, one year after the outbreak in *TLOU*, and federally in 2015, when the United States recognized gay marriage as a fundamental right of the Fourteenth Amendment to the Constitution. While Bill celebrates the Second Amendment by bearing arms, he was never granted the rights of the Fourteenth Amendment. Although gay marriages in the United States are legal under civil law, same-sex marriage recognition by Christianity is "creating much division in the mainline Christian churches."[18] According to Peter Hart-Brinson's research, "judging homosexuality to be morally wrong is the single largest predictor of opposing gay marriage."[19] Specific factors that Hart-Brinson found to be a part in opposing gay marriage were "Political conservatism and the two separate measures of religiosity (attendance at religious services and born-again Christian identity) are the next largest set of influences on public opinion" against it.[20] Many of the people who Hart-Brinson interviewed, "spoke confidently about the inerrancy of the Bible and the sinfulness of homosexuality, while maintaining that lesbians and gays should be accorded equal rights under the law."[21] In combating homophobia in American culture, Jakobsen and Pellegrini state that "no single religion—in fact, no religion at all—is established as the one and true religion" in the United States. American democracy is founded upon the separation of church and state.[22]

Regarding Christian marriages, many mainline churches use the language in the Old and New Testaments to argue that God intended marriage to be between a man and a woman.[23] Genesis states that "This at last is bone of my bones and flesh of my flesh; this one shall be called Woman, for out of Man this one was taken. Therefore, a man leaves his father and his mother and clings to his wife, and they become one flesh" (Genesis 2:23–24). In Paul's letter to the Ephesians, he describes how people should live based on the Gospel: "Husbands, love your wives, just as Christ loved the church and gave himself up for her" (Ephesians 5:25–26). Margaret Farley notes that, "At the heart of Judaism's historical tradition of sexual morality is a religious injunction to marry. The command to marry holds within it a command to procreate, and it assumes a patriarchal model for marriage and family."[24] Like Judaism, the Christian testament "offers grounds for a sexual ethic that . . . values marriage and procreation."[25] Of course, one of the most homophobic quotes comes from Leviticus which does not comment on marriage. It states that gay sex is a sin: "If a man lies with a male as with a woman, both of them have committed an abomination; they shall be put to death; their blood is upon them" (Leviticus 20:13). According to queer theologian David Tabb Stewart, he "*cannot* redeem Leviticus for queerdom,"[26] and I will not attempt to do so either.

However, the Bible also discusses marriage in genderless terms. Marcella Althaus-Reid argues that, "Jesus represents the range, from female to male, of the sexuality of God as it comes from Genesis and the creation of humankind in the image of God. In a way, we all carry phalluses and clitorises at the same time."[27] The gender neutrality that Althaus-Reid calls attention to is confirmed in the Bible. In Paul's letter to the Hebrews, he does not proclaim the union between two people as he writes: "Let marriage be held in honor by all" (Hebrews 13:4). Patrick S. Cheng, moreover, specifies various queer relationships in the Bible such as "Jonathan and David (who made a 'covenant' together) (see 1 Samuel 20:16) [and] Ruth and Naomi (whose vow to follow each other is traditionally used in opposite-sex marriage ceremonies (Ruth 1:16)."[28] Michel Foucault has devoted much space from *The History of Sexuality* (Vols. 1–4) arguing against the mainline Christian doctrine and its interpretation of sexuality. In volume 3, Foucault recognizes the Church's ideology of marriage between a man and a woman,[29] but writes that, "In Christianity, on the other hand, the link between sexual intercourse and marriage will be justified by the fact that the former bears the marks of sin, the Fall, and evil, and that only the latter can give it a legitimacy that still may not exculpate it entirely."[30] In that way, the Fall gives humans the right to procreate, but they need to sin to do so. Agustín Colombo argues that Christian patristics, like Ambrose, Gregory of Nyssa, and Jerome, affirm "that marriage and creation of the family were a 'result of a sad decline, by which Adam and Eve had lapsed from an *angelic* state into physicality, and so into death.'"[31] The concept of marriage seems dependent on how Genesis is read. This creates, as James Bernauer describes it, "combats of interpretation."[32] Such disagreements place the Church in a dilemma, as copulating outside of marriage and procreating are sins like gay sex[33] (Leviticus 20:13).

Foucault's recent posthumous publication *Confessions of the Flesh* (Vol. 4), dives deeper into the ironies of Genesis, specifically about gender. In his book, Foucault addresses this by examining how God created man and woman (Genesis 1:27–28) which

> gave unequivocal authority to the view that the difference of the sexes is present since the Creation. But it immediately raises a difficulty in that it comes directly after the affirmation that man was created in the image and likeness of

God. How could the one and undivided God create man in his likeness and at the same time bearing this duality of the sexes?[34]

If God has created humans in his image, is the Woman not in his image as well? She is an image of God as well.[35] And, as Foucault points out, God can produce humans, so they do not *necessarily* need to copulate, though they do so. For these reasons, "the distinction of the sexes (created by God) is dissociated from their union (which can come into play only after the fall and the separation from God), and how reproduction is split into an angelic multiplication and an animal birth."[36] Foucault addresses the biblical concerns with marriage by writing that,

> if it is also connected to the fall, it's not in the same way. Whereas "multiplication" is ontologically based in the creative act, and it is therefore already present in the earthly paradise, at least as a possibility, and the fall is what gave it its material reality—as well as its image function in relation to the spiritual realities—marriage was completely absent from a human condition that had not yet experienced the fall. The text of *On Virginity* is quite explicit on this point: "Fashioned by God, man lived in Paradise, and there was no reason for marriage." Yet God had created woman before the fall so that she would be man's companion. But companion in the sense of helper, assistant (boêthos), not wife.[37]

Early Christianity uses Genesis to establish the ideology that marriage is necessary for procreation in Western culture. This understanding comes at the expense of interrogating Genesis further and by noting that God never explicitly referenced marriage in Genesis. Moreover, there was no need for marriage in paradise as God could produce people, and in his likeness which is of both genders. If so, *TLOU* TV series then presents an accurate, albeit alternative view to the mainline Christian Churches' comprehension of Genesis and holy unions.

Marriage in *TLOU* signifies a spiritual union between Bill and Frank that can be read as a Foucauldian adaptation of Genesis as God produces humans in his likeness, and God does not need them to procreate. Procreation and marriage come after, namely from the Fall. Frank and Bill exist in the world of the Fall, and they, as children of God, decide to marry. The two are faithful and united to one another as advocated in Christian traditions.[38] Thus, Bill and Frank live a righteous life that is reflective of Christian teachings. They help Tess and Joel. While Joel is morally questionable in *TLOU*, he is not marked as bad like the raiders who shoot Bill to gain access to Lincoln. Bill, while initially selfish, does sacrifice himself to Frank, which is dramatically different from his character arc in the video game. While Bill never meets Ellie in the TV show, she does benefit from the resources that he leaves for Joel after he commits suicide. In doing so, Bill is helping Ellie's journey even from beyond the grave. Indeed, Bill would agree with Joel's decision to rescue Ellie because for both Joel and Bill, the world is not worth saving and especially not at the expense of their loved ones.

Frank's and Bill's arcs and their unseen excursion into the afterlife is representative of the HBO stamp. The purpose of HBO shows, as a premium television service, is to offer characters prominent arcs to convey long form narratives. The show marks Bill and Frank as two characters who will continue their journey into the afterlife. Bill's and Frank's endings bleed out of the narrative and into the unknown as it is unclear as to where their two souls journey after the show ends. Both lived a righteous life, and they devoted their lives to each other. While Frank and Bill exemplify Adam and Eve's Fall, they nonetheless showcase a hopeful (and open-ended) trajectory which stands in contrast to the other character's harsh fates: Tess, for example dies defending Ellie and Joel; Ellie's mother is bitten by an infected amidst giving birth to Ellie. This, as Mazin puts it, is a hopeful union in a world that has very few.

CONCLUSION

This chapter has analyzed how Bill and Frank's relationship was adapted for *TLOU* for HBO. It notes how Mazin expanded upon this companionship from the video game by giving these characters hopeful character arcs. In examining this process, I argued that Bill and Frank's narrative mirrored that of Adam and Eve's story in Genesis. To do this, I used queer theology to explain how Bill and Frank do adhere to God's expectations concerning productive relationships which allow for acceptance of queer unions. Hopefully, this relationship will have a large impact not just on video game (or TV) production, but on the outlook of queer relationships, especially regarding the interpretation of queerness in the Bible.

NOTES

1. While some churches are supportive of gay relationships, many of the Catholic priests who I have spoken with state that God's ideal union is between a man and a woman, and they quote the second creation story in Genesis to support their statement.
2. Banfi, "Ellie's Journal: Para-Narratives in *The Last of Us Part II*."
3. Banfi, "Queer Kiss."
4. Banfi, "Queer Kiss."
5. Ruberg, "Queerness and Video Games," 545.

6. Shaw and Friesem, "Where Is the Queerness in Games?" 3880.
7. Priestman, "*The Last of Us* HBO TV Series Writer Promises Ellie Will Be Gay," n.p.
8. O'Rourke, "*The Last of Us*," n.p.
9. Brettler et al., *The New Oxford Annotated Apocrypha: New Revised Standard Version*. All biblical quotations are gleaned from this edition.
10. Carden, "Genesis/Bereshit," 24.
11. Brettler et al., *The New Oxford Annotated Apocrypha: New Revised Standard Version*, 14.
12. Foucault writes about confession in *The History of Sexuality, Vol. 1: An Introduction*: "From the age of Christian penitence to the present day, sex was a privileged theme of confession. A thing that was hidden, we are told. But what if, on the contrary, it was what, in a quite particular way, one confessed? Suppose the obligation to conceal it was but another aspect of the duty to admit to it (concealing it all the more and with greater care as the confession of it was more important, requiring a stricter ritual and promising more decisive effects)?" (1976, 61). For Foucault, confession is a way in which we are able to act and remain sexual beings. The irony here is that Bill is confessing to having sex but to an encounter that was not natural for him. In that way, he is concealing his sexuality by admitting to having sex.
13. Morrison, "Interview by Banfi."
14. The cherubim are winged creatures who guard "sanctuaries like the one in Jerusalem" (Brettler et al., 2018, 17) (see 1 Kings 6:23–28).
15. The world of *TLOU* is affected by contaminated food with basic ingredients, such as flour which resembles the corrupted edible material in The Book of Joel. In episode 2 "Infected," Ibu Ratna, professor of Mycology at the University of Indonesia, is asked to examine a sample via a microscope and an infected body. She is surprised to learn that the cordyceps can survive in the human body as an infected woman is filled with the fungus. The infected woman was bitten at a "flour and grain factory on the west side of the city." Ratna opines this is a "perfect substrate." The General informs Ratna that they "need a vaccine or a medicine." Ratna informs him that "there is no medicine. There is no vaccine." She recommends that they "bomb. Start bombing. Bomb this city and everyone in it." This assessment follows the previous episode where Dr. Neuman, an epidemiologist, claims on a talk show that it is not a virus (influenza) that will cause the downfall of humans, but rather a fungus that will control the mind with the goal of spreading its infection to every person ("When You're Lost in the Darkness," Ep. 1). The downfall of humanity in the video game also stems from eating. At the beginning of the game Sarah can find a Texas Herald newspaper in the bathroom which states that "The Food and Drug Administration's investigation of crops potentially tainted with mold continues across the country. Initial lists distributed to vendors nationwide warned against crops imported from South America, but now the scope has extended to include Central America and Mexico. Several companies have already voluntarily recalled their food products from the shelves."
16. Ritchey, "Here's What We Know About Frank's Disease in *The Last of Us*," n.p.

17. Jakobsen and Pellegrini, *Love the Sin: Sexual Regulation and the Limits of Religious Tolerance*, 79.
18. Cheng, *Radical Love*, 20.
19. Hart-Brinson, *The Gay Marriage Generation: How the LGBTQ Movement Transformed*, 86.
20. Hart-Brinson, *The Gay Marriage Generation*, 86.
21. Hart-Brinson, *The Gay Marriage Generation*, 114, see 115 and 154.
22. Jakobsen and Pellegrini, *Love the Sin: Sexual Regulation and the Limits of Religious Tolerance*, 79.
23. Farley, *Just Love: A Framework for Christian Sexual Ethics*, 21.
24. Farley, *Just Love*, 35.
25. Farley, *Just Love*, 38.
26. Stewart, Leviticus, 77 (Stewart's emphasis).
27. Althaus-Reid, *Indecent Theology*, 73.
28. Cheng, *Radical Love*, 20–21.
29. Foucault, *The History of Sexuality, Vol. 3: The Care of the Self*, 182–183.
30. Foucault, *The History of Sexuality, Vol. 3*, 183, see 235.
31. Colombo, "What Is a Desiring Man?" 80 (Colombo's emphasis); see Brown, *The Body and Society: Men, Women, and Sexual Renunciation in Early Christianity*, 99.
32. Bernauer, "Foucault's Confessions," 1. Bernauer states that it is not Adam's misdeed that brought on the Fall, but rather a happy fault that established procreation.
33. Chappell, "Vatican Says Catholic Church Cannot Bless Same-Sex Marriages," n.p.
34. Foucault, *Confessions of the Flesh: The History of Sexuality, Volume 4*, 166–167.
35. Carden, "Genesis/Bereshit," 26.
36. Carden, "Genesis/Bereshit," 169.
37. Carden, "Genesis/Bereshit," 237–238.
38. Farley, *Just Love*, 35–38.

BIBLIOGRAPHY

Althaus-Reid, Marcella. *Indecent Theology*. London: Taylor & Francis, 2001.

Banfi, Ryan. "Queer Kiss: An Analysis of the Internet's Reaction to Same-Sex Love in *The Last of Us Part II*." *Media Res*, 2020, https://mediacommons.org/imr/content/queer-kiss-analysis-internet%E2%80%99s-reaction-same-sex-love-last-us-part-ii.

———. "Ellie's Journal: Para-Narratives in *The Last of Us Part II*." *Game Studies* 22.3 (2022), http://gamestudies.org/2203/articles/banfi.

———. "'Authentic' Cityscapes and Violence in 'The Last of Us Part II.'" *Mediapolis: A Journal of Cities and Culture* 7.3 (September 2022), https://www.mediapolisjournal.com/2022/09/authentic-cityscapes-and-violence/.

Bernauer, James. "Foucault's Confessions 1." *Rice University*, May 4, 2021, https://www.youtube.com/watch?v=n4OZ_SY7rMY&ab_channel=NikiKasumiClements.

Brettler, Marc, Carol Newsom, and Pheme Perkins, eds. *The New Oxford Annotated Apocrypha: New Revised Standard Version*. Oxford, UK: Oxford University Press, 2018.

Brown, Peter. *The Body and Society: Men, Women, and Sexual Renunciation in Early Christianity*. New York: Columbia University Press, 1988.

Carden, Michael. "Genesis/Bereshit." In *The Queer Bible Commentary*, edited by Deryn Guest (pp. 21–60). London: SCM, 2006.

Chappell, Bill. "Vatican Says Catholic Church Cannot Bless Same-Sex Marriages." *NPR*, 2021, https://www.npr.org/2021/03/15/977415222/illicit-for-catholic-church-to-bless-same-sex-marriages-vatican-says.

Cheng, Patrick. *Radical Love: An Introduction to Queer Theology*. New York: Seabury Books, 2011.

Colombo, Agustín. "What Is a Desiring Man?" *Foucault Studies* 29 (2021): 71–90, https://doi.org/10.22439/fs.vi29.6215.

Farley, Margaret A. *Just Love: A Framework for Christian Sexual Ethics*. New York: Continuum, 2006.

Foucault, Michel. *The History of Sexuality, Vol. 1: An Introduction*. New York: Pantheon Books, 1976.

———. *The History of Sexuality, Vol. 3: The Care of the Self*. New York: Pantheon Books, 1986.

———. *The History of Sexuality, Vol. 2: The Use of Pleasure*. New York: Vintage, 1990.

———. *Confessions of the Flesh: The History of Sexuality, Vol. 4*. Translated by Robert Hurley. New York: Pantheon Books, 2021.

Hart-Brinson, Peter. *The Gay Marriage Generation: How the LGBTQ Movement Transformed American Culture*. New York: New York University Press, 2018.

Jakobsen, Janet, and Ann Pellegrini. *Love the Sin: Sexual Regulation and the Limits of Religious Tolerance*, vol. 39. New York: New York University Press, 2003.

Morrison, James. Interview by Banfi [phone call], July 22, 2023.

O'Rourke, Ryan. "*The Last of Us*: Craig Mazin on Creating a More Hopeful Ending for Bill and Frank." *Collider*, January 30, 2023, https://collider.com/the-last-of-us-bill-frank-craig-mazin-interview/.

Priestman, Chris. "*The Last of Us* HBO TV Series Writer Promises Ellie Will Be Gay." *IGN*, March 12, 2020, https://www.ign.com/articles/the-last-of-us-hbo-tv-series-writer-promises-ellie-will-be-gay.

Ritchey, Cori. "Here's What We Know about Frank's Disease in *The Last of Us*." *Men's Health*, January 30, 2023, https://www.menshealth.com/entertainment/a42708211/franks-disease-the-last-of-us/.

Ruberg, Bo. "Queerness and Video Games: Queer Game Studies and New Perspectives through Play." *GLQ* 24.4 (October 2018): 543–555, doi: https://doi.org/10.1215/10642684-6957940.

Shaw, Adrienne, and Elizaveta Friesem. "Where Is the Queerness in Games? Types of Lesbian, Gay, Bisexual, Transgender, and Queer Content in Digital Games." *International Journal of Communication* 10 (January 2016): 3877–3889.

Stewart, David Tabb. "Leviticus." In *The Queer Bible Commentary*, edited by Deryn Guest (pp. 77–104). London: SCM, 2006.

Chapter 8

Turning Reconsidered

Sam and Henry and the Futility of Nonviolence amidst Racism and Runners

Adam B. Banks

Amid fierce public outrage in the wake of the murders of Ahmaud Arbery, Breonna Taylor, and George Floyd in the spring of 2020, several government officials and news-media pundits patronized and condemned protestors. One such condemnation was issued by Trey Gowdy, a past Fox News contributor and House Oversight Committee chairman, who insisted that ordinary (Black) "fellow citizens" would benefit from *turning the other cheek* while adding that the rule doesn't apply to police departments.[1] Gowdy asserted that it was the duty of those enraged by these murders—two of which had taken place at the hands of police—to adopt respectable forms of protest which maintained a sense of safety and law-and-order.[2] In this *not-so-coded* language, Gowdy used the Bible to peddle an anti-Black message of peace maintained by an armed police force, claiming the right of officers to uphold order "by any means necessary." Going beyond misconstruing the liberatory themes of scripture, Gowdy also repurposed this latter phrase to support the tactics of a militarized state against a Black population seeking self-determination. That is, the *ends* sought by Gowdy (and the state) oppose the goals sought by Black citizens of the United States, the original context from which the phrase was seized.

Gowdy's gross misappropriation of Malcolm X stands in a long tradition of anti-Black racist rhetoric in response to raucous rebellions. Seen as the "dysfunctional cousin" to the peaceful Civil Rights Movement, Black riots have always been demonized while the peaceful protests of the 1950s and 1960s are raised as the standard for Black expression of discontent.³ Malcolm, however, refused to adopt this logic of peaceful expression, calling out the hypocrisy inherent in such a demand on behalf of defenders of a nation state established through the genocide of Indigenous peoples and the enslavement of Blacks.⁴ Critical of the quotidian violence and social death dominating Black being, Malcolm criticized the systemic anti-Black racism upheld by the same proponents of peaceful protest.⁵

As Nikole Hannah-Jones's *1619 Project* explains, Black people have functioned as the bedrock on which the settler-colonial United States was built.⁶ However, those who comprise that foundation have always been dispossessed of any capacity for self-determination, permanently haunted by death. This haunting manifested through racist public discourse and extravagant violence, but also became institutionally spectral as the education, legal, health, and other systems constructed the plasticity of Black subjectivity; all at once, the Black is sub/super/human at the convenience of whiteness, rendering a perilous state of Black (non)being.⁷ It was this sickening mistreatment as nonbeing which frustrated Malcolm, moving him to argue that Black people were permitted to incorporate the same tactics leveraged by other groups in their pursuit of freedom. He made freedom a task to be acquired and achieved *by any means necessary*.⁸

Opposing Gowdy's blasphemous scriptural interpretation and gross miscontextualization of Malcolm X, Tobe Nwigwe released a humorous yet prophetic track less than two months later. The artist explains that aggressors might be able to get away with attacking Jesus but should refrain from assaulting Nwigwe "because I fight."⁹ Alluding to the scripture cited by Gowdy, Nwigwe provides the grounds for an alternative interpretation, maintaining a desire for peace while introducing a stance of violent resistance. In no way does he promote aggressive, offensive violence; on the contrary, it's a position of closed-fisted defense that the artist describes. However, this Black man's artistic expression sparked viral social media debates regarding the use of violent resistance in relation to the scripture, and, while there were many perspectives shared, three were most striking: (1) passivity, (2) nonviolent resistance/self-defense, and (3) armed/violent self-defense.¹⁰ The first two perspectives overwhelmingly represent traditional Christian interpretations of Matthew 5:39 while the third does not. However, situating the question in the context of ongoing anti-Black violence committed by police (the State) and white supremacists ("fellow citizens") places the third perspective as one worth considering. That is, in light of the longue durée of Black fungible subjectivity made possible through explicit and mundane violence, the question of violent resistance deserves legitimate consideration.

The Last of Us (*TLOU*) contends with the third perspective by depicting situations that call to question the utility of nonviolent versus violent self-defense. In a world of fungal infected undead agents, evaluations of good, bad, right, and wrong in relation to violence become irrelevant as the predominant concern shifts from a moralistic appeal for civility toward survival. Transcending fictive realms, Sam and Henry face circumstances reflective of historical dilemmas encountered by disenfranchised Black communities, rooting the futility of nonviolent Christian morality in the real world. An example of this is found in the lives of Black inhabitants of Lowndes County, Alabama, during the 1960s. In this predominantly Black county, there was zero Black representation in positions of power. This gross lack of representation naturally meant that any Black attempt at enfranchisement was quashed by violent, white resistance. The violence was truly gratuitous, though, in the sense that anti-Blackness was presumed, and attacks occurred at any time, at any place, for any reason. Public displays of collective striving for progress weren't required to attract aggression; being on the wrong road, standing outside after sunset, or simply encountering the wrong person in the wrong mood on the wrong day could be the grounds for obliterative violence. Always haunted by the specter of gratuitous violence, local Black organizers—with national support, having members of the Student Nonviolent Coordinating Committee (SNCC) as co-laborers—regularly gathered for worship while strategically arming themselves, without experiencing moral conflict. Facing a reality like that of Sam and Henry—engulfed in a sociopolitical network dependent on anti-Black violence to the point that the county was known as "Bloody Lowndes"—organizers were willing to employ an ethic of armed self-defense against heartless opposition in service to an ultimate concern that precedes moral civility: endure and survive.[11]

Taking together the strategies for survival portrayed in *TLOU* and those adopted by organizers in Lowndes County, Alabama, this chapter argues for the consideration of an alternative reading of Matthew 5:39—one that includes violent self-defense.

ENDURE AND SURVIVE

Possibly inspired by the history of Black peoples, the directors of *TLOU* present Blackness as synonymous with precarity. Immediately following the opening credits, the title of the fifth episode becomes evident as the viewer is introduced to a violent gang of bandits who have overrun FEDRA, taking over the QZ and the rest of Kansas City. After panning through different torture scenes, the viewer encounters two Black male siblings doing their best to *endure and survive* amidst such violent chaos.

Holing up somewhere in the periphery, evading Kathleen's cronies, Sam and Henry hide for a week before they must venture out in search of food and in hopes of escaping the city. The importance of armed/violent self-defense surrounds the duo as their hideout is decorated with illustrations of supernatural power–wielding versions of the Black boys. Sam draws himself with Cyclops-like abilities, blasting beams from his eyes to defeat the violent assailants he faces in reality: police officers, bandits, and zombies. His child imagination, yet mature intuition, portrays the aggressors targeting the Black youth in their crosshairs, enacting violence to the point that Sam's survival depends on armed self-defense. That is, the violence threatening their survival can only be endured through violent resistance. This is why, right before leaving from the attic, Henry's display of the blade brings the face-painted Sam comfort.

This captures the historical experience of many Black youth whose birth placed them in the crosshairs of anti-Black violence. This threat of systematized infant mortality rang true for Pattie McDonald's son, resident of Lowndes County, Alabama, and victim of white supremacist terrorism. Renting a piece of her property to SNCC leaders in the 1960s, McDonald found that she became more of a target of aggression. Several Klansmen stalked and attempted to assassinate Pattie's husband, Leon. One night, Pattie shares, her daughter assisted in changing her son's diaper, relocating him after finishing the chore. Soon thereafter, they would come to learn that this simple relocation would be a lifesaving act as white stalkers scattered a wave of bullets through the infant's window (which was right above his crib) and several walls throughout the house, including Pattie and Leon's bedroom. Miraculously, no one was harmed.[12]

This reality of Black life in the United States explains why Sam and Henry would hesitantly approach Joel and Ellie; at the same time, this sociohistorical context undergirds the condescending orientation Joel holds toward the youth throughout the episode. Overcoming their initial suspicion, the group proceeds forward with Henry's plan of escape—going down through the tunnels, rising to the surface in the suburbs, and escaping the city. The plan works until they face opposition from a sniper perched in the suburbs. After Joel overtakes the sniper, the fleeting moment of inbreaking freedom is swept away by Kathleen and her henchmen's arrival on the scene. Completely dominated by grief caused by the death of her brother and son, Kathleen is blind to the presence of Ellie (and Joel), the true murderer(s) of her son, and assigns the sum of tragedies she has endured to the Black youth.

Throughout the episode, the viewer finds that each moment that Henry and Sam remain alive, Kathleen believes her world is steadily eaten away. This is seen in the arrest, torture, and murder of all of Henry and Sam's past associates at the order of Kathleen, evincing what João H. Costa Vargas articulates as "epidermalization."[13] This notion asserts anti-Blackness to be constitutive of the modern nation-state, which always relies on the expansion of violence. Through this expansion, non-Black bodies are (unwillingly) made Black through modes of warfare aimed at Black bodies—a forced intimacy with death. Under constant carceral surveillance, violence is aimed at Black neighborhoods, but bullets spill over into surrounding, non-Black areas, creating "black cyborgs." This is what the audience witnesses in the excessive murders of Black and non-Black subjects in Kathleen's hunt for Sam and Henry; the boys' doctor and other past comrades are made Black through the dominating power's warfare directed toward Black bodies. The directors reflect the logics of State domination in the tactics of Kathleen's militia as they yoke white death to Black survival. That is, as long as Sam and Henry are alive, Kathleen's world disintegrates.

Kathleen and her Klan press on hunting for the Black delinquents. And just before she discovers their location, Henry exposes himself, unarmed, revealing his ultimate concern: survival. But not his own; Henry is most concerned with the survival of his brother, and, if he must lay down his life to preserve Sam's, Henry is willing to die. This reveals that his entire being finds purpose in self-sacrifice for the sake of communal survival.

Kathleen's murder attempt is disrupted by an abandoned truck that sinks into the ground, giving way to all hell breaking loose. Mushroom-infected zombies burst forth from the ground attacking whoever they can catch. Bloaters, clickers, even a child zombie, make Kathleen's henchmen their victims while Sam, Henry, and Ellie do their best to evade the monsters. In typical fashion, Joel provides cover fire from his sniper's nest primarily for Ellie, ignoring the Black boys until she makes it clear she's not going to abandon them. This display of anti-Black, patriarchal power further threatens the survival of Sam and Henry as their ontology is most explicitly put on display.[14]

In this scene, Sam and Henry are surrounded by soulless opposition: Kathleen and her bandits, the zombies, and Joel. This is in addition to already having survived the soulless opposition of FEDRA. As he shared with Joel, Henry faced a conundrum of either watching his brother die due to the lack of medication, or turning over Kathleen's brother, Michael, in exchange for Sam's necessary treatment. Seen not only in the rape, extortion, and beatings referenced by Henry earlier in the episode, this soullessness reflects a sort of "slow violence" maintained by FEDRA; in the unspectacular, Blackness is steadily drained of its subjectivity in covert manifestations.[15] In this context, I use soul to signify intellectual or emotional energy which one possesses and recognizes in another, as well as the capacity to possess or extend affectionate compassion. With this understanding, the viewer is confronted with the ethical dilemma engulfing the ontology of Blackness.

This dilemma of institutionalized soullessness is discussed by Elizabeth Hinton as she traces the historical evolution of policies and legislation influencing anti-Black surveillance and incarceration, revealing twentieth-century racialized juridical processes that brought about the contemporary, inequitable prison industrial complex. Daniel Patrick Moynihan is identified as a central figure that influenced presidential/national administrations that tethered delinquency to Blackness.[16] Setting aside research which emphasized the impact of social determinants on poverty and criminality, administrations codified anti-Blackness through pathologizing Black criminality in cultural, familial, and social life. Anti-Black political programs such as the War on Drugs and the War on Crime were implemented, leading to the oversurveillance of ghettos and the extant disproportionate Black representation in jails and prisons. These Wars on Drugs/Crime proved to be Wars on Blackness. Problems framed as racial "deficiencies" became naturalized through the local, state, and federal legislation, absolving systemic disparities of any blame. This disavowal evinces the soullessness of the State.

Beverly Daniel Tatum compliments the scholarship of Hinton showing how the education system perniciously abstracts the value of Black children (especially boys) while ignoring their intellectual development. For example, Tatum details how athletic programs recruit and rely on Black athleticism and benefit from an image of inclusivity and multiculturalism, while ignoring and/or excusing the academic challenges faced by Black students. Achievement gaps are discussed at PTO and school board meetings while districts continue withholding any investment to deconstruct or alter sociopolitical structures of anti-Black annihilation; instead, the school operates maliciously in tandem with capitalism and the criminal legal system.[17]

Reflecting racist U.S. systems, each of the parties hunting Henry and Sam are soulless, as heart and conscience are absent from the scene: the zombies, with their mental and emotional functions incapacitated; Kathleen and her henchmen driven by vengeance and bloodthirst; and Joel, seemingly blinded by his prioritization of escorting Ellie out West as well as his routinized anti-Black orientation toward the world. As Wilderson notes, anti-Blackness takes form in the spectacularly "horrifying and outlandish"—Kathleen and her Klan—as well as the "mundane and quotidian." It's the latter which describes Joel's orientation toward Henry and Sam; while there may not be any spectacular expression of dominance enforced on the brothers, Joel's treatment of the pair as fungible for the sake of his and Ellie's liberation evinces his mindset of superiority.[18]

The mundanity of anti-Blackness was seen in Bloody Lowndes. There, like many places across the South (and implicitly baked into Northern legislation), Jim Crow was codified through juridical codes; however, anti-Black racism found its most menacing source of entrenchment in the threat and reality of everyday violence enacted toward Black people by ordinary white people. It was through microaggressions such as forcing Black people to avoid eye contact, salesclerks extending suspicious looks in stores, and constant police surveillance. These routinized practices functioned to keep the spilled blood in Lowndes at the surface of Black people's minds; death was a constant shadow even in the absence of weaponry.

While challenged with the quotidian anti-Blackness of Joel, Henry and Sam are bound by the lack of institutional protection; no agency, group, or body undertakes the responsibility to protect and serve—certainly not FEDRA or the bandits—so they are left to survive on their own. The brothers' vulnerability matches the Black population in Lowndes who also found themselves not only as targets of routinized violence but having no institutional support. The routine terror inflicted upon Black residents by ordinary white folk was not deemed to be newsworthy, thus sparking no media coverage. One example was the implementation of federalized desegregation being met with anti-Black intimidation efforts to dissuade transferring schools. This vigorous push of coercion was matched by an energetic outreach for white student recruitment; with all the spots for enrollment filled, Black students would be no worry at all.[19] And worst of all, this nonspectacular systematized anti-Black racism didn't warrant the presence of cameras or journalists. Without media coverage, the plight of Black people couldn't be spread or legitimized through authoritative outlets, thus moral objection could be avoided.

In addition to the media not covering such instances of anti-Black violence, the police did not provide protection through defending the lives of Black organizers. On the contrary, as Derecka Purnell argues, police presence often escalates violence rather than diminishes conflict.[20] Similarly, Joy James discusses how the Federal Bureau of Investigation's Counter Intelligence Program (COINTELPRO) stewarded tax payers' contributions to destabilize progressive political movements through targeting, intimidating, and murdering Black efforts for self-determination.[21] Stokely Carmichael provides firsthand testimony to this style of state-sanctioned interference. While he and other leaders were raising awareness about local organizing efforts at the Lowndes County Training School, suddenly the police arrived, having been called to put an end to the unsettling presence of the organizers. The police's primary concern was protecting the interests of white folks, stating plainly to Carmichael that "white people don't like this."[22] Carmichael, though, would not back down, asking if he was being arrested or not, and publicly displaying a relentless commitment to organizing and raising the collective consciousness of Black folks. Absolutely taken aback by such boldness, the deputies left, and scores of students swarmed Carmichael, captivated by his audacity and survival of such an encounter.[23]

Although this audacious display of loyalty to freedom rights won many Black youth to the movement, Lowndes remained riddled with the blood of its Black residents. Without the support of law enforcement and the media's refusal to cover stories of anti-Black terrorism, there was no public agency that provided the means by which Black lives could be protected. Symbolic gestures could disrupt humiliation, as seen with Carmichael standing up against the police, but did nothing to refute the ongoing Black death. Likewise, the media's disengagement offered no platform by which Black organizers could express nonviolent agential resistance to disrupt the terror, leaving no way for them to appeal to the hearts and minds—souls—of the public to affect policy. The Black community found itself without any option for institutional support.

Alas, the sibling duo, sinking in a sea of soullessness, is found without ammunition (and refuse to use their knife), revealing the selection of nonviolence as a strategy of survival. Unfortunately, though, their choice generates their demise as Sam is bitten and becomes a zombie. Ellie's attempt to cure Sam through an amateur blood transfusion proves ineffective, and, after retrieving Joel's gun initially in defense of Sam, Henry recognizes his little brother is gone. Failing to fulfill his purpose, Henry makes Sam's death visible by neutralizing the infected threat.[24] That he pulls the trigger ending his own life after Sam's death makes clear that Henry's purpose for survival was to ensure the survival of Sam. This differs from other characters, such as Joel, as he continues his journey beyond the death of his counterpart Tess. Likewise, Joel is able to navigate a zombie-ridden world beyond the death of his daughter, Sarah, which had happened years ago. As noted by Melvin G. Hill, Joel's continued survival was not dependent on the life of his (TV) Black daughter, but the same would not be true for Henry and Sam.[25] With Sam's end comes the death of Henry's purpose, revealing a multi-layered significance of survival in relation to the Black duo and Blackness as a whole in this fictional world. For them, there is no larger mission such as transporting precious cargo, saving humanity, or creating a vaccine for the infection. Just survival. Joel, on the other hand, lives on, surviving his daughter's death (and murdering Marlene), strongly resembling Kathleen. Does Joel also view white survival as dependent on Black death?

In this episode of *TLOU*, Sam's and Henry's actions reveal that the tactic of nonviolence in response to armed aggression is as good as killing one's own community and oneself. That is, being unarmed while being the target of weaponized anti-Black violence ultimately leads to one end: death. Interestingly, the one time Henry chose violence led to the preservation of Sam's (and implicitly his own) life. While he didn't directly end the life of Michael, he disclosed his location to FEDRA operatives, consequently producing death. Henry's moral purity is certainly compromised. However, as a dominated subject of FEDRA, it's not as though this exchange was a choice, and certainly was not a decision informed by greed; on the contrary, it was out of communal preservation. Before charging Henry as being the reason for his and his brother's constant state of precarity, one must recognize the horror of the status quo instituted by FEDRA, Henry and Sam being targets before the ordeal, during, and after, always already evading negation.

That the purpose of their life is survival equates the ontology of Blackness to precarity as Blackness is portrayed as the constant evasion/invasion of violence. With violence being the number one threat to the purpose and therefore existence of Blackness, there is no means by which existence might continue through acquiescence and nonresistance, nor through symbolic agential action. The disruption of violence and pursuit of communal harmony becomes impossible without having violent self-defense as an option.

Sam and Henry's perpetual scouting of the margins and the constant navigation of the periphery reveal violence to be used only in *defense*; Sam and Henry do not go hunting for threats to neutralize. In other words, they are not leveraging violence for offensive strategies, implying this as the line they aren't willing to cross even in the apocalypse. Instead, having no other form of juridical or physical protection, violent self-defense is used for the sake of survival. It is their last and only option.

Resembling the posture of Henry and Sam, Black residents of Lowndes County fortified their homes to defend their lives, especially as institutions proved unreliable. The prioritized fortification reveals the primary purpose of their action to be defensive survival. Doing their best to bulletproof their homes proves that Black folks were targets of unwarranted violence and, like the brothers, were in no way on the offensive.

"In Lowndes County, no one will protect Negroes," said Frank Miles Jr., an activist in Lowndes.[26] So this is exactly what Black residents of the county did. In addition to fortifying their residences, Black locals began arming themselves with pistols and rifles otherwise used for small game hunting. Stacking weapons on mattresses for occupants to acquire in case of emergency, placing rifles behind doors and pistols on nightstands, going out into the fields with pockets filled with shotgun shells or a revolver tucked in the waistband; being armed for defense became the norm. Stokely Carmichael reflected that the anti-Black terror led him to stop "telling people they should remain nonviolent. . . . This would be tantamount to suicide in the Black Belt counties where whites are shooting at Negroes and it would cost me the respect of the people."[27] Carmichael's words make clear that to refuse access to institutional support by which Black folk could find protection while maintaining an ethic of nonviolence was as good as suicide—as seen with Sam and Henry.

Knowing that certain buildings and individuals were more likely to be targeted, organizers "posted armed sentries outside churches, leaders' homes . . . and . . . provided SNCC field secretaries with armed escorts and guns of their own."[28] When local gun shops refused to sell ammunition to Black residents, networks of ammunition acquisition were established, even reaching as far as Georgia. Nonviolence was popularly understood as a means of getting "yourself killed, and other people too," as one resident said.[29] For people depending on hunting, gun ownership was already widespread, therefore there was no need to train an armed militia. Likewise, anti-Black violence being so unpredictable made armed self-defense necessary in so many different locations; so, organizers could not be limited to the presence of one group; a single militia provided an easy target that could be seen as bombastic pretension, thus providing a reason for annihilation. This was avoided through the democratization of arms; the Black community as a whole knew the necessity of resisting violence with violence for the sake of survival.

Not once were members of the Lowndes County Freedom Organization (LCFO) accused of inciting violence; of course there were accusations of Black folks being the reason violence broke out at various times—for instance, Carmichael passing out fliers—but armed organizers did not go searching for white folks to gun down; neither those that had committed atrocities against members of the Black community, nor those who were prominent members of the Klan; Black people being armed was not used for the sake of offense. Jeffries states that, "Armed self-defense negated the effectiveness of midnight marauding, frustrating the attempt by whites to defeat the movement through violence."[30]

POPULAR INTERPRETATIONS: PACIFISM AND THE "THIRD WAY"

Sam and Henry's navigation of persistent anti-Back negation reflects the experience of Black citizens of Lowndes County, providing a generative framework by which to expand the harmful popular interpretations of "turn the other cheek." The saying is found as a part of a three-chapter unit popularly labeled "The Sermon on the Mount, which functions as the theological foundation for Jesus' teaching and ministry."[31] Following Jesus' proclamation of his mission to "fulfill and not abolish the law," he speaks of six antitheses. Named for their dialogic structure, each saying consists of a reference to Jewish law—"You heard it said . . . "—and a clarification—" . . . but I say to you . . . " For each of the six topics Jesus offers critical reflection on popular understandings of the law, ultimately presenting insight for what is at stake for those seeking to be welcomed into the "kingdom of God/heaven."

The fifth antithesis is concerned with retributive justice, in which Jesus says, "You have heard that it was said, 'An eye for an eye and a tooth for a tooth.' But I say to you: Do not resist an evildoer. But if anyone strikes you on the right cheek, turn the other also."[32] This antithesis has had two major camps of interpretation: pacifism and nonviolent resistance/defense.

Pacifism is the philosophical stance of opposition to violence, militarism, or war.[33] Instead of arming oneself or engaging in battle, the pacifist chooses nonviolence, some believing in its moral superiority, and others considering the loss (economic, political, or otherwise) sustained through retaliation. Though pacifism at times includes nonviolent resistance/defense, it is most commonly used to indicate the position of nonresistance.

A major influence in the interpretive camp of pacifism in relation to Matthew 5:39 is the nineteenth-century writer, theologian, and philosopher Leo Tolstoy. In a commentary on "The Sermon on the Mount," Tolstoy takes a literal interpretation of "turn the other cheek" saying that Jesus means exactly what he says.[34] In a typical *violence begets violence* framework, Tolstoy argues that violent resistance to hostility perpetuates a cycle of evil, restricting humanity to an existence defined by brutality. Equating violence with evil, Tolstoy asserts that violent retaliation in no way stands as a resistance toward evil; instead, it functions as an acquiescence to evil, having no impact on the salvation of humanity. He further claims that the advancement of humanity toward righteousness is not owed to those willing to commit violence but those who are martyrs.[35] In becoming a martyr the pacifist reflects the actions and death of Jesus—the epitome of good. In the end, the best response to violence, according to the pacifist, is no response, as Jesus urges his audience to disrupt evil/violence by refusing to adopt aggression as a tool for survival; death isn't seen as an impediment to (righteous) progress.

Though offering valuable insights into the interpretation of the scripture, making violence inexcusable in relation to Christ-like love, Tolstoy seems to be overly dualistic (gnostic even) in his analysis. Tolstoy was certainly familiar with the notion that salvation was gifted to creation through the incarnation, life, death, and resurrection of Jesus. Therefore, to place the salvation of creation/humanity upon the ability of humanity to accomplish justifiable deeds is to offer a substantial variation of the significance and identity of Jesus as the Christ. James's writings play a significant part of this conversation as he asserts "faith without works is dead"; however, works are situated as accompanying, or springing forth from, a preceding faith.[36]

Furthermore, Tolstoy's dualistic argument begs the question of righteousness's relationship to genocide. According to this logic, would populations be condemned for defending themselves against complete annihilation? Can victims of violent repression find righteousness and salvation within the boundaries of creation, history, and/or mortality? The argument of progress by way of willing acquiescence to violence is the equivalent of telling Sam and Henry, and other post-apocalyptic communities, to pursue utopia by bearing their skin when zombies draw near. Lisa Sowle Cahill points out how an argument for the actualization of righteousness via willing death provides the basis for populations acceding to efforts of annihilation, which is not reflective of God's justice.[37] A righteousness solely discovered beyond this plane of existence is a righteousness not worth pursuing. This is an underwhelming argument for how to interpret this command from the same one who said he came to usher in the inbreaking rule and reign/kin(g)dom of God; this is a kin(g)dom found in our midst.[38]

Rejecting escapist pacifism (as well as violent retaliatory action), Amy-Jill Levine provides a noteworthy argument from the perspective of nonviolent resistance to aggression. Offering an interpretative history of the maxim "eye for eye, and tooth for tooth," Levine explains how this brutal regulation was not a literal tenet for Jewish people from its beginning. Instead, the code represented the legal principle of commensurate restitution. Yet, according to Levine, instead of extending the existing law, Jesus' clarification redirects his audience to a different topic. Levine says "the talion speaks of physical mutilation; Jesus speaks about public humiliation."[39] In the first century Near East, Levine explains, to be slapped (or be demanded of one's tunic or required to travel a distance) was a matter of public humiliation and the expression of one's superiority/inferiority in relation to another. Levine explains further, "To be struck on the right cheek presumes, if the striker is righthanded, a backhanded slap. . . . It is the slap that would be given by a master to a slave, or a soldier to a peasant. A backhanded slap is designed to humiliate, not to injure."[40] Levine argues that in such a humiliating instance, if the victim returns violence, this can have deadly consequences; yet, if the victim cowers, the violence may persist. Instead, highlighting biblical scholar Walter Wink, Levine asserts that the act of turning the other cheek functions as a nonviolent confrontation of the aggression.[41]

By turning the other cheek, the victim calls to question the extent to which the perpetrator is willing to escalate humiliation. If the perpetrator will inflict violence upon the left cheek, they will have to do so in a manner that either brings dishonor to themselves or increases the violence by treating the victim as an equal. In this way, turning the other cheek becomes an effective nonviolent response to aggression which forces the aggressor to acknowledge the agency of the one being attacked. Shifting away from Tolstoy's point of focus—whether to respond or not—Levine shows that it is the type of response that the victim expresses which determines whether they are accurately interpreting the command from Jesus.

While Levine offers a drastically different interpretation from Tolstoy, her argument remains wanting in relation to the specificities of anti-Blackness in the United States, whether related to humiliation or violent mutilation. For Levine, the purpose of the antitheses is to guide Jesus' audience to act in ways that restore or maintain communal harmony (the kin(g)dom of God).

As opposed to becoming complicit with the subjugation one endures, a form of meaningful symbolic resistance is to be shown in a way that does not denigrate the aggressor and leaves room for the recognition of one's moral deterioration. Levine points to Rev. Dr. Martin Luther King Jr. as one who effectively deployed this strategy through public protests.

Representative of many freedom rights activists, Dr. King engaged in nonviolent direct action where the moral integrity of anti-Black assailants was called to question. Often in tandem with different media outlets, public protests were staged in a way that revealed vicious anti-Black resistance to (Black) progress. Appealing to the moral outrage of empathetic white people, organizers expressed full commitment to nonviolent means of resistance through media coverage. Offering his interpretation on "turn the other cheek," King shares:

> We shall match your capacity to inflict suffering by our capacity to endure suffering. We shall meet your physical force with soul force. Do to us what you will, and we shall continue to love you. We cannot in all good conscience obey your unjust laws, because noncooperation with evil is as much a moral obligation as is cooperation with good. Throw us in jail, and we shall still love you. Send your hooded perpetrators of violence into our community at the midnight hour and beat us and leave us half dead, and we shall still love you. But be ye assured that we will wear you down by our capacity to suffer. One day we shall win freedom, but not only for ourselves. We shall so appeal to your heart and conscience that we shall win you in the process, and our victory will be a double victory.[42]

Here King champions nonviolent resistance primarily through the moral appeal to "heart and conscience."

King and other Southern Christian Leadership Conference activists relied heavily on the media; however, the media was not consistent with its presence, as seen with the residents of Lowndes County. Most often, Black organizers were left to deal with anti-Black violence without the attention of the public and the possibility of appealing to white morality. How could Black people appeal to white consciousness and hearts when their suffering wasn't seen? How could hearts and minds be changed in situations where Black suffering was seen but was a source of consumption (lynchings); where Black ontologies stood/stands outside of the register of humanity? How generative is appealing to the hearts and minds of others without first proving their possession of souls?

Levine wisely argues that scriptures must be interpreted for every given context. The same is true for the saying "turn the other cheek." While she might not have intended it, lifting Rev. Dr. Martin Luther King Jr. as the epitome of what it is to follow such a command places her in opposition to and disapproval of those who armed themselves in defense of gratuitous anti-Black violence in Lowndes County (and other locations) as this was a context in which nonviolent resistance to racialized aggression would perpetuate obliteration without any effort toward communal harmony. There are too many contexts, unfortunately, where perpetrators of violence are heartless and have no conscience; infected by the evils of racism and cupidity, they feast on Black flesh like zombies. Sam's and Henry's demises become the story of all Black folk through the adoption of the strategy of nonviolent resistance.

Jemar Tisby raises the question of the condition of the church's soul. Delineating the perpetual structural denigration of Black people, Tisby underscores the faith community's continuous compromise; time and again the church in the United States acquiesced to bigoted legal and social norms, sacrificing its own integrity in the process.[43] Resembling Levine, authoritative voices of the church have told Black folks how to ethically respond to racism, while disavowing the ethical bankruptcy found in the systemic obliteration of Black populations at the hands of integral institutions.[44]

Opposing King and the U.S. Christian tradition, Malcolm X adopted a strategy of violent resistance in response to the anti-Black violence perpetuated by ordinary citizens and hegemonic institutions. The pervading presence of racist carnage was known to Malcolm from birth. In fact, his parents, being members of Black religious organizing groups, became targets of white supremacist terrorism at the hands of the Klan while Malcolm was still in his mother's womb. Again, only at the age of four years old, his family's home was burned to the ground; two years later the same white instigators murdered his father.[45] He, like Sam and Henry, knew firsthand the condescending and life-threatening messages to "turn the other cheek," insinuating he and other brutalized people embrace an uncritical forgiveness and forget the offense. Meanwhile, white people operated by a completely different ethic. Malcolm, rejecting such hypocrisy, argued that violent defense was the only language white supremacist criminals were capable of understanding.[46]

While he was willing to incorporate violence, he did so in service to self-defense, arguing this to be essential to humanity. Whites were unwilling to concede this truth to Blacks, infuriating Malcolm for such blatant hypocrisy; for Malcolm, Blacks were permitted to incorporate the same tactics leveraged by other groups in their pursuit of freedom. In fact, violence leveraged by Blacks would be the same tactic but used differently. Instead of implementing violence for the purposes of genocide and ontological negation in the name of nation building, Malcolm argued for the right of Black people to operationalize violence for the sake of survival. Sounding much like residents in Lowndes County, Malcolm X said that, "If the government does not protect black people, they are within their right to protect themselves."[47]

On the one hand, Levine's interpretation is incredibly helpful for it reveals that Jesus' clarification has more to do with humiliation than violence. That is, Gowdy's insistence that people "turn the other cheek" in response to violence is a misapplication of the scripture. The passage is not relevant to brutally violent anti-Black situations. Levine's genius redirects readers' interpretation of the text to situations of humiliation.

On the other hand, though, the argument to appeal toward moral integrity through nonviolent exercising of agency leaves marginal and disenfranchised Black populations without reasonable solutions. Too often, Black humiliation and brutalization are conjoined twins for which there is no symbolic response powerful enough to preserve life. To what symbols do bullets cower and fall out of the air? What symbolic action resists pistols and rifles aimed at one's parents, partner, and offspring? What symbolic action announces "I am human" amid fire bombings of homes and churches? The sibling duo, the Black residents of Bloody Lowndes, and Malcolm X all make clear that traditional interpretations of Matthew 5:39 fail the racialized subjects of institutional violence. In the context of such dire soullessness, for the sake of survival Lowndes says, "Movement supporters praised the Lord and passed the ammunition without discussion, debate, or the slightest bit of hesitancy." This embrace of armed self-defense on the part of the church broadens the interpretation of the antithesis as it preserves the possibility for communal harmony. This ultimate goal of the Divine command is impossible if the majority of the community is decimated through senseless violence; it remains possible, though, when anti-Black violence is negated, proving violent self-defense to be a sufficient strategy for survival and interpretation of the passage.

CONCLUSION

In discussing the maxim, Levine references Wink's *third way*: "rather than escalate violence, and rather than accept the loss of personal dignity, confront the violence . . . by displaying agency and courage."[48] This may work for the context of harsh public embarrassment, but too often "turn the other cheek" is used to address how someone should respond to violent aggression. So, I propose a *fourth* way in how the text might be interpreted: violent self-defense (emphasis on defense!). A willingness to confront violence with violence does not correlate to confronting evil with evil, as argued by Tolstoy (and less explicitly by Levine). A violence committed in service to domination and subjugation—acts founded upon denigration resulting in hierarchical social arrangements, that is, antithetical to harmony and peace—is certainly evil; a violence carried out for the sake of self- or group-preservation—avoiding obliteration—offers a chance at survival, preserving the possibility of pursuing communal harmony which the antithesis highlights. The latter represents the goal of Sam and Henry, yet their attempt at turning the other cheek (in the Levine sense) came back to bite them.

Plainly, if Jesus willed the obliteration of dominated communities, he neither would have aligned with the people he did nor been devoted to the work of empowerment. Therefore, it is obvious that his message is not to be interpreted literally when it comes to situations of anti-Black violence. Instead, the interpretation of this maxim must be broadened so that the turning of the cheek signifies the adoption of a new posture in relation to a perpetrator; this new posture is one that resists offensive/subjugating violence with life-preserving self-defense. Like the Lowndes County Freedom Organization, this means adopting the posture of a black panther which only shows its claws and bares its teeth after having been backed into a corner by a threat.[49] Having no other option for survival, the panther defends itself "by any means necessary."

In an increasingly militarized State, this proposed fourth way of interpreting the passage requires careful navigation of the line between "suicidal bravado" and "decentralize[d] armed resistance."[50] That is, Sam and Henry couldn't flamboyantly flash weapons in the face of Kathleen and her cronies; this would equate to self-obliteration. Instead, being armed would preserve their likelihood for successful defense and survival. Likewise, I wonder if the presence of a neighborhood association's armed night-watch team would have caused law enforcement to halt their advance on Breonna Taylor's apartment; I wonder if Ahmaud Arbery's armed neighbors' presence would have preserved his life had they been on the scene as assailants cornered him like prey; and I wonder if the officer's knee would have remained on George Floyd's neck for more than eight minutes if cell phones were replaced with weapons in the hands of onlookers. As seen in Bloody Lowndes, the Black Power movement, and the Black Panther Party for Self Defense, Black survival becomes possible through democratized armed self-defense.[51]

This fourth way is found in many of the most cherished scripture narratives: Moses defending his Hebrew kindred through killing the Egyptian slavedriver; Jael's tent-spike tactics to neutralize the cruelly oppressive Sisera; even David and his weaponization of a sling and stones to kill Goliath! With each of these stories, violence is wielded in a defensive, liberatory, and preserving manner; it is the last and most viable choice for survival against unwarranted violence. This very notion is communicated through social media filters, vehicle stickers, U.S. residences, and houses of worship raising the Ukrainian flag; we want those under attack to survive, even if it means "throwing hands."

As an American Baptist pastor, I long for the day described by the prophet Isaiah when weapons will be transformed from that which snuffs out life into that which sustains communal thriving.[52] At the same time, as a Black man, Carmichael's statement resonates with me; as long as perpetrators of anti-Black violence have access to and commit murderous acts with destructive weapons, it is only right for Black people to be justified in defending ourselves from annihilation through the fourth way: violent resistance.

NOTES

1. Garcia, "Gowdy on Trump Church Visit."
2. Matthew 5:39.
3. Taylor, *From #BlackLivesMatter to Black Liberation*, 115.
4. Cone, *Martin and Malcolm on Nonviolence and Violence*.
5. Patterson, *Slavery and Social Death*.
6. Hannah-Jones, *The 1619 Project*.
7. Jackson, *Becoming Human*.
8. Malcolm X, *By Any Means Necessary*.
9. Nwigwe, *Try Jesus*. "Try" signifying experimental assault. To "try" is to test the ethic of "turn the other cheek."
10. A general trend recognized as I mined the comments on Nigwe's post on Instagram, Twitter (now X), and YouTube.
11. This being the name of the episode which features the sibling duo. "Endure and Survive." *The Last of Us*, created by Neil Druckmann, and Craig Mazin, season 1, episode 5, HBO, 2023.
12. Jeffries, *Bloody Lowndes*, 100–101.
13. Vargas, *Can the Line Move?* 66.
14. Salem, *Review: 'The Last of Us' Barely Makes Space for Black Folks in Its Apocalypse*.
15. Nixon, *Slow Violence and the Environmentalism of the Poor*.
16. Hinton, *From the War on Poverty to the War on Crime*, 20.
17. Tatum, *Why Are All the Black Kids Sitting Together in the Cafeteria?* 138.
18. Wilderson, *Red, White & Black*, 88–89.
19. Jeffries, *Bloody Lowndes*, 113–114.
20. Purnell, *Becoming Abolitionists*, 3.
21. James, *Seeking the Beloved Community*, 99.
22. Jeffries, *Bloody Lowndes*, 62.
23. Jeffries, *Bloody Lowndes*.
24. Hill, "Black Deprivation."
25. Hill, "Black Deprivation."
26. Jeffries, *Bloody Lowndes*, 102.
27. Jeffries, *Bloody Lowndes*, 104.
28. Jeffries, *Bloody Lowndes*, 104.

29. Jeffries, *Bloody Lowndes*, 104.
30. Jeffries, *Bloody Lowndes*, 104.
31. Matthew 5–7.
32. Matthew 5:38–39, NRSV.
33. Cahill, *Blessed Are the Peacemakers*, 14.
34. Tolstoy, *My Religion*, 43.
35. Tolstoy, *My Religion*, 48.
36. James 2:26.
37. Cahill, *Blessed Are the Peacemakers*, 161–162.
38. Matthew 16, Matthew 25, and countless other references throughout the gospel pointing to the profound significance of overlooked happenings amidst his first century audience.
39. Levine and Brettler, *The Bible with and without Jesus*, 202.
40. Levine and Brettler, *The Bible with and without Jesus*.
41. Wink, *Jesus and Nonviolence*.
42. King, *Strength to Love*, 51.
43. Tisby, *Color of Compromise*, 22. Mainline protestant denominations being his primary focus.
44. Cone, *Martin and Malcolm on Nonviolence and Violence*, 180.
45. Malcolm X, *The Autobiography of Malcolm X*, 1973.
46. Cone, *Martin and Malcolm on Nonviolence and Violence*, 179.
47. Cone, *Martin and Malcolm on Nonviolence and Violence*, 181.
48. Levine and Brettler, *The Bible with and without Jesus*, 203.
49. Jeffries, *Bloody Lowndes*, 152.
50. Jeffries, *Bloody Lowndes*, 103.
51. The argument can be made that the Black Panther Party for Self-Defense arming its members contributed to its systematic annihilation, which I would rebut by pointing to the political power being acquired by the Oakland and Chicago chapters which led to infiltration, calumniation, and assassination. The arming of chapter members was critical for survival, a precondition for amassing political power.
52. Isaiah 2:4.

BIBLIOGRAPHY

Cahill, Lisa Sowle. *Blessed Are the Peacemakers Pacifism, Just War, and Peacebuilding*. Minneapolis, MN: Fortress Press, 2019.

Cone, James H. "Martin and Malcolm on Nonviolence and Violence." *Phylon* 49.3/4 (2001): 173–183, https://doi.org/10.2307/3132627.

Garcia, Victor. "Gowdy on Trump Church Visit: Jesus Is 'Not a Republican or Democrat,' Should Not Be Invoked in Politics." Fox News, June 2, 2020, www.foxnews.com/media/trey-gowdy-trump-jesus-not-republican-democrat.

Hannah-Jones, Nikole. *The 1619 Project: A New Origin Story*. New York: One World, 2021.

Hill, Melvin G. "Black Deprivation in Naughty Dog's 'The Last of Us' Remastered and 'The Last of Us Part II.'" *Journal of Games Criticism* 5 Bonus Issue A (2022), https://gamescriticism.org/2023/07/26/black-deprivation-in-naughty-dogs-the-last-of-us-remastered-and-the-last-of-us-part-ii/.

Hinton, Elizabeth. *From the War on Poverty to the War on Crime: The Making of Mass Incarceration in America*. Cambridge, MA: Harvard University Press, 2017.

Jackson, Zakiyyah Iman. *Becoming Human: Matter and Meaning in an Antiblack World*. New York: New York University Press, 2020.

James, Joy. *Seeking the Beloved Community: A Feminist Race Reader*. Albany, NY: SUNY Press, 2014.

Jeffries, Hasan Kwame. *Bloody Lowndes: Civil Rights and Black Power in Alabama's Black Belt*. New York: New York University Press, 2010.

King, Martin Luther, Jr. *Strength to Love*. Boston: Beacon Press, 2019.

Levine, Amy-Jill, and Marc Zvi Brettler. *The Bible with and without Jesus: How Jews and Christians Read the Same Stories Differently*. San Francisco, CA: Harperone, 2020.

Nixon, Rob. *Slow Violence and the Environmentalism of the Poor*. Cambridge, MA: Harvard University Press, 2011.

Nwigwe, Tobe. "Try Jesus." The Pandemic Project, 2020.

Patterson, Orlando. *Slavery and Social Death: A Comparative Study, with a New Preface*. Cambridge, MA: Harvard University Press, 2018.

Purnell, Derecka. *Becoming Abolitionists*. New York: Astra House, 2021.

Salem, Merryana. "Review: 'The Last of Us' Barely Makes Space for Black Folks in Its Apocalypse." *Junkee*, 2023, https://junkee.com/longform/the-last-of-us-review-black-death.

Tatum, Beverly Daniel. *Why Are All the Black Kids Sitting Together in the Cafeteria? And Other Conversations about Race*. New York: Basic Books, 2017.

Taylor, Keeanga-Yamahtta. *From #BlackLivesMatter to Black Liberation*. Chicago: Haymarket Books, 2016.

Tisby, Jemar. *Color of Compromise: The Truth about the American Church's Complicity in Racism*. Grand Rapids, MI: Zondervan, 2019.

Tolstoy, Leo. *My Religion*. New York: T. Y. Crowell & Company, 1885.

Vargas, João H. Costa. "Can the Line Move? Antiblackness and a Diasporic Logic of Forced Social Epidermalization." *Critical Ethnic Studies: A Reader* (2016): 66, muse.jhu.edu/book/69008.

Wilderson, Frank B., III. *Red, White & Black: Cinema and the Structure of U.S. Antagonisms*. Durham, NC: Duke University Press, 2010.

Wink, Walter. *Jesus and Nonviolence: A Third Way*. Minneapolis, MN: Fortress Press, 2003.

X, Malcolm. *By Any Means Necessary: Speeches, Interviews, and a Letter by Malcolm X*. New York: Pathfinder Press, 1970.

———. *The Autobiography of Malcolm X*. New York: Ballantine Books, 1973.

Chapter 9

The Road and *The Last of Us*
Failed Fathers at the End of the World

Peter Admirand

In Cormac McCarthy's *The Road* (*TR*), a father desperately seeks to shelter his son from the encroaching and inevitable blight of the apocalypse—"the darkness implacable."[1] In *The Last of Us* (*TLOU*), a father's enveloping body could not protect his daughter from the piercing of fatal bullets. Later blessed with a second chance, this other father initially refuses and squanders the gift of fatherhood and then embraces the role perhaps to the detriment of all other living beings. Both fathers also die before their progeny reach adulthood. To say they left their children orphaned is to overlook all the struggles and trials they endured, and yet, orphans their children become. Do these fathers, then, fail in the end, or is there a moral hope and perhaps theological lesson in these failures? This chapter, while focusing on the man in *TR* and Joel in *TLOU*, will also scour both works for other fathers, named and unnamed, hoping at best to show they are failed, but not false fathers, which I'll explain through Irving Greenberg's assessment of Jesus as a failed but not a false Messiah. But first, images of fatherhood at the end of the world.

FATHERHOOD IN BOSCH'S HELL

Some of the most haunting phrases of the Gospels are Jesus' warnings about the end times. His chilling words follow a series of parables and responses to questions from Pharisees, Herodians, and potential disciples while in the Temple and the Temple precincts, where he challenges paying taxes to the Romans, denounces religious leaders who devour the house of widows, and clarifies what true discipleship entails (love of God and of humankind), among other disputes and queries (Mark 12).[2] Then as he was leaving the temple and the disciples gawked at its beauty, Jesus prophesied its destruction. Later at the Mount of Olives, the curious (and perhaps anxious) disciples wanted to know when such catastrophes would strike. Jesus lists a series of destructive signs and laments: "Woe to those who are pregnant and to those who are nursing infants in those days!" (Mark 12:17). Sadly, many end times have come and gone, and many, many pregnant and nursing women—and their countless children—have perished.

In prophesying what would happen to his followers amidst the persecutions, Jesus foretells that: "Brother will betray brother to death, and a father his child, and children will rise against parents and have them put to death" (Mark 12:12). While too many dire and catastrophic contexts have led otherwise good people to act in this way, we also know of many other cases where a family loves each other until the bitter end, risking everything for one another (as we will see between the man and his son in *TR* and with Joel and Ellie in *TLOU*).

Recently, I winced at a photograph in the *Washington Post* capturing a man, perhaps a father, trying to wrench apart barbed wire so a little child could pass across a border into the United States. Is the child safe now? Did the razors pierce him? Reading or teaching about memoirs from parents who failed to save their children from suffering and death or those reflecting on their childhood and the ways their parents tried to inoculate them from explosions or repression chide me to be silent and to listen. I know nothing of what it means to be a father amidst war, famine, persecution, forced migration, or ecological catastrophe, where hard, difficult choices must be taken; impossible choices. Do you stay where you are with the children or flee to the unknown, danger lurking and penetrating from all sides? I can imagine, as a father of five children, some now young adults, two still in primary school, that I would be as selfless, kind, or supportive in those worlds as I try to be in my peace-filled and plenteous one. But moral failures here make me weary and dismayed. I'm not pleasant around when hungry; I can be anxious or can panic if my emotions run wild; I'm not resourceful outside the classroom or in the written text. How many ways would I fail them in those horrid contexts when I still fail my children in this one?

While many of us have been shielded from dire times, we are familiar with hellish landscape paintings like Giotto's rendering in *The Last Judgment* (for the Arena Chapel, painted from 1304–1313; see Figure 9.3) or Hieronymus Bosch's *Hell*, painted in 1490 (see Figure 9.4). As I inspect the paintings, two initial key points seem dominant: (1) While containing the mythological and grotesque, the paintings' acts of cruelty and nightmarish, poisoned hellscapes mirror life for some on Earth; and (2) those of us who can only see such scenes as imaginary or as horror-fiction need to look more closely at the world outside our little haven. Death, of course, was more of a daily reality for those living in the fourteenth and fifteenth centuries in Europe, from plague, ongoing war, rampant disease, poor understanding of modern medicine, low birth survival, and generally shorter lifespans. But while death remains everywhere, many of us in the so-called first-world can try to hide and obstruct such pervasive death-realities, perhaps reading about them in a newspaper and then turning the page or clicking on another link.

Let's try, then, to place ourselves in such paintings, and for the purposes of this chapter imagine you are a parent or guardian with a child, or children, clasped about you. (In writing these words, I immediately think of the infamous photo of the Nazis and local fascists murdering the few remaining Jews in Miropol, with one mother, bent over toward a little boy—who is slipping on his knees in front of her—as she clasps him with both arms along with another child, mostly obstructed. All are about to drop into the pit of dead or still near-dead bodies below them. The killers, right behind them, have already fired their guns at the mother's head. It is too awful to even think what happened next to the children, if still momentarily alive, tumbling down into that pit with their now pulverized mother [see Figure 9.1].[3] Again, the so-called hellish-imaginary and the hellish-real can be indistinguishable.)

Figure 9.1. Wendy Lower's *The Ravine* Examines This Photo of a Holocaust Massacre Committed by Germans and Locals in Miropol, Ukraine, on October 13, 1941 (USHMM). *Security Services Archive, Historical Collection of the State Security Service (StB) Prague, archival no. H-770-3*

Can we, should we, even envision ourselves amidst such dreads? In Joseph-Désiré Court's depiction of a piteous scene during the Noahide flood (see Figure 9.2), a mother, sinking in the water while clinging to a flimsy branch, desperately raises her naked child above the surging sea toward a man standing on a rock. The man, though, is reaching away, down toward an old man nearly swallowed by the waters, his ghostly face barely visible.

Figure 9.2. *Scene from the Great Flood* (1826), by Joseph-Désiré Court. *Joseph-Désiré Court, Public Domain*

While the painting has been allegorized as the man choosing the past over the present and future, it is another choiceless choice. From the story, we know, they and everyone else—including that baby and who knows how many other innocent babies—would senselessly and unjustly drown—even as no baby is guilty of any sin or deserving the wrath of any impecunious god. Can we imagine, for a moment, what it would be like for those parents—the helplessness of the impending doom, the god who will not hear our piteous cries amidst the raging surf and our faltering hold, the baby already swallowing too much spray? Those of us in Europe read about such stories every day, but we are generally safe and warm, and detached even as we feel badly.[4]

As we turn to the paintings by Giotto and Bosch, let's not delude ourselves by the demons. Such exist but they are very, very human, even as we snicker at the canvas with its plethora of fangs, wings, and snouts or try to disown them as pure evil. They (we?) are usually not demons all the time. In the

Figure 9.3. Giotto's *The Last Judgment* (for the Arena Chapel, painted from 1304–1313). *Giotto, Public Domain*

Figure 9.4. Hieronymus Bosch's *Hell* (1490). *Hieronymus Bosch, Public Domain*

contexts of genocides and mass slaughters, millions of regular people participate in such decapitating, sawing, burning, raping, drowning, and devouring. Examples are endlessly sickening and demoralizing.[5] What do you do if you are a parent in such worlds? I do not know. Again, I may know much about fatherhood, but of that cross of fatherhood, to be a father despite such horrors, I know nothing—save that I would fail my beloved children even while yearning and striving otherwise.

FAILED MESSIAHS, FALSE PARENTS

Earlier I explained that I would look at Orthodox Rabbi Irving Greenberg's notion of Jesus as a failed but not false Messiah and apply that idea to fatherhood here. Greenberg's argument was that Jesus genuinely tried to redeem the world; in this sense he was not a false, or what I would call an imposter Messiah only trying to accumulate personal glory, wealth, or a harem. For Greenberg, despite Jesus' best efforts and intentions, he failed to redeem the world. Imperial Rome still barbarously ruled; injustice still boomed. Trying to appease later Christian complaints, Greenberg argued that he meant it as a compliment, seeing failure in all the great Jewish prophets as a sign of both their fidelity to God and their social justice ambition. They did not redeem the world, but their successes, despite their ultimate failures, still veered the world closer to such a restoration. Without such failures, the world would be worse; or to put it positively, such failures helped instill the later conditions for flourishing. The example of a pacifist, compassionate Jesus, I could argue, inspired those like St. Francis of Assisi (to forge another link with Giotto above) and modern examples like Sr. Dianna Ortiz, Dorothy Day, and Oscar Romero. They all failed as well, but without this chain of holiness and goodness, what then? As Greenberg writes: "Such failures are the key to success of the divine strategy of redemption."[6]

For Greenberg, then, with the inevitable disappointment of even the most holy lovers of God, there can be meaningful failure while trying to usher in the reign of God. These stalwarts fail only in terms of achieving their overall hope and aim, but their lives, marked by the love and grace of God, should be celebrated and imitated. It is in this sense that I predominantly assess the man and Joel as fathers in *TR* and *TLOU*, respectively. But first, a quick comparison of the works.

THE ROAD AND *THE LAST OF US*: WHAT KIND OF MIRROR?

Cormac McCarthy's *TR* was published in 2006 and won the Pulitzer Prize for Fiction in 2007; Naughty Dog's *TLOU* launched on the PS3 in 2013. The influences of the novel are undeniable and cited by both Neil Druckmann, and regarding the HBO Series, Craig Mazin.[7] In *TR*, a father, whom his son calls "Papa," traverses a desolate, post-apocalyptic hellscape with his young son. They are alone because the boy's mother (and the man's wife), fled so she could die and not witness others—especially those against her boy—"rape us and kill us and eat us" (56). She tragically, or realistically, saw no hope in the hopeless world now encircling them.

During the man and the boy's journey together, they scavenge food and find shelter, hide from marauders and cannibals, and endure nature's unforgiving climes. The father cannot fathom helping others in need as they are either threats feigning succour or a burden that cannot also be carried, often to his son's dismay: "Can't we help him? Papa?" (50).

The father finds his will to live through the boy—even seeing him as the only light in an otherwise darkened world. But the boy's suffering sears the father: "The boy was terrified. He put his arm around him and held him. His body so thin" (112). How could it not? Despite this desolation, though, the man teaches the boy survival amidst the "wet ash" (85), the dangers to avoid at all costs. Zombie-like or raging humans violate and infringe upon them; sickness and injury follow. Yet the father still speaks of the light (or fire within), or at least allows the boy to so believe. Inevitably, the man succumbs to death. The boy is left alone but is miraculously adopted by another family.

The parallels with *TLOU* need little elaboration here, but perhaps the most significant differences are the presence (and non-presence) of God, which is explicitly identified, even thirsted for in *TR*, but which is mostly rejected or seems buried within *TLOU*.[8] In *TR*, moreover, the boy is not only younger than Ellie but maintains a purity and innocence that the rebellious (but also world-naïve) Ellie never possessed. Of course, all children are born innocent and the second *TLOU* game emphasizes how much Ellie had grown into a young woman—no longer laughing at stupid jokes or marveling at the world around her. In this regard, Sarah would be closer in spirit to *TR*'s boy than the younger Ellie—let alone the traumatized, bitter, vengeance-obsessed one. While the man in *TR* envisions the boy as light and "a word of God," invoking both the opening of Genesis and for Christians, Jesus as the Word Incarnate (5), it is interesting to apply this idea on Ellie. She is clearly a light to Joel, a type of firefly leading him out of his dark mourning. Marlene and Jerry both believed Ellie could also be the savior of the world with her immunity. Ellie even seemed prepared to make such a sacrifice. "It can't be for nothing" as she tells Joel, who was hoping she'd instead decide to turn back to Jackson. But if one sees Ellie as a potential Christ figure, the father in me also sees an age and maturity difference. Jesus of Nazareth, at the least, was a fully grown man, and in my reading, social-justice focused, not suicidal. In other words, he knew teaching and living the kin-dom of God would have consequences, but he valued all lives, including his own. This is unclear with Ellie, who was not only a pawn in an adult world but seems to think she has no intrinsic meaning or worth—and that this possibility is taken away by Joel's actions in St. Mary's Hospital.

Of the aforementioned three children—Sarah, Ellie, and the boy—I wanted to write: "It is the one who failed the most, especially morally, who can still be such a savior"—meaning Ellie, but there are many ways to save, almost as many as there are to destroy. The boy, especially as a light to the world, can extend horizons of hope, even if cruel reality mocks the efficacy of such kindness and goodness—think of Sarah, for example. Did not Joel become bitter and morally aimless after clasping her bullet-ridden body? How long can the boy in *TR* sustain such optimism amidst catamites and splayed corpses? Isn't Ellie's proficiency with weapons and brutality the only saving we trust in? I'll later touch on such a question as I work through fathers in *TLOU* and *TR*.

FATHERS IN *THE ROAD*

Ironically, in *TR*, the greatest (apparent) sign of true fatherhood is the courage and love to be able to kill your children or to help them do it themselves before unimaginable horrors desecrate and destroy them (113). "Can you do it? When the time comes? Can you?" (29; see also 114).[9] But it is also this unbounded love that wants to avoid such an act at all costs. Like Joel with Sarah, the man would sacrifice anything for his son. In *TR* such acts of love include "wash[ing] a dead man's brains out of [your child's] hair" (74) or using your stomach to warm his nearly frostbitten feet, no matter your own agony and despair (36). It also requires killing other humans, especially those ready to gorge on you and your child. "My job is to take care of you," the man tells his son. "I was appointed to do that by God. I will kill anyone who touched you. You understand?" (77).

All the will in the world is not enough, though. After surviving months together on the road, amidst "One vast salt sepulchre. Senseless. Senseless" (222), the boy's father dies, despite the son's efforts to nurse him through his wounds.[10] Loyal to the end, the boy remains by the dead body for three days before trudging back to the road. He is immediately followed. He flees back to who had been his only protection, now lifeless. The stranger, meanwhile, has a shotgun and evident physical wounds—including a facial disfiguring that would unnerve a child in a less ash-strewn world. He asks the boy if this was his father and tells him the boy should come with him. How likely is it that just as his father dies, in a life of grueling survival-drudgery, the boy finds not just a father but a loving family? Is this not a delusional, traumatic, or guilt-ridden vision?

Regardless, the boy receives the protection another little boy in the novel was earlier denied by the boy's father. When the boy had claimed to have seen this little child (along with a dog), he begged his father to help; that he would even give up half of his own food (86). But the father sensed danger, seeing this supposed other child as a trap, a sign of a gang watching and lurking, poised to attack.[11] He forces his son to flee with him, apparently deciding that even if this other child was really alive and alone or had recently strayed from bloodthirsty marauders, the man could not bring another child with him.[12] The boy cries and protests—"What about the little boy?" (86)—and here I would contend the first death[13] of his father occurs. Such a death may explain the sudden and only shift in point of view in the novel to the first person from its otherwise third person perspective. The shift in authorial voice and in memory seems to signal some kind of acute trauma.[14] According to the first-person voice in this one paragraph, a voice that could be the older boy's, or the father's, or perhaps the father at the end of the novel, the boy remembers the dog but not "any little boys" (87). But the boy does seem to remember, if in fact he is telling the story. And if not the boy, and unless it's the father already dead, again who is left telling this tale?

Returning to the novel's end, the boy initially fears this disfigured man eats other people. Experience has taught him this (198), so the boy is surprised to hear this other man still has living children (284). And he seems to want to help the boy, with two actions—otherwise risks—supporting this hope. He lets the boy keep the gun even after the boy tells him he knows how to use it (285); and perhaps more tellingly, he agrees with the boy's request to cover his dead father with an otherwise needed blanket (286) and keeps his promise in doing so. Keeping promises was something the boy's own father highly valued (34).

Then there is the woman, this other man's partner/spouse. When the boy agrees to go with the new man and meets the woman, the scarred man told the boy they had discussed whether to save him and they had decided to do so. Here both are immediately unlike the boy's own parents. While the boy's own mother said her "heart was ripped out of me the night he was born" (57) and can only see death as an option, this woman embraces the boy. She even talks to him of God and encourages him to pray. And when the boy says he "tries to talk to God but the best thing was to talk to his father," she replies: "that the breadth of God was his breadth though it pass from man to man through all time" (286). In a world of cannibals eating their own children, this boy had not only been raised by a father with strong moral principles, embedded in the notion that his boy remains linked to a God of light, and they should carry this fire within them, but the same boy finds even a more loving and complete family sustained by belief in God. Here, we could not be further from *TLOU*—though stories of betrayals and treachery or parents eating their children are not fiction[15]—nor is it impossible or unrealistic for strangers to save others as memoirs attest of righteous people[16] who risked their lives and the lives of family members to save strangers, neighbors, or acquaintances despite scarcity and reprisals. But it remains rare, and seemingly, miraculous if not dumbfounding.

FATHERS IN *TLOU*

Most fathers in *TLOU* and its sequel are dead, missing, or killed during the game, Joel and Dr. Jerry Anderson being the most prominent.[17] Other fathers are unknown—like Ellie's biological dad. Likewise, we never learn about the father of Sam and Henry, while Jesse is killed before he can meet JJ, his son with Dina. Riley must even kill her own father after he had become infected and had killed Riley's mother.[18] Outside Joel and Sarah (and Ellie), and Abby and her father, the only other father and child who interact in the game is Manny Alvarez and his ailing dad, whom we briefly meet in the stadium as Manny is helping him to eat. While Abby comforts Mr. Alvarez that she'll keep Manny safe, the son is later shot and killed by Tommy.

Fathers referred to in notes or artifacts found by players in *TLOU* reinforce tragedies and senseless deaths. In the sewers, Joel finds a series of notes that fill in the story of Ish, a fisherman/survivalist, who harbors a family (a father, Kyle, wife Susan, and children) that soon grows with other survivors to form a small little community led by adult protectors. There's even a school and playroom. Tragically, it also succumbs to the infected. One mistake, a door left ajar, sends children and adults scurrying. Kyle, one of the fathers and adult protectors of the children, got bit as he was trying to lead some "little ones" to safety. Like Papa in *TR*, he then prepared himself to mercy-kill the children to prevent worse from happening before he turned. "If it comes down to it, I'll make it quick." When playing as Joel and exploring the room, the player sees little bodies covered in a white sheet and the words "They didn't suffer" scrawled on the floor. After finding and reading the note, Joel mutters: "Jesus." We don't know the status of Ish and some of the others, though a note Joel later finds reveals Ish and Susan and some other children survived the escape from the sewers though their status since is unknown.

Whether to stay or flee to protect one's children, as noted earlier, is a harrowing choice for many in our own world during government instability, natural disasters, war, and food shortages. The games reflect this. While rummaging through some houses in Pittsburgh, Joel/the player can find another note written by Kyle before he fatally brought his family to Ish in the sewers. Joel's comment—"Now, that wasn't a good idea now, was it?" belies the fact that fathers in such situations never can know what path will keep their child safe. His lack of empathy here is revealing. In applying Greenberg's false/failed vocabulary, these are all failed (even heroic), but not false fathers. Unlike Lev's mother who was willing to turn Lev over to the Seraphite elders no matter his fate, these desperate fathers did everything to try and keep their little ones safe, but like millions of others, premature, violent death still followed.

Sadly, it is the murder of fathers (or father figures) in *TLOU* that spur the revenge cycle and desultory and parallel paths for retribution chosen by Ellie and Abby. While both daughters blame themselves for their fathers' homicides, neither is responsible, and nothing will restore their fathers to them. Killing others will only slowly kill themselves—the essence of what those fathers adored and loved. In this sense, flashbacks in *TLOU* are a common feature to uncover pivotal past events that reveal current motivations or character. The zebra scene with Abby and her father (and Owen) is particularly telling, for example. We immediately see their closeness and mutual love in their dialogue and trust—and if Abby's father is willing to take risks to save a zebra, how much more would he do for his child, his "Abs"? As a father, we learn how he painted a "colorful jungle" scene in the walls of her room and how much he loves her.

As the second game tries to portray Jerry as compassionate, honorable, brilliant, and conscientious, would Abby have been as driven to revenge if Jerry were a false father? Is it their legitimate love that fuels the later violence? This is an uncomfortable question to consider. My only issue for Jerry, and it is also a discomforting one, is his seeming eagerness to operate on Ellie knowing he would have to kill her in the process. Was their hubris in his belief in himself or just hope to end the world's evident demise?

If the basic requirement of fatherhood is to save and not destroy one's offspring, how do we assess acts of destruction of others (especially otherwise innocent or mistaken others) to save our children? Again, while Jerry was willing to sacrifice Ellie—someone else's child—in the hope of a greater cure for others, Joel was willing to sacrifice himself to save Ellie from that fate. Which father is best acting the part here? Even as some of us grapple with whether Joel committed what Ellie calls an "unforgivable" act by taking away the chance for her life to have meaning, his intention to save her, or at least prevent someone else killing her (especially without her adult consent) is commendable. Where things get morally muddled is in his extreme violence (some of which the game "forces" you to do for progress like killing Jerry (or in a cut scene, Marlene[19]) while other actions the gamers choose, like whether to murder the unarmed medics cowering in the room. Especially pernicious for Ellie, though, are all the lies Joel maintained to defend his actions and shield her from the full truth. Such extreme violence and layers of lying adulterate whatever noble intentions had been present—turning Joel into a false and not just a failed father—a notion I'll return to later.

To be clear, Joel did not fail Sarah in her final moments of her life. Like Kyle in the sewers, he did everything he could, even guarding her with his own body—willing to die for her. That is not a failure; but is emblematic of what a father should do. In the few interactions we see between Sarah and Joel, they are playful, intimate, and caring to one another. Just as he carries her gently from the couch to the bed, so he later carries her while she is wounded (and likewise carries Ellie from the operating table). As a single, working dad, Joel evidently needs Sarah to be independent, but as his "baby girl" she knows she is loved. He later proudly tells Ellie that Sarah "dragged" him to "every damn museum in Texas."

But her death shatters something within him, leading to a suicide attempt and morally indefensible actions in the name of survival.[20] Before her death, Tess admits what she and Joel had become: "We're shitty people." Without a purpose as a father, Joel is lost without anyone to protect, whether his brother

Tommy or Tess—or uses them as an excuse to occlude his immoral actions. If Joel had died with Sarah or instead of Sarah in that fatal moment, we would not speak of him as a false father. When Joel rejects a vulnerable Ellie's stirring for fatherly protection, though, he embodies a false father. After Ellie first mentions Sarah to him, he sullies Sarah's memory by scorning Ellie. "You're right," he coldly tells her, too afraid to admit his own fears, "You're not my daughter and I sure as hell ain't your dad." It is Joel's fatherly nadir. Despite this failing, though, can we still highlight a redemptive arc for Joel from a failed to a false and then back to a failed (but ultimately, good) father? Perhaps, and I'll return to the above scene in the conclusion, but it should be noted in comparison, that in *TR*, Papa is never a false father.[21]

Consider, for example, how Joel's actions and prevarications at the end of the first game are agonizingly revealed in *TLOU2*, leading to Ellie and Joel's rupture. While Joel's murder occurs early in the game, flashbacks enable the player to relive some key moments between Ellie and Joel prior to his death. Though softened by happy memories, especially the great effort Joel made for her sixteenth birthday, Ellie slowly learns what happened at St. Mary's Hospital. She pleads to hear the truth from Joel. He struggles to find the right words, though, finally rasping: "Making a vaccine would have killed you. So I stopped them." As in *TR* and *TLOU*, when your child's life is endangered by someone else, you stop that threat. Whether a God-given role of not, that is what these fathers are ready to do. But with this truth confirmed by Joel, Ellie spasms and cries, shaking. Joel reaches out to console her. She lashes out: "Don't you fuckin' touch me!" She says she'll go back to Jackson, "but we are done." She walks away.

CONCLUSION: NICKNAMES

Nicknames are often a sign of endearment, especially between parent and child (or among adult lovers). While Sarah is Joel's "baby girl," "honey," or "baby," his preferred pet name for Ellie is "kiddo."[22] She also has her own names for Joel usually making fun of his age, calling him "old man" or referring to him in her journal as a "smug old fogey"—or hinting he's a dinosaur in their birthday museum excursion.[23] These are all silly or touching words only meant for them. In their last conversation together, she also calls him an "asshole"—notably after he sweetly compliments her—but the anger expressed was also an outlet to restore their fractured relationship—especially after his lies.

While the boy in *TR* calls his father, "Papa"; and Sarah calls Joel, "Dad" and "Daddy"; and Abby calls her father "Dad," Ellie never explicitly names Joel with any fatherly term. But it's understood—though not without some painful moments. When Ellie first mentions Sarah to Joel, as touched on earlier, she only does so as a means of expressing a shared sense of loss. She reaches out with empathy, but he replies with bitterness, seething: "you have no idea what loss is." But Ellie, whose life has been immersed in loss, and who has never known fatherly love, further opens her heart: "Everyone I have ever cared for has either died or left me . . . everyone"—she pushes him away—"fucking except for you." Exposing her vulnerability and dread, she explicitly admits her burgeoning devotion for Joel. But again, Joel only thinks of his own fears (which is also the fear of loving and then losing someone else)—and his words to her, especially at that moment, are almost as unforgivable as his actions as a hunter or in St. Mary's Hospital. With these transgressions in mind, I again ask: Is Joel's character path, then, stagnant, especially as a father?

In general, Joel, like the man in *TR*, shows his love through actions. After his cruel words to Ellie and after they overcome a threat, Joel tells Ellie to get off her horse and onto his. He pretends the reason is that he doesn't want Tommy's wife to be mad at him for having his little brother go on the mission with Ellie. Joel asks Ellie if she's good. Her smile and her holding on to him point to her acceptance of his change—and that she sees this as his apology, maybe even refutation, of the hurtful words he had spoken. To show his love, Joel tries to do and find things that make Ellie happy, whether comic books or a tape of the Apollo lift-off. Joel's love for Ellie is also expansive, not possessive. He is happy when he thinks she has potential love interests, even if he mistakenly thinks it's Jessie.[24] And when Ellie later admits that she kissed Dina, he tells her he doesn't know Dina's intentions, "but I do know that she would be lucky to have you."

Returning to my earlier introduction of Irving Greenberg's failed and false Messiah distinction, what made Jesus, in Greenberg's estimation, a failed but not a false Messiah, was that he tried to change the world as the Messiah was expected to do, but he failed. The Roman Empire continued its violent rule for another few centuries and power politics and corruption continue to this day. Yet, even to non-Christians, Jesus' life still deserves praise, unlike a false Messiah who "has the wrong values, i.e., is one who would teach that death will triumph, that people should oppress each other, that God hates us, or that sin and crime are the proper way."[25] Likewise, a failed father, though not perfect, genuinely loves his children, seeks what is best for their development and growth, and lives with integrity, but can't shield them from some of the injustices and pains in this world or keep them or him safe. A false father, though, betrays his children by his own selfishness or hypocrisy, caring little about their welfare or how his actions negatively impact them.

In the end, the father in *TR* and Joel in *TLOU* are failed fathers, with Joel even slipping into falsity and betrayal of what fatherhood means. He turns narcissistically inward and even his acts of kindness can seem focused on the self—yet he loves deeply. It is the love of these fathers for their offspring, biological or otherwise, that cohere and link these works in prominent ways. In *TR*, the son and father are "Each the other world's entire" (6), while in *TLOU*, Joel sings to Ellie: "If I ever was to lose you, I would surely lose myself"—a Pearl Jam song she later learns and plays in mourning Joel. Prominently, it is the memory of Joel with his guitar on his porch that prevents Ellie from drowning Abby and gives her the space to let Abby and Lev go. His memory prods Ellie toward some path of healing and redemption. Here, Joel, even as a failed father, nurtures Ellie's stumbling toward renewal because his love for her reaches beyond and after his death. Likewise, in *TR*, the boy continues to "carry the fire" (83; see also 128–129) and to speak to his dead father, a speaking that his new mother sees as the breadth of God. While the hope hinted at in *TR* remains mostly unaddressed in *TLOU*, perhaps the love Ellie and Abby felt from their fathers can now fuel a greater good—and not simply vengeance. Daddy, baby girl, Papa, kiddo—these are the talismans that speak beyond and despite inevitable fatherly failures—bonds of intimacy and love despite even the end of the world.

NOTES

1. McCarthy, *The Road*, 130. All subsequent citations from the novel will be cited in the main text.
2. For a social justice reading of these scenes, along with the praise of the widow for giving away all her pittance, which precedes Jesus' prediction of the destruction of the Temple (which implies money the widow needs to live is being spent instead on lavish upkeep of the Temple), see Myers, *Binding the Strong Man*, 308–323.
3. For a moving and important analysis of the photo, see Lower, *The Ravine*.
4. See Hayden, *My Fourth Time, We Drowned*.
5. See Admirand, *Amidst Mass Atrocity and the Rubble of Theology*.
6. See Greenberg, *For the Sake of Heaven and Earth*, 178.
7. Radish, "The Last of Us."
8. Joel is portrayed as a nominal Christian: his tombstone has a cross and his pleas usually reference God/Jesus (especially after the death of Sarah). Dina's Jewishness is reflected upon and explained in the synagogue scene with Ellie, though her belief in any God, as opposed to continuing her links with Jewish ritual, need further scrutiny, as does the initial beliefs of the Seraphites.
9. For an examination of this motif through the lens of sacramental theology, see Potts, *Cormac McCarthy and the Signs of Sacrament*, 158–159.
10. While Ellie nurses Joel through his wounds suffered on the University Campus, she is helpless during Abby's torture and death of Joel.

11. In *TLOU*, hunters feign someone in need of help to then capture, loot, and kill passers-by as Joel and Ellie experienced in Pittsburgh. Joel also later admitted he sensed it was a trap because he had once done similar things—"I've been on both sides." When Ellie asks if he killed "a lot of innocent people," and he just grunts a "hmm," she replies: "I'll take that as a yes," and he tells her to "Take it however you want."

12. When they later find a charred baby on a spit, his face munched away (198), the man tells the son he would have saved and brought such a little baby with them (200).

13. I would contend the father's second death is when the father punished the man who tried to steal their cart by making him strip down naked, a scene which haunts the boy: "but we did kill him" (256–260).

14. A similar shift, but to the second person, occurs after the man and the boy come across a group of cannibals imprisoning half-eaten and still alive human beings. The man has just given his son a gun to shoot himself with in case they are found. The passage not only plays on the firing of a gun as killing the child but echoes the fire of goodness said to be in the boy. And if the gun doesn't fire, "Could you crush that beloved skull with a rock?" (*TR*, 114), perhaps referring to Psalm 137:9.

15. See Yarov, *Leningrad;* and Jisheng, *Tombstone.*

16. In the Shoah, see Gilbert, *The Righteous.*

17. Manny Alvarez was an eager member of Abby's revenge group against Joel, even spitting on his dead corpse and prepared to kill a captive Ellie.

18. We learn this in issue four of the comic, *The Last of Us: American Dreams.*

19. Marlene justifies Ellie's likely death by saying: "This isn't about me—or her," while Joel, despite his obsession to protect others, often inordinately focuses on himself. Recall his words to Sarah while she's dying: "don't do this to me." And yet, as an interesting foil or perhaps parallel to Joel, Marlene could be considered a false mother-figure for the way she was willing to sacrifice Ellie without her full consent or knowledge. We can still ask: what if we were Marlene? But while Marlene kept Ellie safe, she always did so at a distance. Joel might have feared getting close to Ellie but still provided a space for this to blossom. That space may have been the difference in their decisions in St. Mary's Hospital.

20. When Ellie and Joel encounter a dead couple in a bathtub and she says they took the easy way out, Joel replies: "It isn't easy, trust me." While Joel's comment is ambiguous, the HBO version later expanded and confirmed that he had tried to kill himself after Sarah's death and has a head scar as a reminder (episode 9, "Look for the Light").

21. For an account rightly nuancing claims of redemption in *TR*, see Rambo, "Beyond Redemption"; and for a charged critique of Joel, see Ramirez, *Rules of the Father*, 131.

22. Powerfully, Joel calls Ellie "baby girl" when comforting her after the traumatic David episode.

23. When Abby is torturing Joel, she calls him "stupid old man."

24. Abby's father correctly recognizes Abby's feelings for Owen: "I'm your dad. I see things. Like the way you both try really, really hard not to look at each other when you're around me."

25. Greenberg, *For the Sake of Heaven and Earth*, 153.

BIBLIOGRAPHY

Admirand, Peter. *Amidst Mass Atrocity and the Rubble of Theology: Searching for a Viable Theodicy*. Eugene, OR: Cascade Books, 2012.

Gilbert, Martin. *The Righteous: The Unsung Heroes of the Holocaust*. London: Doubleday, 2002.

Greenberg, Irving. *For the Sake of Heaven and Earth: The New Encounter between Judaism and Christianity*. Philadelphia, PA: Jewish Publication Society, 2004.

Hayden, Sally. *My Fourth Time, We Drowned: Seeking Refuge on the World's Deadliest Migration Route*. London: 4th Estate, 2023.

Jisheng, Yang. *Tombstone: The Great Chinese Famine, 1958–1962*. Translated by Stacy Mosher and Guo Jin. New York: Farrar, Straus and Giroux, 2012.

Lower, Wendy. *The Ravine: A Family, a Photograph, a Holocaust Massacre Revealed*. London: Head of Zeus, 2021.

McCarthy, Cormac. *The Road*. New York: Vintage, 2006.

Myers, Ched. *Binding the Strong Man: A Political Reading of Mark's Story of Jesus*. Anniv. ed. Maryknoll, NY: Orbis, 2008.

Potts, Matthew L. *Cormac McCarthy and the Signs of Sacrament: Literature, Theology, and the Moral of Stories*. New York: Bloomsbury, 2017.

Radish, Christina. "'The Last of Us' Co-Creators Break Down Season 1 Finale and What Fans Can Expect from Season 2." Collider, March 13, 2023, https://collider.com/the-last-of-us-season-finale-craig-mazin-neil-druckmann-interview/.

Rambo, Shelly L. "Beyond Redemption? Reading Cormac McCarthy's *The Road* after the End of the World." *Studies in the Literary Imagination* 41.2 (2008): 99–120.

Ramirez, J. Jesse. *Rules of the Father in The Last of Us: Masculinity among the Ruins of Neoliberalism*. Cham: Palgrave, 2022.

Yarov, Sergey. *Leningrad 1941:1942: Morality Under Siege*. Translated by Arch Tait. London: Polity, 2017.

PART III

Redemption?

Chapter 10

God's (Non)Presence, Interdependence, and Hope in *The Last of Us*

A Theological Reflection

Pavol Bargár

In[1] the post-apocalyptic landscape of the HBO series *The Last of Us* (*TLOU*),[2] it is no easy task to find images, or even traces, of God's presence. More often than not, actually, God seems not to be present in that bleak world. However, even instances of divine non-presence can be telling and theologically nourishing. The present chapter explores three such images, focusing on the themes of power dynamics in the relationships within human communities, the distorted *imago Dei*, and queer romance. Engaging dialogue partners from the fields of postcolonial, feminist, and queer theologies, this chapter will seek to reflect on how these images can engender, or else disable, hope. It will be argued that even in post-apocalyptic settings, authentic relationships can represent loci of hope and transformation. As such, the chapter aims at showing that even if non-present in the world, God can be effectively working through people. In principle, therefore, the chapter strives to make a contribution to the field of theological anthropology.

A TALE OF TWO COMMUNITIES: SILVER LAKE AND JACKSON

God seems to be readily absent from the world of *TLOU*. And so are largely absent the doctrinal, liturgical, and ethical implications of faith in God, at least explicitly. After all, what would be the point of still nurturing faith in God after the apocalypse has broken in? And yet, God nevertheless seems to be present and effective here, even in the midst of, or perhaps despite, God's non-presence. In this section, two contrasting examples of such divine (non)presence will be explored by zooming in on two different communities.

First of all, there is Silver Lake, a town in Colorado that Joel and Ellie stumble upon in episode 8. That episode opens with images of a snow-covered landscape and a settlement, accompanied by a male preacher reading the passage from the biblical book of Revelation on a new heaven and a new earth. The camera soon turns to the preacher and his congregation. The faces of some congregants are pious, others seem worn down by life. There is a big banner hanging up in the community hall saying: "When We Are in Need, He Shall Provide." A young girl is shown crying because, as the viewer will find out, her father recently passed away. The pastor responds to the girl's cry by citing the passage from Revelation 21 about God wiping every tear and death having no more bearing on human life (Revelation 21:4).

Shortly after, there is an encounter between Ellie and the preacher as both of them need to go hunting in the woods; Ellie needs to provide food for herself and for Joel, who is down with a fever after being stabbed at the university campus. The preacher needs to provide food for his community. Ellie has more luck as she both shoots a deer and catches by surprise the preacher and his companion who are just about to claim her deer. After the other man returns to their village to bring antibiotics for Joel in exchange for half of the deer, Ellie and the preacher engage in conversation. His name is David and he is the leader of the community in Silver Lake but, as he emphasizes, not of his own will but because the people have elected him. In addition, David describes himself as a "standard-type Bible preacher" to his community. When Ellie asks why he still believes "that shit" after the world ended, David responds by saying that he actually only found God after the apocalypse. Then David invites Ellie to join his community.

Involuntarily, Ellie must accept the "invitation," as she falls captive to David and his men who are on a mission to kill Joel who, as it turns out, killed Alec, one of their group and the father of Hannah, the girl who cried during the service. While in custody, Ellie discovers that David has been feeding human flesh to his community, most of whom remain unaware of the fact. David admits it, saying that he is ashamed but insisting that he has had no other option as the community is running low on supplies and the people love him and wait on him to provide for them. This, I would suggest, implies that David effectively self-identifies as a God vis-à-vis other people. On such reading, the banner in the meeting hall is then to be interpreted as referring to David, rather than the biblical God. There are also other examples to support this claim. For instance, when Hannah publicly calls for having both

Joel and Ellie killed to revenge the murder of her father, David slaps her on the face only to immediately stretch his hand toward Hannah to lift her up. He tells Hannah she perhaps thinks that she has no father anymore, but the truth is she will always have a father. Again, though it might seem that David refers to the God of the Bible, it is likely that he has himself in mind as the one who cares and provides for the people in his community. Furthermore, he stylizes himself in the divine-like position of the one who can offer Ellie a new beginning as he believes the current phase of her life with Joel is coming to an end. To be sure, in a post-apocalyptic context where God is apparently not present, space emerges for "false prophets"—preachers who seek to control people by peddling hope through faith in the God in whom they do not believe in themselves.[3]

When Ellie accuses David of being an "animal," he agrees with that judgment, albeit countering that "we all are, that sort of is the whole point." He confesses to Ellie that he had struggled with his "violent heart" for a long time but then, after the world ended, he found the truth. However, that truth, for him, was not to be found in God but rather in cordyceps—in its fruitfulness, its drive toward multiplication and expansion, its single-minded commitment to protect its "children" and secure a future for them, even if it involves resorting to violence. David sees such a violent heart in Ellie as well, in addition to her natural leadership, intelligence, and loyalty. In David's mind, this makes Ellie similar to him and sets her apart from the other people in the community: "They need God, they need heaven, they need a father . . . you don't." David feels that he is a shepherd surrounded by sheep and that all he wants is an equal, a friend—whom he believes to have found in Ellie. David wants Ellie to be his partner helping. In his mind, the two of them would lead the people so that the community could grow and expand. However, Ellie resists this temptation. After David chases her in the burning meeting hall and tries to rape her, uttering the words that "there is no fear in love," she kills him.

The story of David and the Silver Lake community is, I argue, one of failed interpersonal relationships due to one man's delusion of his own grandeur in an attempt to fill the vacancy for God. It is a story of domination and subjugation. The theme of domination and subjugation is helpfully theorized, from a theological perspective, by postcolonial theology. To go beyond the discourse of empire and colony to include broader power dynamics, Robert Heaney turns to the concept of *coloniality*, rather than colonialism. In his view, this category helps us understand the relationship of theology to particular exercises of power in encounters between and among humans; it acknowledges the need for deeper critical awareness, especially from those in privileged positions; and it accentuates a recognition that the ultimate "end of theology is conversion."[4]

However, domination and subjugation is not all there is to power dynamics. Theological discourse, in particular, insists that resistance is another crucial dimension of these dynamics. So, what is then the way out of this straitjacket? How can stories like David and his Silver Lake community be challenged and overcome? Theologizing from a postcolonial and Asian feminist perspective, Wonhee Anne Joh shows one possible way. In her book *Heart of the Cross*, Joh uses Korean notions of *han* and *jeong* to develop both a postcolonial Christology and a theology of love to navigate people's lives today.[5] *Han* refers to loss and suffering. It is a sense of helplessness and unresolved resentment; it entails "frozen energy" that can negatively implode into fatalism and revenge.[6] *Han*, however, can be transformed. Such transformation creates space for *jeong* and, for Joh, the cross of Christ as a symbol of this transformative grace. *Jeong* is linked with "compassion, love, vulnerability, and acceptance of heterogeneity as essential to life"; it "embodies the invisible traces of compassion in relationships."[7] In this hermeneutical framework, Jesus as the Christ is not a heroic figure standing on his own. Rather, the interplay of *han* and *jeong* problematizes a clear distinction between self and other. The Christ of *jeong* is both Jesus and the community of Jesus.[8] The solidarity of the cross captured through this postcolonial Christology is between Jesus as a colonized and suffering Jew and colonized and suffering others. Rejecting the option of constructing one's identity over against the identity of the other, Jesus' way is one of "transformation through the power of *jeong* in connectedness."[9]

Evaluating the potential of *han* and *jeong* for providing a fresh perspective on human existence today, Grace Ji-Sun Kim asserts that they provide us with a new terminology to verbalize "the pain and love we carry in our hearts and community."[10] She calls us away from "ways of thinking and life choices that are ultimately self-destructive" and toward the ways to "love ourselves and embrace the Other because the Spirit of God flows through all of us and the whole community of creation."[11] This dynamic shows how *han* and *jeong*, suffering/pain/loss and compassion/care/love, can foster transformation to enable new ways of living together in what Willie Jennings calls "a revolutionary intimacy."[12] The focal point here is *interdependence*, which I would suggest, is one of the key ideas in *TLOU*.

This brings us to Jackson, the second community to be considered as an antithesis to Silver Lake. Jackson is a town located in Wyoming and inhabited by some 300 people, including children, where Ellie and Joel find Joel's brother, Tommy, in episode 6. Tommy now resides here with his wife, Maria, who is pregnant. The people in Jackson form a true community. The town has a school, a community hall, a movie theater, and a prison, though, Maria is quick to add, there is no need for the latter. There is also a multi-faith church, an interesting feature in the post-apocalyptic context of explicit divine non-presence. Unfortunately, a lack of further elaboration on this fact in the show prevents ruminating on the theological significance of religious faith and its practice for the people at Jackson. However, what one can conclude is that religion still plays a role in the life of at least some of them. And, since there is no evidence to the contrary, one can perhaps see religion as one of the issues on which Jackson diametrically differs from Silver Lake where religion was the way to exercise power over people.

In the Jackson community, no particular individual(s) is in charge. Rather, there is a democratically elected council that makes decisions on behalf of the whole group. Plus, everyone takes turns in community work and service. While the Jackson community does not advertise itself, it is in principle open to accepting newcomers. It operates on the principles of egalitarianism and shared ownership, though no common housing and familial structures are maintained.[13] This is important to note in order to underline the importance of the intimate dimension for the web of relationships that the Jackson group seeks to pursue.

To build on our previous discussion, the people at Jackson have gone through painful experiences in their lives and are still at a loss (*han*)[14] but, unlike the Silver Lake community, they are also willing—through what we could call the power of *jeong*—to open themselves to the other, including strangers, and to build truly reciprocal relationships. This is interdependence, a *modus vivendi* that brings into the world and makes effective God's logic, even if God is not readily visible.

OF CLICKERS AND HUMANS: *IMAGO DEI* AND LIFE IN FULLNESS

In this section, I would like to particularly focus on responding to the question of what it means to be a bearer of God's image in the world where God is not (visibly) present. Christian tradition maintains that the image of God (*imago Dei*) in human beings has been distorted after the fall, yet not completely lost. Irenaeus of Lyons taught that the whole human has been created in God's image as "the union of the soul receiving the spirit of the Father, and the admixture of that fleshly nature."[15] If being created in the image of God has implications for the way one navigates through the created world, as I believe Irenaeus's insistence on the unity of the soul, spirit, and flesh suggests, then the fact that such creation involves being a bodily creature must necessarily play a role in this process.[16]

It would seem as natural to argue, therefore, that "clickers," the infected in *The Last of Us*, symbolically stand for a prime example of how the image of God in humans is not only corrupted but perhaps even lost due to cordyceps taking over both their bodies and minds.[17] This theme is pertinently expressed by Sam, an eight-year-old boy whom Ellie and Joel meet in Kansas City together with his older brother, Henry, in episode 5. After being bitten by a clicker, Sam asks Ellie whether it will still be him inside after he turns into a monster. Does a clicker bear the image of God? However, before one goes into drawing clear borderlines between clickers and humans, it is good to remember how *TLOU* portrays humans. Certain moments in episode 4 suggest that survival is seen as the main driver of human behavior in the post-apocalyptic world. Specifically, this idea is foregrounded in the scene when Joel tells Ellie that he, Tess, Tommy, and the people they were with in Boston did everything it took for them to survive, with an implication that it might have involved killing innocent people. At that point in the story, Joel still has no expectations from, commitment to, and hope for human existence in the world, apart from providing for the family.[18]

In the world of *TLOU*, therefore, humans might not necessarily differ from clickers as the former, too, are shaped by loss, lack, suffering, and trauma. In the previous section, I have argued this point by employing the terminology of *han*. Here, it will be helpful to elaborate on this line of thought further using Judith Gruber's concept of "spectral theology." Drawing on Gregor Hoff's understanding of "ghosts" as a narrative symbol standing for that which is unredeemed and perhaps irredeemable, Gruber asserts that "haunting . . . is the occupation with a troubled past that opens the imagination for a fragile future, knowing that the experience of suffering, but also the hope for healing, disorders time."[19] Haunting turns to a "hermeneutic of wounds and tears" to enable transformation by rupturing the conventional patterns of power and success.[20] Gruber reads Jesus' story as one that is characterized both by suffering and the overcoming of death. Yet, haunting persists. The wounds on Jesus' resurrected body remain and are real (John 20:27). As a result, and significantly for our reading of *TLOU*, when told as a ghost story, "cross and resurrection disrupt a triumphalist teleology from death to life,"[21] providing space for coming to terms with the messiness of life and the continued reality of sin in the world. Ultimately, then, spectral theology allows us to interpret life's messiness and ambiguities as "manifestations of God's salvific presence in the mode of hopeful yearning."[22]

Such spectral theology resists the temptation to strive for completeness in life. To make her case, Gruber draws upon Achille Mbembe's principle of "compositional logic." Rejecting the ideal of self-mastery, Mbembe proposes that working for life vis-à-vis death pertains to "the capacity to assemble and to compose, including things that at first do not appear to be compatible." The aim of such an endeavor is not completeness but rather "a kind of radical openness . . . and the disposition towards the encounter with the unknown."[23]

The argument against human self-sufficiency and in favor of openness toward the other is made from yet another perspective by Willie Jennings in his book *After Whiteness*. Reflecting on the state of theological education today, Jennings contends that the image of the "white self-sufficient man" has taken deep roots in educational institutions around the globe and has a decisive impact on how we perceive the ideal of (not only theological) education.[24] This so-called ideal is to master knowledge in order to control the world and become independent from others.

In contrast to this concept, Jennings emphasizes the crucial role of formation in the educational process; for him, it is "the art of cultivating belonging."[25] Jennings's deeply theological argument is founded on the dream of a God who comes to the world (through the people of Israel and through Jesus) to offer people a share in divine life. Here, the focus and ultimate purpose is communion, as evidenced by both the gospel story and the feminist concept of eros as, in the words of Rita Nakashima Brock, "the power of our primal interrelatedness."[26] Jennings succeeds in unmasking the logic of "whiteness," a concept that has implications far beyond skin color, when he shows that colonialists have deluded people into believing that there is no community; there is, purportedly, only capital and profit. Thus, human beings, with their bodies and souls, have been reimagined as commodities, freely disposable for those in power to make money. This paradigmatic shift has far-reaching consequences for the understanding of humans as the image of God.

In *TLOU*, it can be rendered through the contrast between David and his Silver Lake community, on the one hand, and the relationship between Ellie and Joel, on the other. As we have seen in the previous section, David admires cordyceps for its care for and protection of its "children," that cordyceps created in its own image. David even sees it as love. Analogically, David wants to love his "children," protecting them and providing for them, so that they can grow and expand. His action toward both Hannah and Ellie shows that David wants to mold them in his own image. A theological problem with this understanding of "*imago Dei*" and its pursuit is that David, like cordyceps, acts parasitically. They both prey on their host to indulge their will to power. David cannot resist his desire to control others, denying them the freedom that is necessary if one is to bear the image of one true God. David's idea of "love" is "monstrous, toxic, and self-serving."[27] Furthermore, another theological problem is that David fosters a purely centripetal conception of growth. In other words, the blossoming is for the community of the like-minded only. It is tribalism. It is a glorification of sameness. Such an understanding and practice of *imago Dei* leads to bondage and exploitation, effectively disabling the pursuit of life in fullness.

In contrast, the relationship between Ellie and Joel gradually develops throughout season 1, so that they now truly belong with each other. In a beautiful scene in episode 9 that depicts Ellie and Joel feeding a giraffe in a neglected sports field, a close-up of Joel looking at Ellie with affection shows how much his relationship toward her has changed. He now wants to teach her how to play the guitar, engages in word games with her, and is excited when he can offer Ellie her favorite food. Joel even assures Ellie that she does not have to go to the hospital if she does not want to (an idea she resolutely rejects). For her part, Ellie says that after the surgery she will follow Joel wherever he will go—"Tommy's, a sheep ranch, the moon." They now truly belong together. Moreover, Joel confesses to Ellie that he tried to commit suicide by shooting himself the next day after Sarah, his daughter, had died, adding that he was ready to die then but is not now. To Ellie's words that time has healed the loss, Joel responds by asserting that it was not time. Ellie has become a gift providing his existence with a new justification and meaning. They both agree to be happy that Joel's suicide attempt did not work out. Their belonging together is one of interdependence, mutual support, and purpose.

As far as the understanding of *imago Dei*, the crucial difference between David as the leader of the Silver Lake community, on the one hand, and Ellie and Joel, on the other hand, lies in the difference between Jennings's "white self-sufficient man" and an intimate community that cultivates belonging and interdependence. Hence, the image of God through the lens of *TLOU* is relational. In Christian tradition, such relational images flow from the understanding of the triune God as "the perfect fellowship of love, acceptance, inclusion, and creativity."[28] Moreover, this divine fellowship is like a fountain of meaning and potentiality that springs forth on to God's creation inviting it "to join a fellowship of souls and bodies on a journey toward joyful consummation."[29] The triune God is fundamentally relational, and so people as bearers of the image of this God are also relational beings. However, one must go deeper still. In its study document *Christian Perspectives on Theological Anthropology*, the Faith and Order commission points out that human existence bearing the image of God takes place within the twofold dynamic of both "dignity, potentiality, and creativity" and "creatureliness, finitude, and vulnerability."[30] The final scenes of episode 9 especially remind us that the image of God can be distorted and there is still violence, self-interest, and lies. Nevertheless, there is also hope that authentic relationships can be sustained, pointing toward life in fullness. Being a bearer of the image of God in the context of *TLOU*, therefore, means pursuing life in fullness through authentic interpersonal relationships, despite the losses, wounds, and traumas that continue to be real and present. From a theological perspective, such reading opens up a hermeneutic potentiality to trace God's presence in a world where God is otherwise absent.

LONG, LONG TIME: QUEER, VULNERABLE, AND HUMAN

This section will further develop the "spectral" theological anthropology of interdependence introduced in the previous sections by examining one particular case of a nurturing human relationship. Episode 3 tells the story of Bill. Bill is a survivalist who decides to stay at home following the outbreak. After everyone else leaves the town escorted by FEDRA, Bill makes various adjustments to his already well-equipped house and its surrounding to provide him not only with safety but also give him a sense of enjoyable life in which gourmet dinners play an important role. At that point, Bill thinks of himself as a "white self-sufficient man." After four years, however, Frank comes along. After saving Frank from one of his traps, Bill lets Frank come into the house, have a shower, give him some clothes, and serve him a fine meal with wine. Was Bill lonely after all? Did he long for human company? In a decisive scene, both men take turns playing the piano Bill's mother left him and singing "Long, Long Time" by Linda Ronstadt. When Franks asks Bill what girl he was singing about, Bill replies that there is no girl in his life. Frank says that he knows and subsequently kisses Bill. Before they make love, Frank makes clear he is no "whore" and if they are to sleep together, he will stay with Bill "for a few days."

Three years later, Frank and Bill are shown to be caught up in a "married couple" argument. Frank wants to make their home beautiful and to invite some friends. He seeks to pursue a fulfilling life. The next scene portrays the two men having Joel and his companion, Tess, over for a meal in their garden. While Frank and Tess are obviously enjoying this opportunity to feel like "civilized human beings" again, Bill remains disapproving, unambiguously stating that he feels Frank and him are self-sufficient and not in need of other people. Bill wants to protect their "private paradise." A change in Bill becomes evident soon after in a scene that depicts Frank giving Bill a surprise he prepared for him: a bed of strawberry plants full of fresh red strawberries. It is a beautiful intimate scene indicating Bill's vulnerability and humanity as he giggles with happiness while enjoying strawberries, apologizes to Frank for aging faster than him, and admits that he often feels afraid now that he loves and cares for Frank. Bill has clearly been transformed through their relationship. To take the point further, in the following scene, Bill is shot during a raiders' attack one night and although Frank is treating his wound, Bill thinks at the moment that he is going to die. He therefore pleads Frank to call Joel to look after Frank when he is gone. That is a clear sign of Bill's gradual growth into trust and interdependence. And interdependence is also the driving factor at the end of their story, ten years after, when Bill decides to make an "incredibly romantic" move and accompany the now paralyzed Frank on his journey to euthanasia.

Insights from queer theology can help us make sense of Bill and Frank's story. Linn Marie Tonstad suggests that queer theology invites us to resist the temptation that much of so-called T-Theology has fallen prey to, namely, of participating in a "process of abstraction that moves away from real, suffering bodies, which are particular and concrete."[31] Instead of justifying and safeguarding the abstraction of meticulously defined patterns of belief and behavior, we are led to learn and accept that "God is in and with unruly bodies."[32] Indeed, the logic of God's economy in the world goes beyond conventional logic. It is a logic of grace working in and through all the concreteness, fragmentation, and messiness of human existence. It is kin-dom.[33] Because of this material and dynamic nature of human existence, a human being is never a "finished project." We are surprises to ourselves, and queer theology calls us to be open to such surprise.[34] And being open to the possibility of surprise within oneself also implies, I would suggest, being open to a surprise within the other, both human and divine; it means leaving room for a "strange God."[35] This dynamic is, I believe, what Rita Nakashima Brock refers to as "erotic power" which "creates and connects hearts, involves the whole person in relationships of self-awareness, vulnerability, openness, and caring. . . . Erotic power is the power of our primal interrelatedness."[36] Now, admittedly, this power needs to be navigated in order to work toward transformation.[37] In Christian tradition, at least through the lens of queer and postcolonial theologies, the process of such navigation can be rendered via the symbol of God's dream for God's creation. It is the dream of the God who aims for "ecstasy in the body of the creature," striving, ultimately, for communion of all God's creation.[38]

As she concludes her book, Tonstad maintains that queer theology affirms finitude by acknowledging the inevitable tragedy of human existence. Importantly for Christian tradition, that finitude is profoundly malformed by sin.[39] However, Christianity also believes that "the last enemy to be destroyed is death" (1 Corinthians 15:26, NRSV). Tonstad deems the attempt to grapple with "the orientation of a life lived under the shadow of death" to be an "irresolvable dilemma."[40] Going against the grain of images about the normativity in human relationships, the story of Bill and Frank can perhaps shed some light on this dilemma by celebrating vulnerability and interdependence. As such, it finds a power and meaningfulness in relationships that, despite their oddity and elusiveness, have the potential to be transformative, indeed, life-changing. And, seen through the perspective of faith, they might perhaps enable us to see glimpses of that "strange God," even if God is not readily visible.

CONCLUSION

In the post-apocalyptic context of the first season of HBO's *TLOU*, God is not readily present. Still, there is space left for moments of surprise and genuine encounter. Moreover, a hope is fostered here for transformation, meaning, and authentic life. It emerges and is driven through deep and self-less human relationships, no matter how short-lived, fragile, and broken they may be. There is a potential that people may become a gift and a blessing for each other. As such, the series gives us insight into the nature of human existence in relation to other people, the world, and God. In particular, and in a significant way for Christian theology and existence, we are thus provided with some hints for the call to construe one's life in terms for a preferential option for freedom in interdependence.[41] From a theological perspective, then, *TLOU* can be interpreted as an invitation to "convivial recovery"[42] which lies in a creative response to various forms of our persisting intoxication with power and the myth of self-sufficiency, that is, our addiction to the delusion of our own independence and individual accomplishments. In other words, it is an invitation to turn one's life into a "consistent presence"[43] before the face of the anthropic, non-anthropic, and divine others.

NOTES

1. This chapter is a result of the research supported by the Charles University Research Center program.
2. This chapter only engages with the HBO series (in particular, season 1, as no other seasons were yet available at the time of writing), and not *The Last of Us* video games or shorts. For more details on the HBO series, see "The Last of Us," IMDb, accessed August 15, 2023, https://www.imdb.com/title/tt3581920/?ref_=fn_al_tt_1.
3. See Forasteros, "Apocalypse Stories," 45.
4. Heaney, *Post-Colonial Theology*, 69. See also Heaney, "Coloniality and Theological Method," 55–65.
5. Joh maintains that every attempt to translate the two terms into English will necessarily remain lacking. Therefore, she refrains from such an endeavor, leaving the words untranslated.
6. See Joh, *Heart of the Cross*, xxi.
7. Joh, *Heart of the Cross*, xxiv, xxi.
8. See Joh, *Heart of the Cross*, 98.
9. Joh, "Transgressive Power of Jeong," 157.
10. Kim, *Embracing the Other*, 111. For a more extensive theological discussion on *han* and *jeong* as two dimensions of human existence, see also Kim, *Colonialism*.
11. Kim, *Embracing the Other*, 113.
12. See Jennings, *Acts*, 29.

13. There is an amusing scene in episode 6 having to do with the social organization of Jackson. When Joel opines that the people at Jackson are basically communists, Tommy vehemently dismisses the term. However, when Maria willingly agrees that it really is communism that they practice, Tommy also accepts the idea.

14. This is symbolically expressed through the monument at the fireplace of Maria and Tommy's house, dedicated to their deceased beloved ones—Maria's son (named Kevin in the HBO series), and Tommy's niece, that is, Joel's daughter, Sarah.

15. Irenaeus, *Against Heresies*, V.VI.1.

16. See Bargár, *Embodied Existence*, 26.

17. I am aware that *TLOU* fandom distinguishes at least six consecutive stages of the infected, namely: runners, stalkers, clickers, bloaters, shamblers, and rat kings. However, it is not necessary to follow this distinction for the purposes of this chapter.

18. This attitude will change radically as becomes clearly evident especially in episode 9.

19. Gruber, "Salvation in a Wounded World," 383. See also Hoff, *Religionsgespenster*, 17–18.

20. Gruber, "Salvation in a Wounded World," 385.

21. Gruber, "Salvation in a Wounded World," 386.

22. Gruber, "Salvation in a Wounded World," 387.

23. Mbembe and Goldberg, "The Reason of Unreason," 226.

24. See Jennings, *After Whiteness*, 6.

25. Jennings, *After Whiteness*, 10.

26. Brock, *Journeys by Heart*, 26.

27. Mooney, "When We Are in Need."

28. Bargár, *Embodied Existence*, 108.

29. Bargár, "Toward Comm/unity," 236.

30. Faith and Order Commission, *Christian Perspectives*, art. 81.

31. Tonstad, *Queer Theology*, 87. The term T-Theology, coined by Marcella Althaus-Reid, refers to theology as ideology; that is the theology that makes the claim of being "the one and only." See Althaus-Reid, *Queer God*, 172, n. 4.

32. See Tonstad, *Queer Theology*, 87.

33. The term "kin-dom of God" comes from Ada María Isasi-Díaz, whose preference for this neologism is motivated by the reasons that are both deconstructive (rejecting the patriarchal connotations of the term "kingdom") and constructive (underlining the relational nature of God's [new] creation). See Isasi-Díaz, "Solidarity," 304.

34. See Tonstad, *Queer Theology*, 91.

35. See Althaus-Reid, "Queer I Stand," 104–105.

36. Brock, *Journeys by Heart*, 25, 26.

37. See Kim, *Embracing the Other*, 142.

38. See Jennings, *After Whiteness*, 143, 152.

39. See Tonstad, *Queer Theology*, 130.

40. Tonstad, *Queer Theology*, 131.

41. See also Ewell, *Faith Seeking Conviviality*, 22.

42. The term comes from Ewell, *Faith Seeking Conviviality*, chapter 8.

43. The phrase comes from Willie Jennings in his foreword to Ewell, *Faith Seeking Conviviality*, xix.

BIBLIOGRAPHY

Althaus-Reid, Marcella. *Queer God*. London and New York: Routledge, 2003.
———. "Queer I Stand: Lifting the Skirts of God." In *The Sexual Theologian: Essays on Sex, God and Politics*, edited by Marcella Althaus-Reid and Linda Isherwood (pp. 99–109). London and New York: T&T Clark, 2004.
Bargár, Pavol. "Toward Comm/unity amidst Brokenness: Christian Mission as (a Pursuit of) Theological Anthropology." *International Review of Mission* 110.2 (2021): 231–245.
———. *Embodied Existence: Our Common Life in God*. Eugene, OR: Cascade, 2023.
Brock, Rita Nakashima. *Journeys by Heart: A Christology of Erotic Power*. New York: Crossroad, 1992.
Ewell, Samuel E., III. *Faith Seeking Conviviality: Reflections on Ivan Illich, Christian Mission, and the Promise of Life Together*. Eugene, OR: Cascade, 2020.
Faith and Order Commission. *Christian Perspectives on Theological Anthropology: A Faith and Order Study Document*. Faith and Order paper no. 199. Geneva: World Council of Churches, 2005.
Forasteros, J. R. "Apocalypse Stories—Both in the Bible and on HBO—Reveal How to Create a World Worth Saving." *Sojourners* 52.5 (June 2023): 39–40, 45.
Gruber, Judith. "Salvation in a Wounded World: Towards a Spectral Theology of Mission." *Mission Studies* 37.3 (2020): 374–396.
Heaney, Robert S. "Coloniality and Theological Method in Africa." *Journal of Anglican Studies* 7.1 (2009): 55–65.
———. *Post-Colonial Theology: Finding God and Each Other Amidst the Hate*. Eugene, OR: Cascade, 2019.
Hoff, Gregor Maria. *Religionsgespenster: Versuch über den religiösen Schock*. Paderborn: Schöningh, 2017.
Irenaeus of Lyons. *Against Heresies*. Grand Rapids, MI: Christian Classics Ethereal Library, https://ccel.org/ccel/irenaeus/against_heresies_v/anf01.ix.vii.vii.html.
Isasi-Díaz, Ada María. "Soidarity: Love of Neighbor in the 1980s." In *Lift Every Voice: Constructing Christian Theologies from the Underside*, edited by Susan Brooks Thistlethwaite and Mary Potter Engel (pp. 31–40, 303–305). San Francisco, CA: Harper, 1990.
Jennings, Willie James. *Acts*. Louisville, KY: Westminster John Knox, 2017.
———. *After Whiteness: An Education in Belonging*. Grand Rapids, MI: Eerdmans, 2020.
Joh, Wonhee Anne. "The Transgressive Power of Jeong: A Postcolonial Hybridization of Christology." In *Postcolonial Theologies: Divinity and Empire*, edited by Catherine Keller, Mayra Rivera, and Michael Nausner (pp. 149–163). St. Louis, MO: Chalice, 2004.

———. *Heart of the Cross: A Postcolonial Christology*. Louisville, KY: Westminster John Knox, 2006.

Kim, Grace Ji-Sun. *Colonialism, Han, and the Transformative Spirit*. New York: Palgrave Macmillan, 2013.

———. *Embracing the Other: The Transformative Spirit of Love*. Grand Rapids, MI and Cambridge, UK: Eerdmans, 2015.

Mbembe, Achille, and David T. Goldberg. "'The Reason of Unreason': Achille Mbembe and David Theo Goldberg in Conversation about Critique of Black Reason." *Theory, Culture, and Society* 35.7–8 (2018): 205–227.

Mooney, Darren. "'When We Are in Need' Finds *The Last of Us* Putting Its Own Spin on Post-Apocalyptic Tropes." *Escapist*, March 5, 2023, https://www.escapistmagazine.com/the-last-of-us-episode-8-review-when-we-are-in-need/.

Tonstad, Linn Marie. *Queer Theology*. Eugene, OR: Cascade, 2018.

Chapter 11

The Last of Us and Eschatology for a Post-Apocalyptic World

Flora x. Tang

What does it mean to speak about eschatology *after* the end of the world? To speak of eschatology in the post-apocalyptic world of urban ruins, cordyceps brain infections, and military dictatorships in *The Last of Us* (*TLOU*) is an ironic, if not risky, task. In *TLOU*, the world as people knew it had already ended. Whatever beliefs in a future that is always brighter are now but a remnant of naïve pre-outbreak memories. Life in both the QZs and outside is the daily task of narrowly escaping the many imminent threats of death. It is the raw human desire for subsistence and survival that drives life forward in this post-apocalyptic world, rather than any collective hope in a triumphant future or a pre-outbreak past. The video game and TV show's itinerant, adventure-based storyline also rid the characters and the audience of any substantial hope in any NPCs and side characters' ultimate survival: we know soon after the TV show's second or third episode that every NPC-like character we encounter in this post-apocalyptic game-world will most likely meet an untimely death at the conclusion of their particular storyline.

This chapter nevertheless attempts to speak about eschatology from this very future-less landscape of destruction. I contend that speaking about eschatology from *TLOU* is a necessary corrective to the often harmful (if not outright violent and colonial) potentials of dominant narratives within Christian eschatology. These same narratives of domination have been echoed in the U.S. self-narrative as a nation, which also associates futurity with triumph and expansion. While much of mainstream contemporary theologies have imagined eschatology using the language of temporal finality and triumphant futures, this chapter explores various spatial dimensions of eschatology that may redirect human hope in a different direction. While

TLOU is not an explicitly theological or religious work, threads of these alternative imageries of the eschaton and eschatological hope may be found in the story and its characters' journey in a post-apocalyptic world. I read these threads of eschatological hope through the theologies of various decolonial theologians who write on eschatology such as Vine Deloria Jr. and Vítor Westhelle, as well as the theocentric eschatology of Kathryn Tanner. Reading these scenes and theologies together point toward different answers to the question: What do we hope for—what can we hope for—when there is no future? While the majority of the chapter remains in the game-world of *TLOU* and the theoretical world of contemporary theology, the answers to the question can and should undergird our responses, hopes, and activism in light of contemporary issues of climate change, war, and other catastrophes that foreclose our earthly futures.

Eschatology, which originates from the Greek word *eschatos*, meaning "last," is conventionally invoked in Christian theology as the study of "the last things" at the temporal end of individual human lives and at the cosmic end of the world. For many, Christian eschatology is a theological task of profound hope in a world where "all things are made new" (2 Corinthians 5:17; Revelations 21), where joy prevails and sufferings cease, where goodness triumphs while evil fades away. Throughout history, especially during times of trial, Christians turn to eschatological visions as both a cause for hope in a future that looks radically different from the present *and* as a guidepost for ethical action of love and justice that may bring about signs of this future on earth.[1]

Eschatology and the concept of hope have also been widely critiqued for their idealistic and escapist nature. These critiques are present both from within Christian theology and from theorists who engage with nonreligious concepts of hope from a critical lens. For many, the Christian eschatological talk of futures is escapist at best, and detrimental to marginalized people's present-day material struggles at worst.[2] This chapter engages with the many decolonial and liberationist critiques of Christian eschatology and its secular political counterparts, but retains the language of eschatology to consider what alternative conceptions of hope, eschaton, and reign of God can be harnessed.

JOURNEYING AGAINST MANIFEST DESTINY

TLOU follows Joel and Ellie's transcontinental journey from the Boston QZ to the American West in search of Joel's brother Tommy and the Fireflies' medical team. It is perhaps theologically revelatory for a story taking place temporally after the destruction of the world to take the shape of a journey across the ruins of a country that no longer exists. The episodic storyline is driven by the two main characters' location and the different people they encounter in each location, rather than by a purely progressive plot and its typical narrative arc. Every final destination they seem to reach turns out to not be the final destination or the redemptive triumphant ending (for themselves and for the world) they had hoped to be. In the end, no vaccines are made—the entire purpose of Ellie's journey westward now void—and the world they had hoped to restore merely continues the way it is. Joel and Ellie's relationship fractures upon Ellie's faint awareness of Joel's lies about what had taken place at the Fireflies' hospital. In the end of a game-TV show about "the end," life merely continues, without the resolution of a final tragedy or triumph.

Triumph has always been central to the language of Christian eschatology. Triumph, too, has been the central imagery associated with early American nation-building narratives: Joel and Ellie's fictional transcontinental journey recalls various hope-filled, political-eschatological transcontinental journeys throughout American history, from manifest destiny–inspired westward settlement to the building of the transcontinental railroad. The nineteenth-century doctrine of manifest destiny refers to the United States of America's territorial and ideological expansion as divinely ordained. White, English-speaking Protestant Americans, favored by God, were to expand westward into a land that in their imagination was both empty and brimming with threats at the same time. This doctrine of manifest destiny envisioned American movement toward the West as a benign movement of spreading progress and prosperity for the religious and political salvation of people who dwell in these lands.[3] Later, the same doctrine expanded into a sense of democratic messianism, which believed that America, via spreading its democracy, would redeem the world from tyranny and evil.[4]

In these American self-narratives about its journey from New England to the frontiers of the Wild West, eschatological and soteriological undertones abound. Theological and "secular" (the two categories more intertwined than entirely diametrical) narratives of triumphant redemption become the drive behind such treacherous journeys toward the West. Apocalyptic narratives of an eschatological battle between good and evil are invoked in American self-imagination of its treacherous battles against barbarism, heathen religions, and undemocratic forms of governance.

The coloniality of American expansionism and of Christian eschatology has already been widely critiqued by decolonial theologians and scholars of religious history alike. The drive toward finality and triumph—words that have concrete violent impacts upon conquered land and their people—marks many dominant Christian eschatologies throughout the history of

Christianity's deep embeddedness in empire. In some sense, a desire for a triumphant ending and a completion (or at least resolution) of narrative drives our relationship to stories, literature, TV shows, and video games.

The limits of such triumphant redemptive endings in both literature and theology have been discussed by feminist theologian Shelly Rambo. Rambo reads interpretations of post-apocalyptic novels such as Cormac McCarthy's *The Road*, noting how many commenters fixate upon the question of whether the book, in the end, offers a picture of redemption.[5] A similar desire for a redemptive ending is found in the American national story as it is in the ways that Americans narrate their own individual stories. Americanized theological concepts of divine sovereignty, providence, and manifest destiny fuel American exceptionalism and other political-theological violence especially in the face of tragedies such as the attacks of September 11th. Hence, Christian readers may find it difficult to grapple with a novel about post-apocalyptic survival that does not conclude—nor hope for—redemption. This sense of unresolvedness may likewise be troubling to any reader who is used to a redemptive narrative arc in their storytelling, whether it be Americans with a firm belief in American exceptionalism or anyone who is used to stories with a happy ending that resolves it all. In this post-apocalyptic setting, however, Rambo argues that survival does not look like the triumph over death. Rather, the persistence of death remains in the experience of survival, marking the experience of survival to be a liminal space.[6]

This is not a moral or normative claim of what survival should look like, but a descriptive claim of how survival after trauma or violence is often experienced by the survivor—the shadow of death looms large, unable to be immediately repaired by even the firmest beliefs in hope. Drawing from trauma theory, Rambo turns to the experience of Holy Saturday as a theological corrective to the often-redemptive readings of the Paschal Mystery as a swift movement from death to triumphant resurrection. For her, Jesus' descent into hell on Holy Saturday, an often-ignored part of the Christian narrative, symbolizes life that persists and survives amidst the continual threat of death. Such theology of a life that "remains" provides a testimony of what theology could look like without the false promise of deliverance and with no assurance of a viable future. While the majority of contemporary theologies of suffering attend to important questions of theodicy and justice for victims, Rambo's post-traumatic theology attends to what happens theologically when mere survival after trauma is the only foreseeable path given the gravity of destruction or of ongoing structural injustice. God's presence in the persistence of life amidst death itself is salvific, even when this salvation looks nothing like a triumphant victory.

Whereas Rambo critiques the desire to swiftly turn toward redemption in Christian soteriology and American national narratives from a feminist and post-traumatic perspective, other theologians critique the eschatological dimension of such tendencies from their decolonial commitments. Overly future-oriented eschatologies, these theologians assert, have colonial implications. While it may seem like an oxymoron to speak of eschatologies without speaking of the future, these decolonial and indigenous theologians suggest that we can, and we must.

Indigenous theologian Vine Deloria Jr. compares North American indigenous religions' primacy of sacred space to Christianity's over-emphasis on time and temporal finality. Christian eschatology speaks of the history of the world in terms of the overarching history of salvation: in this language of temporal eschatology, all people are the same, and all geographies, spaces, and lands share the same narrative arc from fall to redemption to eschatological kingdomhood. This dominating temporal language of Christian eschatology holds concrete spatial impacts through the history of Christian missions, colonization of indigenous land, and degradation of the earth's environment.[7] The European Christian vision of creation and eschatology as the two temporal endpoints of universal salvation history has led to the disregard of the land of the earth and the desire to expand spatially to subsume the rest of the world into this linear timeline of salvation. Meanwhile, indigenous religious beliefs hold their lands and places as having the highest possible meaning. In indigenous thought, creation is seen as an ecosystem, rather than the beginning event of linear time, whereas eschatology is better viewed as a return to right relations with God, humanity, and the earth.[8] This spatial view of creation and eschatology offers an alternative to Western Christianity's emphasis on the triumphant linearity of salvation history, as well as Christianity's narrative emphasis on eschatology as the future of human redemption. The indigenous Christian view on space and time also mirror some of Western philosophical theology's own emphasis that God transcends time and stands outside of time. By turning to the importance of embodied space and ecology, Deloria's theology offers a concrete alternative to popular notions of creation and eschatology—and by inference, God's existence in general—as bound by human conceptions of temporality.

Drawing from Deloria's critiques of the temporal emphasis of Christian eschatology, South African liberation theologian Victor Westhelle proposes a spatial alternative. He asks: Why does eschatology speak about temporal finitudes of human history, but not about—or from—the various spatial margins of the world? Westhelle notes that *eschatos* in Greek holds a spatial meaning, "end of the earth," as much as a temporal one. The spatial margins and liminal realms of the world, especially the Global South, can interrupt Western Christian complacency in a way that eschatological futures have historically been imagined to do.[9]

These theologians writing from decolonial commitments encourage a turn toward the spatial over the temporal in Christian eschatological thinking, hoping that such a turn would also prompt more honest reflections on the coloniality of a unified salvation history that ends in triumph. In doing so, theology would become more open to honoring the various sacred spaces, kinships, and ancestral land of Indigenous people and all those who hold strong ties to the earth and to the geographical spaces they call home. A spatial eschatology also unveils categories beyond future, hope, and success as meaningful categories to look toward in times of world-ending catastrophes. In a violent world where futility is often the norm and the narrative, perhaps such eschatologies offer more resources to wrestle with these events than an eschatology that focuses too much on a future that redeems the present, or an ending that redeems the middle spaces of suffering. While the belief in a God who raises the dead in the eschaton (especially those who have suffered unjustly during their lifetimes) remain critical to a Christian theology of hope in a world of suffering, these aforementioned theologies offer—perhaps as an additive source of hope—times and spaces beyond "the future" as spaces where salvation and divine presence are found.

In *TLOU*, Joel and Ellie's journey from the American East to the American West echoes (as noted) the familiar, American journeys inspired by the doctrines of manifest destiny. Yet drawing from the above feminist and decolonial theological lenses (all of which write, in some way, against the theological implications of manifest destiny), I read such a journey as precisely a reversal of the triumphant violence of manifest destiny. This reversal offers us an alternative theological language to conceive of eschatology in the face of future-less futility. Ellie's journey toward the Fireflies' medical team was initially set out to be one that ideally would lead toward triumphant reversal of the horrors of the cordyceps-infected world. It was a journey driven by the hopes of her elders who were raised in the before times, who have survived Outbreak Day, and who long for a future of a world where some resemblance of the "before" could return. The post-apocalyptic desire to return to a world of normalcy echoes the Christian theological story of human salvation as return to a pre-fall state of bliss, accompanied by redemption of sin and evil. However, the already-ended world of *TLOU* cannot be easily healed and restored, as new structures of violence spring up and cycles of individual and political revenge foreclose the possibility of a clean return to the past even if a vaccine were to be made and cordyceps defeated. It is not that hope and goodness no longer exist in this post-apocalyptic world, but that no matter how one tries to foresee the future, no viable path or storyline toward a future of peace and human flourishing seem to reasonably exist. This echoes the predicament of many postcolonial or war-torn places in our world today, where decades of intricate and lasting human conflict, oppression, and revenge preclude the imagination of a possible path toward lasting peace. In some sense, the failure of a triumphant restoration of the world of *TLOU* is not just a plot twist of the final episode of the show, but perhaps the storyline's very premise.

Joel and Ellie's journey to the West, despite this premise, is perhaps to follow this glimmer of hope for the salvation of humankind. During their journey from east to west, the two discover an American land that is not empty and not *just* full of threats against their survival, but a land that is spatially marked by human kinship that endures and survives despite the looming dangers around them. This stands in direct contrast with historical U.S. American westward expansion and conquests, which are often premised upon the theological and legal doctrine of *terra nullius* (Latin for "nobody's land") where indigenous land is considered vacant if not yet occupied by European Christians. The post-apocalyptic land and its many "dead cities" turn out to be anything but vacant. Instead, the journey and the land are marked by stories of families, siblings, partners, and communities whose kinship have, thus far, emboldened them with the will to survive. In *TLOU* episode "Kin," the protagonists' trek through the wilderness of Wyoming led them to the doorsteps of a Native American couple, Marlon and Florence, whose grumpy humor and hunting skills have allowed them to survive together in relative isolation from the cordyceps-infected world. The brief addition of these grumpy indigenous characters to one of the TV show's longest depictions of the post-apocalyptic American Wild West distinguishes this journey from other American westward exploration travels. The land, even after a world-ending catastrophe, is not an empty land waiting to be revived by the efforts of Joel's fighting spirit, Ellie's immunity, and the Fireflies' possible vaccine. While it would be easy for the protagonists of the story and the viewers alike to assume that all who survived in this post-apocalyptic setting desired a future that looks like the pre-outbreak American past, the stories of the individuals Joel and Ellie encountered in the land proved otherwise. Some people, such as Marlon and Florence, prioritized their land, home, and kinship over a future-oriented definition of salvation. Others, such as Henry in the TV show, saw the protection of his sickly younger brother as more important than ensuring the success of the resistance movement that may or may not end the militant FEDRA rule in his town. In all these characters and their small pockets of kinship, we see a reversal of the logics of triumphant (and perhaps colonial) eschatology and a turn toward alternate eschatologies and sources of hope that do not revolve around the maximum temporal extension of life, the defeat of enemies, or a nostalgic desire to return to a pre-apocalyptic past.

ESCHATOLOGY AND FAILURE

Often, failure and untimely deaths meet these characters who seek to live according to a logic that resists triumphant hopes in the face of a world-ending tragedy. However, *TLOU* reminds that in this world of precarity, perhaps failure and untimely death are better options than a long life preserved by cannibalistic violence and abuse of power. Human failure, likewise, remains a prominent theme in today's world as humans grapple with their minute individual ability to confront climate change and other ecological disasters, or when peacebuilding movements fail and violence rises again. In both Christian theological language and our human imagination, failure and death are often juxtaposed to salvation, eschatology, and hope. By bringing together various imageries of failure and eschatology together, this section does not strive to glorify failure and human suffering either in *TLOU* or in this world. Rather, having critiqued the motifs of triumph in Christian eschatology in the previous section, I consider the possibility of eschatological hope beyond temporal futurity or the lengthening of life. I also explore how hope may lie beyond the dichotomy between triumphant success and disastrous failure. Furthermore, in a world where colonial eschatology is historically associated with images of triumphant expansion (on the part of those who conquer) and surrender of one's life and land in exchange for salvation (on the part of those who are conquered), perhaps an alternative spatial hope exists for people who seek neither to conquer nor to be conquered.

This section turns to contemporary Protestant theologian Kathryn Tanner's eschatology, which engages deeply with questions of human failure, to consider how *TLOU* and its portrayals of post-apocalyptic kinship can offer different sources and temporalities of eschatological hope. In the final chapter of *Jesus, Humanity, and the Trinity*,[10] Tanner begins her eschatology from the human experience of futility and failure, as well as the now widely accepted scientific fact that this earth one day will cease to exist. What should eschatology do, Tanner asks, in light of the immanent end of the physical world, especially when so many theologians argue for the historical-material continuity between this world and the world of the eschaton?[11] Tanner turns to Thomas Aquinas's view of creation, which is similar to Deloria's indigenous intervention, as a relationship of dependence. In light of scientific understandings of evolution, more Christian theologians have embraced a reading of Creation as not necessarily about humanity's temporal beginning, but more about human beings and the ecosystems' dependence on God. Along the same vein, what if eschatology can also be interpreted apart from its location as a temporal endpoint of the world?

Tanner conceives of the eschaton as a competing spatial sphere (not a temporally future occurrence) with this current material world's sphere of greed, futility, and death. She looks to both the Old Testament and New Testament's gradual de-emphasis of physical death as the most important category of nonexistence, and argues that it is not physical death itself from which we need to be saved. Death is a simple fact of existence—the world as we know it is constructed in a way to ensure temporal finitude. Instead, eternal life is primarily life in God, while death is separation from God. In other words, eschatological hope need not stand in contrast with the reality of the physical death of human beings or of the earth itself. The biological reality of death as the mere cessation of the length of life can be made good by God, who operates in a different time-space that is simultaneous with our world of death and suffering. It is more important for humanity to be delivered from the negative consequences of death, such as alienation, disintegration, and separation from others. These negative consequences of death also include those whose lives are disproportionately cut short by war, violence, and poverty. The eschaton is such a space where despite and through the real, scientific possibility of physical death and decay, the disintegrating effects of death can be healed by the fact that the dead now live in the relational space that is the presence of God. For Tanner, this healing does not only occur in the temporal future—whether in this life or in a post-death future—but occurs also in the present, in an alternate, life-giving eschatological space that competes with the death-driven space of this world. This eschatological space is present and real, sustaining us in our daily encounters with the death-dealing violence and forces of the world, rather than a space that lies in the temporal future.

Eternal life, under this view, is less a matter of duration, but a matter of a new *quality* and *mode* of existence in relations to God. This way, eschatology avoids giving theological primacy to a coming future over present and past time, as it has in much of existing Christian history. Eternal life is hence a realm or a sphere that currently exists in competition with the structure of futility and hopelessness, the realm of death. The eschaton or the sphere of eternal life infiltrates this present world to bring life and purpose to it, without being fully present within this world. Putting Tanner's theocentric eschatology in conversation with Vítor Westhelle's liberationist eschatology, we can also say that this competing spatial sphere of the eschaton is not merely an otherworldly spatial sphere. Rather, this competing spatial sphere can be found too on this earth, in the margins of empire where people live in hope-filled resistance against domination and violence.

Here, Tanner's eschatology takes a spatial and more theocentric turn, arguing that after our individual deaths and after our material world fades away, God becomes our dwelling space and the source of our eternal life. In her theology, God is not merely a (divine) person, but a space itself made possible by inter-Trinitarian relationality and divine-human relations. Space is created through mutual relationships, Tanner would argue, echoing Jürgen Moltmann's eschatology which also defines space as "mutual in-existence" and "mutual indwelling."[12] Mutual indwelling and relationality, such as that of the Trinity, creates space. As a result, space is not an empty void to be filled by human beings and our infrastructures alike. Instead, the experience of being in space is the experience of being within another. Human beings are at once inhabited and inhabiting one another. This different view of space in Tanner's eschatology allows for Tanner to claim that human beings' eschatological selves are thus not enclosed selves, but selves constituted by relationality with God and others.

This view of space allows for a further reversal of eschatologies that fuel political movements of manifest destiny, westward expansion, and colonization. Eschatological space, formed by human relationality, mutual indwelling, and dependence, is distinctly different from the colonial view of space as an empty (barbaric) land to be conquered and converted. Eschatological space is also not evaluated on the physical size or geographical completeness of such space, but the quality of relationships that form it. While a surface level read of the narrative arc of *TLOU* parallels a manifest destiny–like journey through an empty land for the purpose of saving it, a deeper reading in conversation with decolonial theologies and Tanner's eschatology uncovers a storyline in which a temporal, triumphant, and expansive view of space is gradually reversed through encounters with various NPCs or side characters who exemplify a different view of space, kinship, and post-apocalyptic survival.

In episode 6 of the TV show, the protagonists' initial hopes in a post-post-apocalyptic temporal future begin to fuse with their turn toward a spatial-relational hope. Striking up a conversation with Joel, Ellie initiates: "So I've been thinking, let's say we find the Fireflies, it all works, they draw my blood and put it through some of their fancy machines and make a cure. Then what? Like, what do we do?" To which Joel retorts, "Oh, it's 'we'?" Ellie responds: "Okay, fine, whatever. You. You can do anything you want. Where are you going? What are you doing?" This conversation corresponds to Ellie's return to the question in the final episode of the show, where several scenes prior to their arrival at the Fireflies' hospital, Ellie assures Joel that wherever he goes "after this is all over," she will go with him also. In these conversations about future hopes in the face of a future that may never arrive, it is the theme of relationality and friendship—the relational space of "we"—that undergird the conversation. The acknowledgment of the "we," in some sense, mattered more than the specific plans the two characters had or their certainty that a cordyceps-less world would eventually arrive.

For many characters in the show, however, failure, danger, and death haunt the relational spaces of kinship that the characters had built for themselves and their loved ones. Joel and Ellie's relationship concludes at the end of *TLOU* in a state of broken trust and a failed mission, while other characters' narratives have largely ended in untimely death. Tanner's spatial eschatology here offers an alternate view of human failure and inevitable defeats that one experiences when leading a life that prioritizes love and justice. If the eschatological realm is not bounded by ideals of temporal triumph, but is instead a spatial realm that exists simultaneously and in contrast with this world and its death-dealing forces, then we are empowered to radically seek kinship, communion, and justice in a way that is unaffected by considerations of success. Under this view, a transcendent eschatological present, rather than a transcendent eschatological future, inspires ethical action today. Tanner thus concludes her eschatology by claiming that it is better to prefer defeat over success in the world, if failure means to cling on to the eschatological realm of life in God and others, and success means being favored by the death-dealing forces of the world. This is evident in the lives of many historical and contemporary figures who chose to resist war and injustice despite being aware of the magnitude of systemic violence and the comparative futility of their efforts. I think of Oscar Romero and Rutilio Grande who preached messages of justice against an oppressive government despite knowing the imminent risk of their own assassination and death, or the many anti-Vietnam activists who continued in their protests despite knowing that war will most likely continue anyway. For them and many others, the possibility of a failed movement, in terms of its end result, looms large. In the post-apocalyptic world of *TLOU*, where the forces of death take on a heightened and hyper-visible role in life, worldly success looks like the commanders of FEDRA who obeyed orders throughout their careers to climb up the social ladder and avoid sewage duty, or perhaps the ringleaders of the cannibalistic cult of Silver Lake who prefer survival and power at all costs. A voluntary turn toward the possibility of our own powerlessness and failure according to worldly measures—and away from the false eschatological hopes of triumph and total redemption—is perhaps the more ethical path. This turn toward failure does not mean giving up on one's own life or choosing not to protect one's loved ones in the face of danger. Nor does it glorify every human failure as good or honorable. Rather, it means the recognition of a reality in which actions of hope and justice may be futile given the magnitude of injustice. Instead of looking only to a temporal future of social change (or only to an eschatological future of post-death redemption), we place our trust in a "transcendent eschatological present," where our prioritization of love, kinship, and relationality create literal and metaphorical spaces where eschatological hope is found. We turn away from the mere longevity of life or expansion of our earthly kingdoms and powers as metrics of success and turn instead to the little pockets of relational-space that sustain humanity in the face of destruction.

The world of *TLOU*, especially after its post-COVID TV-show production and release, in some ways parallels the various catastrophes and crises of this world, from climate change, pandemics, to ever-rising global authoritarianism and militarism. These global catastrophes challenge our existing conceptions of eschatology and hope, oftentimes preventing us from even speaking about our futures. This chapter suggests that speaking of questions of eschatology, hope, and futures in this world means rethinking the very foundations of these categories and delinking them from their colonial, theo-political implications that have inflicted so much violence throughout history. While *TLOU* never explicitly endorses the language of theology, let alone eschatology, threads of a more decolonial, more honest, and more spatial eschatology are nonetheless present as a counternarrative to the triumphant eschatologies that dominate the American Christian narrative. In a story where the world has already ended, it is the middle-spaces of kinship, rather than an endpoint of salvation or success, that have the last word.

NOTES

1. One of many short theological histories of the evolution of Christian eschatology is Fletcher, "Eschatology."
2. For an excellent summary of queer critiques, Black/Afropessimist critiques, and other liberationist and liberative theological critiques of eschatology, see Maia, *Trading Futures*, 11–14.
3. Wrobel, *Global West, American Frontier*; Babík, *Statecraft and Salvation*.
4. Gomez, "Deus Vult."
5. Rambo, "Beyond Redemption?" 100.
6. Rambo, "Beyond Redemption?" 106.
7. Deloria, *God Is Red*, 61–77.
8. This view on eschatology is found in Tinker, *American Indian Liberation*. Tinker draws from Deloria's thought in his spatially oriented indigenous eschatology.
9. Westhelle, "Liberation Theology"; Westhelle, *Eschatology and Space*.
10. Tanner, *Jesus, Humanity and the Trinity*, 97–124.
11. Tanner, *Jesus, Humanity and the Trinity*, 97.
12. Moltmann, *The Coming of God*, 301.

BIBLIOGRAPHY

Babík, Milan. *Statecraft and Salvation: Wilsonian Liberal Internationalism as Secularized Eschatology*. Waco, TX: Baylor University Press, 2013.

Deloria, Vine. *God Is Red*. New York: Grosset & Dunlap, 1973.

Fletcher, Jeannine Hill. "Eschatology." In *Systematic Theology: Roman Catholic Perspectives*, 2nd ed., edited by Francis Fiorenza and John P. Galvin (pp. 622–651). Minneapolis, MN: Fortress Press, 2011.

Gomez, Adam. "Deus Vult: John L. O'Sullivan, Manifest Destiny, and American Democratic Messianism." *American Political Thought* 1.2 (2012): 236–262, https://doi.org/10.1086/667616.

Maia, Filipe. *Trading Futures: A Theological Critique of Financialized Capitalism*. Durham, NC: Duke University Press, 2022.

Moltmann, Jürgen. *The Coming of God: Christian Eschatology*. Minneapolis, MN: Fortress Press, 1996.

Rambo, Shelly L. "Beyond Redemption? Reading Cormac McCarthy's *The Road* after the End of the World." *Studies in the Literary Imagination* 41.2 (2008): 99–120.

Tanner, Kathryn. *Jesus, Humanity, and the Trinity a Brief Systematic Theology*, First Fortress Press edition. Minneapolis, MN: Fortress Press, 2001.

Tinker, George E. *American Indian Liberation: A Theology of Sovereignty*. Maryknoll, NY: Orbis, 2008.

Westhelle, Vítor. "Liberation Theology: A Latitudinal Perspective." In *The Oxford Handbook of Eschatology*, edited by Jerry L. Walls (pp. 328–342). Oxford, UK: Oxford University Press, 2008.

———. *Eschatology and Space: The Lost Dimension in Theology Past and Present*, 1st ed. New York: Palgrave Macmillan, 2012.

Wrobel, David M. *Global West, American Frontier: Travel, Empire, and Exceptionalism from Manifest Destiny to the Great Depression*, Calvin P. Horn Lectures in Western History and Culture. Albuquerque: University of New Mexico Press, 2013.

Chapter 12

Carrying the Fire and Finding the Fireflies

Hope, Despair, and Godtalk in the Dystopian Stories of Naughty Dog and Cormac McCarthy

Matthew C. Millsap and Ched Spellman

This chapter compares and contrasts the function of theological discourse in the dystopian narrative world of Naughty Dog's *The Last of Us* (*TLOU*) and Cormac McCarthy's *The Road* (*TR*).[1] In both stories, the main characters find themselves struggling to "endure and survive" in a world that is in decay. The major themes in both works organically unfold within the relational dynamic of the travelers that the story follows (Joel and Ellie and the father and his son). These stories are as much about the pursuit of meaning as the pursuit of any destination or objective.

Alongside the collapse of society in light of destructive events, the socio-linguistic structures that shaped the way meaning functioned in that world are also in shambles. These semiotic boundaries are now in a constant state of flux. In this context of relational and cultural disorder, characters in these stories discuss the meaning of life, the existence of God, and the nature of humanity. Examining the distinctive ways that this discourse about theological anthropology and theology proper functions in the various mediums of these stories provides an informative angle into the sophistication and thematic depth of these cultural texts.

THE ILLUSION OF A FINAL DESTINATION IN A DYSTOPIA

Destinations matter. For characters, they provide external goals and fuel internal motivation that is necessary in order to endure any number of painful experiences. For stories, destinations also structure the shape of how literary elements function and the manner in which a narrative unfolds.

In *TR*, McCarthy tells the story of a father and son who strive to survive in a world that is both unnervingly mundane and breathtakingly violent. Significantly, the cause of this destruction is left largely unspecified.[2] The narrative focus is on the effect that this apocalyptic shift has on survivors and more specifically what happens to those who have no memory of any other way of being. "The road" implies a destination, and in the early phases of the story, the father tells the son that they are headed to the coast.

Though this direction drives them forward and structures the unfolding plotline, they both sense that even the dim hope that this destination represents is a bitter illusion: "He said that everything depended on reaching the coast, yet waking in the night he knew that all of this was empty" and had "no substance to it" (29).[3] There was a good chance that they would not make it through the mountain path that they were on, "and that would be that" (29). Later, they find food and shelter but "were still a long way from the coast" (213). At this point, the man "knew that he was placing hopes where he'd no reason to. He hoped it would be brighter where for all he knew the world grew darker daily" (213). When the man and the child eventually do arrive at the coast, the experiences they have in this place mirror the ones they have already had on their journey South. After the father's death, the son does not begin anew but rather continues his path along the road he's been on his entire life. This tense dynamic between grim reality and the glint of hope is a key feature of the story's presentation.[4]

In *TLOU*, Naughty Dog also presents the player with a destination whose finality is questionable. While the premise of the game is straightforward, in that the story revolves around a smuggler, Joel, being tasked with transporting a fourteen-year-old girl, Ellie, across a post-apocalyptic United States, the ambiguity surrounding the destination begins almost immediately. At first, it is unclear to the player why it is so important that Ellie be delivered to the Fireflies, a revolutionary militia. Over the course of the game, the player learns that Ellie has immunity to the fungal infection that produced the apocalypse the world now faces and thus she may be the key to scientists within the Fireflies developing a cure. However, the "destination" Joel and Ellie seek is nonetheless still unclear in two key respects.

First, Joel and Ellie's journey is marked by ambiguity in their search for the Fireflies, whose location remains elusive over the course of the narrative. Their original meeting point outside the Boston QZ (Quarantine Zone), yet still within the city, quickly proves fruitless. When they arrive, they find all the Fireflies dead. Tess, Joel's dual smuggling/romantic partner, reveals she was infected on the way there, and, in her dying wish, tasks Joel with transporting Ellie to Joel's brother, Tommy, a former member of the Fireflies. With this request, Tess maintains hope that Ellie truly is the means of developing a cure. This is no easy task, however, as Joel and Tommy are estranged. Joel no longer knows Tommy's exact location, because after their falling out, Tommy had moved from Boston to the western United States. Later, when Joel locates Tommy and reunites with him, Tommy sends Joel and Ellie to the fictional University of Eastern Colorado ["Go Big Horns!"], where he thinks that the Fireflies have a working science lab. Joel and Ellie eventually find the lab abandoned but also discover clues that lead them to another possible Firefly location: a hospital in Salt Lake City. Repeatedly throughout the game, Joel and Ellie arrive at a destination only to have it lead to another, the illusion of finality becoming ever more palpable the farther they travel.[5]

Second, the precise details of Ellie's immunity remain unclear. Joel and Tess recognize that, given the apparent age of the bite mark scars on Ellie's arm, she should have "turned" long ago but has not. Ellie herself recognizes this anomaly but has no idea how she is immune or how this immunity might be transmitted to others. Ellie represents an ember of hope burning in a dark, despairing world—an ember that she and others want to fan into flame. Yet because no one knows exactly how to do so, the hope that Ellie represents is potentially overshadowed by an ethos of doubt that permeates the narrative. Where is Tommy? Will Joel even know how to find the Fireflies and their scientists? Can Joel successfully transport Ellie there alive? Is it even scientifically possible to use Ellie to develop a cure?

In McCarthy's story, what keeps the father and the boy motivated and imbues them with purpose is their journey down "the road" to the coast, even if they ultimately sense only emptiness awaits them upon arrival. Joel and Ellie are likewise motivated by a hope for what their final destination might produce. The ever-present possibility of failure, though, also gathers like a cloud that darkens their pursuit of the Fireflies.

THE COLLAPSE OF THE WORLD THAT WORDS INHABIT

Within this narrative structure of shifting destinations and shattered hope, characters not only face the challenge of knowing *what to do* but also the challenge of knowing *what to say*. The destruction of the natural order and the structures of society has triggered the slower loss of cultural memory among survivors. This situation has also led to the destabilization of post-apocalyptic discourse. How do you communicate when the ostensive referents of core concepts are no longer in existence? The dearth of physical resources is matched by the lack of linguistic resources needed to achieve shared communication. The presuppositional pool shared across generations has dried up along with the clean sources of drinking water.[6]

In *TR*, this semiotic loss is referenced at several points of the story. The father notes that "sometimes the child would ask him questions about the world that for him was not even a memory" (54). In these moments, he would consider how to answer. He must function in conversations as if "there is no past" and then he simply plays a game of make believe (54). This destabilization extends to the present as well: "No list of things to be done. The day providential to itself. The hour. There is no later. This is later" (54). In this atemporal progress, "the days sloughed past uncounted and uncalendared" (273). As the father muses at one point, "there is no other tale to tell" (32).

The father reflects directly on this unsettling situation one night after making camp in a muddy field. The man tries "to think of something to say but he could not" (88). He senses a familiar feeling "beyond the numbness and the dull despair" (88). This dread centers on "the world shrinking down" around a "raw core of parsible entities" (88). In this situation, "the names of things slowly following those things into oblivion. Colors. The names of birds. Things to eat. Finally the names of things one believed to be true" (88). "More fragile than he would have thought," the man contemplates. He asks, "How much was gone already? The sacred idiom shorn of its referents and so of its reality" (89). The fading memory of the former ecosystem and its living inhabitants prompts existential angst. Here the man contemplates the brutal reality which has lost its ability to articulate the full scope of its tragedy.

The world that Joel and Ellie inhabit has experienced a similar loss in linguistic referents, yet perhaps not as extensively as that in *TR*. As Joel and Ellie make their way through cities, through towns, through businesses and homes, they encounter cultural relics, many of which fascinate Ellie, as she uses them to peer into a past in which she has never lived, yet in some sense, feels as though she has. Whereas for the boy, the previous world seems astigmatic—a blur that cannot ever be fully focused regardless of how distant or how near one is to it—for Ellie, the previous world is largely a wonder whose artifacts become lenses used to give sight to a former life rhythm not of survival, but of work and leisure.

McCarthy directs his narrative in such a way that though the reader may presume the boy has encountered cultural artifacts over the course of his young life, McCarthy seldom, if ever, presents them to him, let alone has him comment on them or inquire about them. As the father and the boy comb their way through the various structures they find, they maintain almost laser-like gazes for items that aid in survival. Indeed, the father has taught the boy to live in this manner, and at multiple points in the narrative, McCarthy makes clear that the duo is near the point of starvation.

In contrast to the boy, Ellie is frequently transfixed by what she finds as she journeys across the post-apocalyptic landscape. While some of this contrast may owe to the player being able to infer that Joel and Ellie have found the means of meeting their basic survival needs without severe difficulty, it also owes to Ellie's personality and the curiosity with which Naughty Dog's narrative team has written her. Ellie, though understanding the gravity of the stakes involved, is not as serious as the boy and thus more open to the effects the "frivolity" of cultural artifacts may have on her.

One of the earliest indicators of Ellie's positive relationship to cultural referents of the previous world in *TLOU* is found while she and Joel make their way through "Bill's Town." In a long-abandoned restaurant, they come across an arcade cabinet for the fictional game, *The Turning*. After explaining to Joel some details about the game despite having never actually played it, Ellie then admits wistfully, "I wish I could play it."[7] Shortly thereafter, as they walk through an abandoned record store, they have the following exchange:

Ellie: Man, this is kinda sad.

Joel: What is?

Ellie: All this music that's just sitting here. No one's around to listen to it.

(Ellie pauses, then sighs.)

Ellie: I don't know, doesn't seem right.

On the other hand, there are occasions in which the previous world feels foreign and distant to Ellie. After Joel and Ellie have met Henry and his little brother, Sam, and the four of them make their way through the neighborhood of a Pittsburgh suburb, they encounter a dilapidated ice cream truck among other abandoned vehicles. Joel explains to Ellie what an ice cream truck used to do in the old world—that children would hear the music of the truck and would come running out of their homes to buy ice cream—and the innocence of such routine behavior is so alien to her that she can scarcely believe it to be true. She offers her judgment to Joel: "Man, you lived in a strange time." Much later, when Ellie has run away from Joel and Tommy in Jackson, Joel finds her in a ranch house, sitting in a teenage girl's bedroom and reading the diary the girl left behind years ago. As Joel walks into the room, Ellie asks,

"Is this really all they had to worry about? Boys. Movies. Deciding which skirt goes with which shirt?" She then scoffs and concludes, "It's bizarre."

Ellie longs for the previous world in a way that the boy does not. This difference exists not only because Ellie still has access to cultural artifacts with the power to facilitate discourse, but also because Ellie desires such discourse.[8] The boy's communication with the father is consumed almost entirely by matters of survival and the gravity of "carrying the fire" on their journey. Ellie carries "fire" of her own (i.e., the potential of a cure to save humanity), yet she has—and actively cultivates—the ability to communicate with others from a world in which she never lived. Her fascination with this previous world and the ways she finds to interact with it animate her to a degree that keeps her motivated toward a goal whose stakes could not be any higher. Why does she want to be the means of saving the world? Because she understands what was lost.

THEOLOGICAL DISCOURSE AS PLOT AND COMMENTARY

In a world that has lost any sense of cultural mooring and societal stability, what would this lead you to say about God? In both *TR* and *TLOU*, theological discourse reflects the disarray of the narrative setting and also informs the meaning of the story's plotline.[9]

At strategic parts of *TR*, the characters express both their hope and despair in the midst of theologically informed discourse. In a sparse narrative setting, this godtalk is particularly prominent. On the one hand, a common theme in post-apocalyptic stories is present, namely, the absence of God. The land is after all, "Barren, silent, godless" (4). Beyond the argument against either God's existence or goodness, godtalk also postures toward something that transcends in some way this desolate landscape. The father assigns his life's purpose to his son. The man "knew only that the child was his warrant" (5). The mere living presence of his son in this world is for him theologically articulate: "If he is not the word of God God never spoke" (5). This assertion contrasts the later reflection on the man during a fever dream. "On this road," he insists, "there are no godspoke men. They are gone and I am left and they have taken with them the world" (32). In a moment of danger, part of what haunts the man are lingering echoes of some of his wife's final words. She had argued against keeping their son alive in this brutal world and urged the man to "curse God and die" (114).[10]

In this vein, a paradigmatic sequence occurs as the man and the boy come upon an isolated old man shuffling down the path with a cane. At the boy's insistence, they give the man some food and allow him to stay with them for the night. At their camp, their conversation veers theological. The old man says that he "knew this was coming" (168) and mentions the possibility of being the last person left alive. The father asks, "How would you know if you were the last person on earth?" After the old man surmises that you wouldn't know this, you would "just be it," the father suggests that God would know. To this the old man states directly, "There is no God and we are his prophets" (17). This statement is both a paradox (how can one speak on behalf of a God who doesn't exist) and also the counterpoint to the father's insistence that the boy is "his warrant" (5). In both cases, the existence of human life embodies an articulation of life's possible purpose.

The final scene of the story returns to these themes. After the father dies and the son joins a group of other travelers, the woman in the group "would talk to him sometimes about God. He tried to talk to God but the best thing was to talk to his father and he did talk to him and he didn't forget" (286). The woman adds that this "was all right" and that the "breath of God was his breath yet though it pass from man to man through all of time" (286).

Whereas, in *TR*, McCarthy is inclined to bring theology and godtalk to bear on his characters overtly, the narrative team at Naughty Dog appears to present much of its godtalk in *TLOU* as subtext. In the game's prologue, the player experiences the tragedy of Joel losing his twelve-year-old daughter, Sarah, at the beginning of the cordyceps infection outbreak (September 26, 2013). In their escape from Austin, Texas, Sarah is shot and killed by a U.S. military soldier with orders to shoot anyone attempting to leave the city. As Joel holds his dying daughter in his arms, he sobs, "Oh no, no, no.... Please. Oh, God. Please, please, please don't do this. Please, God."

One reading of this scene may be to understand Joel as simply engaging in a common expression of grief that might naturally extend from a basic theistic worldview, one in which the holder occasionally appeals to a higher power or (lowercase "g") god. Like with a "there are no atheists in foxholes" mentality, one might conclude here that Joel, amid personal tragedy and racked with grief, begs for the intervention of a higher power with whom he has an abstract relationship.

Conversely, one might perceive Joel as being at least nominally Christian. Given the context of Joel living in an Austin suburb in a Bible Belt state, and considering his age (born in 1981, per game canon), it is possible that Joel possesses a Christian cultural awareness that may be foreign to many today, and indeed would be foreign to most in the post-apocalyptic United States of 2033 in *TLOU*. While claiming that Joel is a devout Christian would be going too far (and perhaps also contrary to the behavior Joel exhibits at different points in the game's narrative), one could view him as implicitly holding to a "Christian" version of what sociologist Christian Smith identified as "moralistic therapeutic deism" (Smith 2006). In this case, Joel's appeal for intervention in his daughter's death is an appeal to the Christian God, a God to whom he might have infrequently prayed at various times in his life.[11]

This second reading of Joel appears to be the more convincing when one additionally looks further into the narrative to the sequences that occur after Joel reunites with his estranged brother, Tommy, who was formerly a Firefly and believed in the Fireflies' efforts to restore a functionally healthy, nation-wide government. Tommy introduces Joel to his wife, Maria, and the two of them walk Joel and Ellie through their Jackson settlement, showing them what life in a safe society within this chaotic world can be. Joel later meets with Tommy privately to try to convince him to take Ellie to the Fireflies and that his part in transporting her is finished, which then leads to this heated exchange:

Tommy: What makes you think I'd do this for you?

Joel: This isn't for me, Tommy. This is for your damn cause.

Tommy: My cause is my family now. You ain't talking about some walk in the park here.

Joel: Jesus, boy . . . have Maria get some of your born-again friends to do it.

Here Joel uses the phrase "born-again"—common in evangelical Christianity to describe someone who has placed saving faith in Jesus Christ and experienced spiritual rebirth (John 3:3–8; 1 Peter 1:22–23)—derisively as means to mock Tommy and his Jackson community, for in an earlier conversation, Tommy had described Jackson and its civilizational amenities to Joel as a place that "gives us all a second chance." Joel's awareness of the meaning of this terminology and his implicit assumption that Tommy will understand he intends it as an insult serves to communicate to the player a shared background between the two in which they likely came of age within the milieu of a Christian culture. In sum, though Joel is not a Christian, he nonetheless demonstrates familiarity with Christianity and its language. Joel's use of godtalk is thus more utilitarian than it is theological.

Shifting to characters beyond Joel, Ellie appears to have some basic understanding of the concept of an afterlife, thus indicating that the people who inhabit the post-apocalyptic world of *TLOU* likely do still have some theological mooring, unsystematic though it may be. During the Pittsburgh sequence with the brothers Henry and Sam, Ellie and Sam become friends with each other, given the nearness of their ages. As the four traverse an abandoned suburban neighborhood, a horde of infected attacks, and Sam is bitten in the ensuing fight (though unbeknownst to the player and to the other characters). Later that evening, Ellie and Sam have a private conversation in a room away from Joel and Henry, and the conversation shifts from small talk to something more profound:

Sam: How is it that you're never scared?

Ellie: Who says that I'm not?

Sam: What're you scared of?

Ellie: Let's see . . . scorpions are pretty creepy. Um . . . being by myself. I'm scared of ending up alone. What about you?

Sam: Those things out there. What if the people are still inside? What if they're trapped in there, without any control over their body? I'm scared of that happening to me.

Ellie: Okay, first of all, we're a team now. We're gonna help each other out. And second, they might still look like people, but that person is not in there anymore.

Sam: Henry says that, "They've moved on." That they're with their families. Like in heaven. Do you think that's true?

Ellie: I go back and forth. I mean, I'd like to believe it.

Sam: But you don't.

Ellie: I guess not.

Sam: Yeah . . . me neither.

After the remainder of the conversation, when Ellie leaves the room, the camera lingers on Sam and eventually reveals that he has been bitten by an infected. The player thus learns at this point the context of why Sam took the conversation in the direction he did: He was bitten, the rest of the characters don't know that he was bitten, and he is terrified of the fate he knows awaits him.

Henry and Sam apparently have had conversations in the past in which Sam inquired of his older brother as to what happens to the person someone was before becoming infected. Henry must have drawn upon the concept of an afterlife, explaining to Sam that who a person was—perhaps the equivalent of a "soul"—is no longer present in the body of an infected. That person has "moved on" to a peaceful afterlife where they are now present with their family members who have gone on before them. To have been infected, then, is to have died. Sam reveals his brother's theorizing to Ellie yet receives little comfort—neither of them truly believes that an afterlife, like heaven, is real.

Godtalk in *TLOU* is not limited to the strictly verbal, however. In a post-apocalyptic landscape, among the vestiges of society lie the remains of sacred spaces that the practices of religions once inhabited. Early in the game, as Joel, Ellie, and Bill traverse "Bill's Town" together, Bill leads Joel and Ellie through his own abode: a small, abandoned church. The trio begin by entering the cellar from outside. As they make their way upstairs, the darkened halls eventually open into the sanctuary, which in stark contrast is lit by the rays of the afternoon sun emanating through stained-glass windows. A dusty pulpit sits empty. On the central table for the Eucharist stand only candles. In the back of the room, sheet music still lies in its proper place on an organ as though yearning for someone to play notes fit for God's ears once again. The golden glow of the scene punctuated by hints of various stained-glass hues offers a moment of beauty amid the darkness of the world the characters inhabit.[12]

Bill presses forward through the room as though the church is any other abandoned building, but the reverence of this once-sacred space impresses Ellie to stop and comment breathlessly, "Wow." Joel says to Bill matter-of-factly, "Nice place you've got here," to which Bill replies, "Well, if you got anything to confess, this'd be the place to do it." If the player, as Joel, chooses to explore a side room, it becomes apparent from the bed and personal effects that the room is where Bill rests and sleeps, his own private "sanctuary" within a world of unspeakable evil. Bill then objects loudly to Joel's intrusion, "That's not the confessional booth, that's my room."

The most fascinating element of this scene in the game is that the space itself must first wordlessly communicate godtalk to the characters before they utter godtalk as human speech in response. Ellie's godtalk is simply to exclaim "wow," perhaps an implicit acknowledgment that no words with more specificity are adequate to describe the sacredness into which she walks. Joel recognizes the sacredness, yet downplays it to a degree in his response, possibly in recognition of his own lagging or abandoned faith. Ironically, Bill, a crass and irreverent character one would not expect to be prone to matters spiritual, nonetheless acknowledges the serious purpose the space once held, maybe even hinting at having confessed sins of his own within the very walls of this church.

In sum, the godtalk of *TLOU*, though often not as explicit as that of *TR*, is multifaceted. While none of the characters speak freely of God or of theological concepts, the remnants of Christianity—both tangible and intangible—endure and survive in such a way that they nonetheless seep into the worldviews of the characters who live in a reality in which God presumably is dead.[13]

CONCLUSION

The basic premise of this chapter is that *TLOU* and *TR* have similarities and differences that can help illuminate the literary sophistication and thematic depth of their individual stories. For example, the brutality and seriousness of *TR* resonates with the destructive world of *TLOU*. This broad connection helps players appreciate the shared features of this genre of creative work. The laconic narration of the former also makes the gameplay exploration and energetic dialogue of the latter stand out. The juxtaposition of McCarthy's novel and Naughty Dog's story provides a hermeneutical framework that can help readers and players process the meaningful effect that these cultural texts are capable of producing.

More specifically, these stories address in their own distinctive ways the nature and function of both hope and despair in the context of a world that has encountered cataclysm. Both stories explore what it takes to understand and articulate both of these themes. Theological discourse formed part of the linguistic frame utilized by characters in their grasp for meaning. The godtalk that is present in these stories is clearly connected to the nature of humanity and the purpose an individual person or society might possess. Talk of the existence or relative goodness of a transcendent being accompanies the attempt to assign value to human life. In this sense, "carrying the fire" relates directly to maintaining one's humanity and seeing its capacity to embody some transcendent element in the most dire circumstances: To both speak of God and thereby signify in some way God's existence.

In the end, the most powerful element of both *TR* and *TLOU* is human relationships. For Joel and Ellie and the father and the boy, these relationships are worth preserving by any means necessary. Even with theological ambiguity about the existence of God and even without the necessary linguistic resources for a full articulation, the presence of human life, however tragic, means that hope is still possible. As Joel tells Ellie, "I struggled for a long time with survivin.' And you—No matter what, you keep finding something to fight for." And as the father tells the boy, "All things of grace and beauty such that one holds them to one's heart have a common provenance in pain. Their birth in grief and ashes. So, he whispered to the sleeping boy. I have you" (54).

NOTES

1. All quotations from *The Road* in the main text will be in-text citations.
2. The relevant passage notes that "The clocks stopped at 1:17. A long shear of light and then a series of low concussions" (McCarthy, *The Road*, 52). The power went out

at that moment and "a dull rose glow" was then "in the windowglass" (52). No further details of the destructive event are given.

3. In addition to being "on the road," the man and the boy's relation to "the coast" is one of the structural elements of the story (see McCarthy, *The Road*, 29, 156, 181, 213, 260). Cf. the father's comment that "the child has his own fantasies. How things would be in the south" (54).

4. As Noble observes, readers of this novel "face a challenging thematic and philosophical balancing act: if they acknowledge the novel's weightiness, they must reckon with its stark, unrelenting fatalism and its profound and yet complex hope for a better future" (Noble, "The Absurdity of Hope in Cormac McCarthy's *The Road*," 93). Noble further characterizes this dynamic as "the absurdity of hope."

5. One might also argue that the illusion of finality also metatextually translates over to the act of playing the game itself, for the player is not simply watching Joel and Ellie on their journey from destination to destination, but is actually controlling Joel and Ellie on their journey through player agency.

6. Kunsa also examines the phenomenon of "post-apocalyptic naming" in the novel. She views the novel as "a linguistic journey toward redemption" and a "search for meaning and pattern in a seemingly meaningless world" ("Maps of the World," 57). Kunsa also connects this linguistic struggle to the story's theme of fledgling hope.

7. On this theme, a significant part of the story in *The Last of Us: Left Behind* (the game's DLC expansion) centers on Ellie and her friend Riley's trip to an abandoned mall where they try to play an arcade game (it no longer works and they use their imagination to imagine what playing it would have been like).

8. Interestingly, Joel recognizes this desire in Ellie as well. For example, as their relationship grows over the game, Joel (through the player's optional actions) begins collecting old comic books he finds in the detritus left behind in abandoned spaces, as he knows Ellie has developed a love for that particular comic series.

9. The theme of morality and its connection to theological concepts is an often analyzed feature of *TR*. For just one example, see the discussion of "God, morality, and meaning" in Wielenberg, "God, Morality, and Meaning in Cormac McCarthy's *The Road*." Wielenberg makes the case that the novel implies the use of a "moral code" apart from any belief in the existence of God.

10. This phrase is also a clear allusion to the biblical story of Job. In this story, Job experiences the loss of his family, his fortune, and his health. The rest of the book is essentially the speech of Job and his friends as they seek to make sense of this seemingly meaningless suffering. See Job 1–2, esp. 2:9. On the connection between Job and *TR*, see Vanderheide, "Sighting Leviathan."

11. Further details from *The Last of Us Part II* (*TLOU2*) resonate with this basic characterization of Joel's connection to a nominal Christianity. For example, when Ellie visits Joel's grave, his tombstone has a cross on it alongside other crosses in the backdrop of the cemetery. In one of their final conversations during one of Ellie's flashbacks, Joel also employs godtalk as he reflects on his decision to rescue Ellie at the expense of everyone else at the Firefly hospital: "If somehow the Lord gave me a second chance at that moment, I would do it all over again."

12. This moment in the game's storyline is also an instance where narrative storytelling is coordinated with gameplay mechanics. A distinctive feature of video games is that they are by nature a participatory medium. There are certain scenes that the game forces players to encounter in certain ways, and there are also places where players can choose how they interact with a space. The sanctuary scene in Bill's town blends both of these elements: Players must enter the church in a certain way and exit through an upper-level window. In the story, the church is a "sanctuary" from the harsh and gray world outside its walls. For the player, too, this moment in the game is a respite from furious chases and forthcoming fights. The player might choose to immediately leave and enter the next sequence of combat, or they may choose to linger and explore the carefully curated beauty of the space. In this sense, the sanctuary scene anticipates the giraffe scene later in the game (where Ellie is once again awestruck by an element of the natural world that implies the enduring beauty of life rather than the death of a previous mode of existence). The blend between narrative pacing, overheard dialogue, player agency, and visual contrasts are part of what make *TLOU* powerful both as a story and as a gaming experience.

13. An interesting parallel to the interlude in the sanctuary in Bill's town in *TLOU* is the synagogue scene in *TLOU2*. During their first day in Seattle, Ellie and Dina find temporary shelter in an abandoned Jewish synagogue. The gameplay mechanics of this scene also require the player to explore different areas of the space and encourages lingering exploration. In these quiet moments, Dina talks about her family (e.g., her fervently religious sister Talia) and her past experience with Judaism. Her sister had consistently encouraged Dina to join her in prayer and dialogue about God and various aspects of the Torah (the girls come across a Torah Scroll in one of the rooms). Dina also mentions some of her participation in Jewish holidays (e.g., observance of the new year according to the Hebrew calendar). Even though she tells Ellie that she's "not much of a believer," Dina alludes to the history of her Jewish heritage by noting that she likes "coming from a long line of survivors." When Ellie curses later, she also playfully responds, "Hey! Language. House of worship here." Dina also notes that she occasionally still prays, though mostly as a way of staying calm, dealing with grief, and maintaining contact with the rituals of her earlier life (she mentions praying as they left on their trip, during a visit to Joel's grave, etc.). Though minimal in relation to the scope of the full game, this scene also shows the way that theological discourse is part of the plotline and a key feature of a character like Dina's way of interacting with the world and its occasions for hope and despair.

BIBLIOGRAPHY

Kunsa, Ashley. "Maps of the World in Its Becoming: Post-Apocalyptic Naming in Cormac McCarthy's *The Road*." *Journal of Modern Literature* 33.1 (Fall 2009): 57–74.

McCarthy, Cormac. *The Road*. London: Vintage International, 2006.

Noble, Alan. "The Absurdity of Hope in Cormac McCarthy's *The Road*." *South Atlantic Review* 76.3 (Summer 2011): 93–109.

Smith, Christian. *Soul Searching: The Religious and Spiritual Lives of American Teenagers*. Oxford, UK: Oxford University Press, 2005.

Vanderheide, John. "Sighting Leviathan: Ritualism, Daemonism, and the Book of Job in Cormac McCarthy's Latest Works." *Cormac McCarthy Journal* 6 (Autumn 2008): 107–120.

Wielenberg, Erik. "God, Morality, and Meaning in Cormac McCarthy's *The Road*." *Cormac McCarthy Journal* 8.1 (Fall 2010): 1–19.

Chapter 13

"Save Who You Can Save"
Soteriology in The Last of Us

Rebecca Chapman

Soft golden sunlight pours into the huge open room, falling upon either side of the pillars that surround the central space. But this is no church. We hear a gunshot, followed by a terrifying silence, then the disturbing growls and groans of an army of infected growing nearer. As episode 2 of *TLOU* draws to its horrifying climax, we see Tess looking into Joel's eyes one last time before her suicidal sacrifice, as she whispers to him, like a prayer, "Save who you can save."

This phrase—save who you can save—becomes like a mantra in the HBO version of *TLOU*. From the symbiotic relationship that develops between Joel and Ellie as the two main protagonists/characters, to gun-toting Bill's protection of his beloved Frank, to David's twisted leadership of his "flock," we see physical salvation played out in a variety of ways. Some of what is offered is sacrificial, like Tess's death and Anna's request to die, while others "save" others for self-centered reasons. But physical protection and safety are not the only games in town. The word "salvation" comes from the Latin *salvus* meaning "healthy," "untouched," "saved," "salvaged," "unspoiled," "undamaged." In a devastated world where people and places have been devastated, surely saving those you love from pain and loss seems impossible.

Born in 1886, the German theologian Paul Tillich was no stranger to pain and loss. His mother, who he adored, died of cancer when he was a teenager, and, in 1914, he joined the Imperial German Army as a Lutheran chaplain. He served in the trenches, burying many men, his closest friend among them, and sometimes digging their graves. He was "expected to encourage the men and show their efforts to be in line with God's will."[1] He was hospitalized multiple times for combat trauma.

Returning home after the war, he began his academic career at the University of Berlin. His experience of the Great War had led him to the view that there was a God who makes all things work together for good was no longer viable for him. In *On the Boundary*, he observed the experience had shown him "an abyss in human existence that could not be ignored."[2] He wrote at the end of one age and the start of another—the world could never be the same after the devastation brought by the Great War.

Returning to civilian life, Tillich began to pull together different aspects of human experience—religion, culture, sociology, science, philosophy, psychology, even poetry—and to look at the relationship between them. Many of his resulting observations strike at the heart of our twenty-first-century life. Before either COVID or cordyceps, there might have been a temptation to become so comfortable in our modern lives that we forgot the reality of death and our finite existence. We think of our modern age as one of anxiety and division—all highlighted truly horribly in *The Last of Us* (*TLOU*) in its post-apocalyptic world. Yet way back in 1952 in his book *The Courage to Be*, Tillich noted, "today it has become a truism to call our time 'an age of anxiety.'"[3] The author of Ecclesiastes might remind us that there is nothing new under the sun!

In amongst the horror of the post-apocalyptic world that we are shown in *TLOU*, what shines through is love—and the choices we make because of it; to save or to destroy. Love changes everything in this show. Here it is not saccharine, nor straightforward. We see that to love is to be vulnerable—"I was never afraid before you showed up"—and love is a choice. Our choices to connect, to build community, and to love are the very things that make us human. Yet we fear not being able to provide for those we love, nor protect them.

We are right to fear. Facing her own imminent death after being bitten, Riley tells Ellie in the episode "Left Behind" that, "it ends this way for everyone sooner or later, right, some of us just get there faster than others." Tillich too was deeply aware that if we exist, our time on earth is limited. Humanity is fallen and finite, and he argued "finitude in awareness is anxiety."[4] Anxiety abounds in *TLOU*, and death is ever-present. The threat of death comes not just from the infected who seek to replicate their cordyceps fungus, but from what is left of humanity in struggles for power and control. This chapter will reflect on the soteriology of *TLOU*, considering, in particular, the work of Paul Tillich, using the model proposed by Clive Marsh[5] as a lens to consider what characters are saved from, saved for, saved by, and finally saved into.

SAVED AGAIN AND AGAIN—BUT FROM WHAT?

Throughout the nine episodes of *TLOU* season 1, the two protagonists, Joel and Ellie, keep each other alive in different ways again and again, saving one another from physical threats. As they make their cross-country journey, Joel protects Ellie physically from threats—from beating an armed soldier to death with his bare hands as they initially flee the quarantine zone, to destroying everyone in his path to prevent Ellie's fatal surgery in the final episode, with many more moments in between. The threats he saves her from are not merely those infected with cordyceps, but other people from different tribes and factions. Yet there are many times he fails, and she steps in to physically save him—she provides the night watch when he falls asleep, and then most obviously she saves his life after he is stabbed at the university, both featured in the episode "Kin."

Many of Tillich's writings look at what it is to be physically finite in an imperfect world. That "finitude in awareness is anxiety."[6] That very finitude is also vital to the way that we see those shown as saviors in *TLOU*. Vulnerability in heroes is key to their humanity. In "Infected," we see Joel flinch as Tess steps towards him, having just informed him that she has been bitten. Showrunner Craig Mazin was clear that to keep the show grounded and real, viewers had to see Joel being afraid, for if we see heroism "on screen in the absence of vulnerability then you begin to become unmoored from reality."[7]

But salvation is about more than just physical safety in the face of vulnerability. Marsh reflects at length on the nature of salvation[8] as potentially encompassing "ultimate well-being," forgiveness, happiness, contentment, and acceptance. In Christian theology, salvation is set out as Jesus offering "propitiation for our sins, and not for ours only, but for the sins of the whole world" (1 John 4.10 and 2.2). For Tillich "sin" is about estrangement—from self, from others, and from God, who he sees as "the Ground of all Being."[9] More than that, Tillich sees sin as "the element of personal responsibility in one's estrangement" and "the personal act of turning away from that to which one belongs."[10] We see this turning away, this hardening of heart to others, at the start of *TLOU* from Joel and from Bill. After losing his daughter Sarah, Joel dumps a child's body in "When You're Lost in the Darkness," detached, seemingly devoid of feeling, perhaps even devoid of humanity. In "Long, Long Time," while it is hard not to enjoy the sight of gun-toting Bill creating his isolationist compound, as he cooks ornate meals and enjoys his red wine, he is always alone. Everything about his life is designed explicitly to keep other people out.

Yet just as Joel physically saves Ellie, and Bill physically saves Frank, so we see how the power of love can break through these saviors' hardened exteriors and gradually remove their separation and estrangement, enabling them to build new relationships. Ellie's innocent enthusiasm and even wise-cracking puns come to bring Joel joy, and a reason to keep going; Bill tells Frank, "I am old, I'm satisfied, and you were my purpose." Tillich observes that "love overcomes separation and creates participation"[11] and Joel and Bill do connect, and participate, with their love for one another restoring them to a community and a connection with the wider world in a new way. Joel and Bill's isolationism is tempered by Frank and Ellie's desire to love and to share with others. Joel tries to protect Ellie from further loss of innocence, when in "Long, Long Time" he tried to prevent her from seeing an open mass grave on the road. Even at this early stage in their relationship, where she is still supposedly "cargo," saving her is about more than physically protecting her from bullets, knives, and infected.

For Tillich, the fallenness from which humanity needs saving is filled with this anxiety, estrangement, and fear of meaninglessness together with the threat of non-being. Anxiety in particular was a key feature of Tillich's writings. In *The Courage to Be*, he sets out three kinds of anxiety: first, the anxiety of fear and death; second, the anxiety of meaninglessness and not having purpose; and finally, the anxiety of guilt. As characters are brought back from estrangement and alienation and regain their sense of purpose, so the anxiety about fear and death duly returns. In "Long, Long Time," Bill admits to Frank "I was never afraid until you came along." Bill is afraid he is going to let Frank down, to fail to save him. For Joel, when his relationship with Ellie moves from being one of cargo to being paternal, alongside those feelings we see him beginning to suffer from panic attacks ("Kin"). He is terrified Ellie is going to die and it will be his fault. Tillich describes these feelings beautifully, writing how "anxiety grasps us whenever we feel the limits of our strength, our lack of efficiency . . . the danger of failure . . . the anxiety about losing them, about having hurt them, about having let them down, creeps into our hearts."[12]

SAVED TO BRING HOPE—OR TO LIVE IN COMMUNITY?

Clive Marsh observes when presenting his salvation framework that what we are saved *for* in this life has been underplayed in the Christian tradition in favor of a focus on the next world[13]—something more pertinent to the future than the present. He suggests that we are saved for a life of flourishing in this life, in addition to the next. For fulfillment or flourishing to happen, health, safety, and shelter would be expected to be present, and Jesus himself was aware of humanity's material needs, providing loaves and fishes for his followers while on this earth, in a practical act of love.

As Joel saves Ellie during their time together, she is being saved physically to be allowed to continue their journey towards the Firefly hospital. The expectation, that the viewer is encouraged to share, is that she will indeed be able to herself be a savior, not just of Joel, but of the world. Her immunity is humanity's last hope against the fungus. She starts off seemingly fairly dismissive of this, but as she grows to love Sam, we see her move from almost idly wondering if she will provide a solution, to almost praying that she can offer hope and healing to her new friend. When she had no one left to care for, she also had no purpose. With someone to look after in Sam, to try to protect herself, she too puts her hope in her own blood. Sadly, we see it isn't enough this time. But it shows us that she is beginning to have hope in her own purpose. As her relationship with Joel develops, we see a father-daughter bond mature, bringing a daily engagement from a parent figure that she has not had previously. When the pair finally reach Jackson, Wyoming, we see her wide-eyed surprise and joy at finding a community that "actually fucking works." Jackson appears to be a functioning democracy, men and women working side by side, with enough for everyone to not only survive but engage with culture; there is even a movie theater, which is showing *The Goodbye Girl*, itself a film looking at a man defined by his past failures and a woman who has been abandoned multiple times. Tillich describes how "hope never dies, because it is the application of the venturing 'in spite of' to the tragedy of historical action."[14] Dare we hope that Ellie could be saved to be a part of this new creation, this community, after offering hope for salvation for humanity through her immunity?

Both Ellie and Tess want the pain and trauma they have suffered to mean something—to have contributed in some way to the world's salvation, and thus perhaps their own redemption. When Joel offers Ellie a way to escape whatever is ahead in "Look for the Light," she responds that "after everything I've done, it can't be for nothing." In Tess's final moments, just before her whispered words described at the start of this chapter, she implores Joel to help make a better future for those who will come after them—to create something for others to be saved into, saying: "this is your chance. You get her there. You keep her alive, and you set everything right. All the shit we did." There is a desire from both Ellie and Tess to have the future look different from the past. Tillich describes this acknowledgment as repentance clarifying that "we are not inescapably victims of our past. We can make the past remain nothing but *past*."[15]

As Joel saves Ellie moment by moment, so she slowly brings him back from the dark place of grief he has been in for the twenty years since his daughter Sarah died in his arms. She gives him purpose and meaning again, which he states implicitly in "Look for the Light" when he tells her about his suicide attempt after Sarah's passing, but now the pain is healing and "it wasn't time that did it." She has idolized him for so long, but never realized she might be saving him in return. He needs to have a purpose, to have meaning to his life—this is what he needs to be saved to, saved for—to be brought out of what Tillich calls the "dark valley of a meaningless and empty life."[16]

TLOU is also a show that unpacks purpose, considering what characters are surviving for—to save, or to be saved? In "Long, Long Time," Bill's letter to Joel spells this out plainly for Joel, Ellie, and the viewer as he explains his life's purpose—"There was one person worth saving. That's what I did. I saved him. Then I protected him, that's why men like you and I are here, we have a job to do." Even for apocalypse-prepper Bill, who thought he was ready for a life alone, another person was needed to give his life fulfillment. This desire for meaning was something that for Tillich would be fulfilled in what he called the New Being, which would bring self-acceptance and "a centre, a direction, a meaning for life."[17]

SAVED BY SACRIFICE

Salvation is so key to the show that the soundtrack from Gustavo Santaolalla and David Fleming even features a track called "Salvation." For Christians, salvation comes from God, especially through the sacrificial death of Jesus of Nazareth, who Christians worship as God Incarnate. Tillich held that Christ, as "the New Being," overcame the existential estrangement he descibed, and was able to challenge the anxiety and fear that accompanied our awareness of our own finite being. Like his reflections on separation, and on types of anxiety, Tillich saw the effects of salvation as having three parts. First, participation was needed—"the saving power of the New Being in Jesus as the Christ is dependent on man's participation in it."[18] Second, acceptance was required—faith provided the ability to receive the message that one had been accepted. Third, there would be sanctification, transforming an individual or even community. Tillich was clear that it was having "the courage to face one's own guilt" that would lead to salvation.[19] Courage certainly isn't lacking in many of the characters' sacrifices as they save those they love—whether this then contributes to their own salvation is more debatable.

Of course, not everyone can be saved. Tess sacrifices herself, having been infected, to an end both unpleasant and yet intimate enough for it to be nominated for an MTV Movie Award in the category of Best Kiss. Firm from the start in her belief that Ellie had a greater purpose, her last words encourage Joel to "save who you can save." While he could not save Tess any more than he could have saved Sarah twenty years ago, he could save Ellie, and through that perhaps give hope to the world.

In *TLOU*, characters are frequently saved by actions motived by love. Much of the show is an exploration of what parents or parent figures will do to protect their children as a result of that unconditional love, and the morals and ethics around this. Why is one child more worth saving, or worth sacrificing, than any other, even if they are yours? *TLOU* writer and director Craig Mazin noted that when looking at any intractable conflict, "at some point you're gonna find somebody doing something because of love. That love manifests as fear, hatred, xenophobia, racism, religious superiority."[20] We think of love as a positive and beautiful thing, but here we see that unconditional parental love takes characters to a primal place that can lead to intense fear and extreme behavior.

That kind of love comes at a cost. Joel violently murders man after man (and woman!) in "Look for the Light" to save Ellie from a fatal brain operation. We see his face set, as if in a dissociative state. He is like a killing machine. Joel physically saves Ellie from surgery, but at what cost? Could anyone be deserving of this manner of saving and sacrifice? Equally, can it ever be right to take someone's life as a sacrifice without their consent? As an innocent child (if that is how one sees Ellie) she is arguably not able to give true informed consent even if she wanted to. From a utilitarian perspective, the impact of her death leading to a cure cannot be underestimated—it could itself save society and secure the future of humanity. Marlene is ready to break promises made to her lifelong friend, Anna (Ellie's mother), in sacrificing Ellie for what she sees as the greater good of saving more people. Is Joel saving Ellie or being selfish in his attempts to prevent her sacrificing herself? There is an ambiguity to what is right or just here. Neil Druckmann, co-creator of *TLOU* video games and the show, has said when they were testing the game, parents almost 100 percent of the time said that Joel "did exactly what he was supposed to do" while much of the time those who didn't have children said he was a monster.[21] Either way, Ellie is saved by Joel's love, and his willingness to sacrifice other people for her.

Parental love is seen resulting in extreme actions repeatedly in that final episode. When Anna is bitten in the final stage of labor, she begs Marlene to kill her to ensure Ellie's safety. But she also risks Marlene and her companion's life by lying to them about when Ellie was bitten. Whatever it takes to save her child is a price worth paying.

Emotionally, Joel has been saved by Ellie, and as mentioned above, he indicates that she brought him to more of a place of healing and wholeness after his daughter's death. But by this point, in saving her physically from surgery, he has had to lie to her about what transpired. Her face and reactions tell us she knows he is lying. She has been rescued, but their relationship may be the other sacrifice that Joel must make in order to keep her alive. Like the lyrics of the moving Linda Ronstadt song that we hear twice in "Long, Long Time": "You warned me of the price I'd have to pay . . . and life's full of loss, who knows the cost."

TLOU's narrative makes it very clear that there is a price to pay for love, and a cost attached to saving people. There is even a cost to saving yourself. To defend herself from David, Ellie kills him in a manner so brutal that when she staggers out into the snow it is clear that without Joel reappearing to support her, she might not have mentally survived the trauma, whatever her physical state. And whatever was left of her innocence, much of it has surely now gone.

Tillich's concept of "dreaming innocence,"[22] unpacked in his *Systematic Theology II*, is one of essential being, of potential. Innocence, then is not purely something that others destroy, but something that can be lost as we become more aware of the world around us and its temptations. For Tillich, the word *innocence* had three connotations; "lack of actual experience, lack of personal responsibility, and lack of moral guilt."[23] As Ellie staggers away from her final encounter with David, the weight of what she has done—the experience of what she has done, her personal responsibility and potentially guilt—together with her physical wounds and the shock of it all, combine to remind the viewer of the cost of self-preservation.

SAVED INTO ACCEPTANCE

Finally, we turn to consider what is it that those who receive salvation are saved into. In being saved from separation and alienation, to different kinds of hope and community, it could be argued that they are saved into relationship. We see characters move from isolation and independence into connection with other people, and shift from initial tentative, hostile connections to caring for others. Other people, initially a source of fear and mistrust, become not only the channel for this change, but the intense connection that they will be saved into. The relationships that are formed are not only restorative but redeeming. Joel's relationship with Ellie grows to become paternal, helping to heal his past hurt and grief, and giving him something to fight for and believe in again. After preparing for a life alone, Bill is unexpectedly brought into a life of love and joy through his relationship with Frank and has a clear purpose again as Frank's protector. Survival might be possible alone in *TLOU*, but salvation is experienced through relationships, through community.

Christian belief is that Christ and his death enable his followers to be a special part of the Kingdom of God—both in the next life, and in building that Kingdom on earth, in particular through the church. Marsh notes that salvation can be found in a range of communities that enable human flourishing as "the salvific communities in which we found ourselves do not all become 'churches.'"[24] In *TLOU* the faith community depicted instead offers a sickening perversion of such a community, run by an abusive narcissist, who quotes Scripture, and insists his followers "need God, they need heaven, they need a Father" even while forcing them to become unwitting cannibals.

David may initially appear to be a savior, leading his community, but there is no acceptance of others' needs here, no real relationship or love. He has contempt for those around him. He even sees cordyceps as fruitful, providing salvation for its own kind as "it multiplies. It feeds and protects its children. And it secures its future with violence, if it must." His acceptance of cordyceps needing to secure its future with violence mirrors his own approach to "saving" his followers, but more importantly, saving himself and his power.

As mentioned earlier, for Tillich salvation includes first participation, then acceptance and then transformation. We experience this through grace, which Tillich wrote powerfully about in his sermon "You Are Accepted": "Simply accept the fact that you are accepted! If that happens to us, we experience grace. After such an experience we may not be better than before, and we may not believe more than before. But everything is transformed."[25] As they grow to love and care for one another, we see Joel and Ellie, and Bill and Frank, accept that they are accepted. They did not ask for those relationships, nor expect them, nor even initially welcome the arrival of Ellie and Frank into their lives. But they have come to love them, they have accepted that they are accepted, and been transformed as a result. As Tillich notes, through salvation "one accepts one's self as something which is eternally important, eternally loved, eternally accepted. The disgust at one's self, the hatred of one's self has disappeared."[26] Any negative or anxious feelings Bill may have had about his sexuality are dispelled by Frank's love; Joel is able to heal, perhaps even to start to forgive himself for Sarah's death, through the presence of Ellie in his life.

Culturally today, we can see that self-forgiveness and self-acceptance are often seen as a key part of secular "salvation" when the phrase is used. Self-love, previously seen as somewhat of a moral failure of selfishness or vanity, is now perceived more as something necessary in the modern Western world. In 1978, the German-American poet Charles Bukowski wrote: "If you have the ability to love, love yourself first."[27] More recently we have Meghan Markle writing an open letter to herself and her fans in 2014, declaring, "You need to know that you're enough."[28] The Beatles may have sung that all you need is love, but John Lennon reportedly also said: "We need to learn to love ourselves first, in all our glory and our imperfections. If we cannot love ourselves, we cannot fully open to our ability to love others."[29] Without the grace that Tillich describes coming to us like a wave of light breaking into our darkness, it is perhaps unsurprising that anxiety about not being enough persists so much in our world today.

Just as our world is broken, so we are clearly shown how broken the world that Joel and Ellie inhabit during *TLOU*'s closing episode. Marlene reminds Joel that even if he physically saves Ellie in the immediate future, he is saving her into a broken world, one where it won't be long until she is torn apart by infected or murdered by raiders. Without the hope of Ellie sacrificing herself to help the fight against cordyceps, the battle for humanity to survive will remain. She, and everyone else, will face a battle just to exist, much less to thrive, or be fulfilled or happy. In physically preventing Ellie's death, Marlene implies that Joel is preventing the salvation of everyone else.

TLOU is a broken world, overrun with infected. And yet, we also see clues that this world also contains great and subtle beauty. Humanity is broken, but nature has flourished and is reclaiming what people have had to leave behind. As Joel and Ellie make their way through an abandoned bus depot, they see a wild giraffe. The camera shifts and a wider shot shows us that many giraffes have made their home in what was once a city baseball field. With humanity forced to retreat, the wildlife, and nature itself, have reclaimed the urban landscape for itself. The humans are so busy fighting each other, destroying their own with inhuman violence, that the natural world has been able to start a process of restoration to what once might have been. It's a beautiful moment, and a beautiful sight, and it's a theme we see throughout *TLOU*. On the show's official podcast, Neil Druckmann describes how, in this moment with the giraffes, when Joel cannot pull Ellie back to the light after her trauma; after she escapes David and his followers, she remains distant and disengaged from him. His efforts to jolly her along achieve little. Just when the viewer fears hope might be lost, it is the magic of nature, as she sees the giraffes in Salt Lake City, that brings her back to a child-like wonder and joy, and enables Joel and Ellie to connect again as they start talking about the animals but transition to a much deeper conversation. In Salt Lake City, like so much of the show, we see "nature reclaiming its domain."[30] The natural world has been saved, liberated from humanity's once crushing dominion over it.

Back in the 1950s, Tillich observed that "nature has lost its religious meaning and is excluded from participation in the power of salvation,"[31] highlighting a contrast to the over-riding anthropocentric theology of his day, although today climate justice is increasingly an area of theological reflection. "Cli-Fi" is an abbreviation now sometimes used for "climate-fiction," a term used to describe media that shows climate change through a science-fiction lens,[32] often attempting to warn viewers to heed the warning scientists offer. Has the anxiety about our finite nature that Tillich described now become climate-anxiety[33] as young people in particular grow up learning that the whole world itself is so clearly finite?

The opening credits of *TLOU* show us a pattern of fungi spreading across the screen—beautiful and a part of nature, but in this show, something so natural can also be deadly. *TLOU* poses the question, can the natural world and humanity co-exist in such a way that both can be truly saved, or can one only thrive at the cost of the other?

CONCLUSION

This chapter has used Clive Marsh's framework, alongside the theology of Paul Tillich, to explore what those in *TLOU* are saved from, saved for, saved by, and finally saved into. Characters are saved not only from physical threat, but from the estrangement and separation that Tillich describes so well, of alienation from others. In particular, the anxiety described by Tillich powerfully echoes the feelings shown by Joel as he grows to love Ellie but struggles to accept his feelings. Characters are saved to fulfill their purpose, which is to care for and love another, whether as part of a father/daughter relationship, a romantic partnership, or a fully functioning community (complete with streetlights and a bar!). Ellie, in particular, appears to be saved to be a hope for humanity, until the final episode at least, when the moving depiction of nature provokes ponderings that human domination may not be the only way after all.

The characters we see are saved by love, or at least by actions motivated by love, often but not exclusively by a terrifying unconditional parental love. Salvation is shown as coming at a cost, and often a heavy price must be paid, and those saved are often saved through some sort of sacrifice. This might be characters becoming vulnerable, opening their hearts, or hardening their hearts to enable them to commit terrible acts of violence to protect those they love. The salvation they come into fits with what Tillich described as to "simply accept the fact that you are accepted." Characters come to accept themselves, to be able to accept and connect with others through relationships. They are saved into community, albeit community in the midst of a broken world. To humanity at least this is a broken world, but it is also a world where nature is being restored to something of its former glory. Must saving one always be at the expense of others?

As viewers, watching all this on the edge of our sofas, what are we saved into through our experience of *TLOU*? Reflecting on the power and potential for violence that lives within love, are we saved from seeing the world in black and white? The show has provoked fierce debate online about Joel's actions in "Look for the Light" in particular. In watching *TLOU* and its two very different protagonists, we are surely drawn to an acceptance of our own moral ambiguity. Salvation comes through a love that saves, but it is clear also that love can also bring about destructive behavior and violence. Is it really love that brings about such hatred, or are such strong negative feelings a warping of what real love ought to be, into abuse? What is the kind of love that makes people human, and what kind of love makes us inhuman? Which sacrifices are selfish, and which are worth it to save others? In a post-apocalyptic world, moral standards might look different to the ones we are accustomed to, but surely there should still be some sort of ethical framework—a moral map to help chart a course when faced with even the most challenging choices. Yet by the end of *TLOU* we see Joel directed only by his desire to keep Ellie safe. Is this desire to save her genuinely for her benefit, or for his own, because he cannot bear to lose her?

From watching Joel with a dying Sarah in his arms in a paternal pieta in the first episode, to carrying an unconscious Ellie away from the hospital they had fought so hard to reach by the final episode, the viewer is left unclear if this is the end of their relationship or a new beginning. We are left wondering—although players of the game have of course had a preview of what is to come!—if salvation in *TLOU* is about acceptance and relationship, then the close of the first season leaves us wondering what price is worth paying for another person's salvation—and if this will include the very relationship that brought about your own. Tillich argued that "all creatures long for an unambiguous fulfilment of their essential possibilities,"[34] and yet *TLOU* leaves us with both ambiguity and possibility. Ellie lives still, Joel loves again, and a functioning community in Jackson awaits their imminent return. But Joel has broken trust, Ellie knows it, and that community sits in a broken world where Marlene's prophecy will surely come to pass. In the end, each of us must choose to save who we can save in the contexts we are in—and accept the ambiguity inherent in having to make that choice.

NOTES

1. Thompson, *Through Mud and Barbed Wire*, 59.
2. Tillich, *On the Boundary*, 53.
3. Tillich, *The Courage to Be*, 35.
4. Tillich, *Systematic Theology I*, 212.
5. Marsh, *A Cultural Theology of Salvation*, 230.
6. Tillich, *Systematic Theology I*, 212.
7. "The Last of Us Podcast, Episode 2."
8. Marsh, *A Cultural Theology of Salvation*, 219.
9. Tillich, *The Shaking of the Foundations*, 46.
10. Tillich, *Systematic Theology II*, 46.

11. Tillich, *The New Being*, 70.
12. Tillich, *The New Being*, 62.
13. Marsh, *A Cultural Theology of Salvation*, 216.
14. Tillich, *The Protestant Era*, 119.
15. Tillich, *The Eternal Now*, 108.
16. "You Are Accepted (Paul Tillich's Famous Sermon)."
17. Tillich, *The New Being*, 12.
18. Tillich, *Systematic Theology II*, 176.
19. Tillich, *The Courage to Be*, 16.
20. "The Last of Us Podcast, Episode 1."
21. "Exit Interview—We Have to Interrogate How We Feel about Our Heroes."
22. Tillich, *Systematic Theology II*, 33.
23. Tillich, *Systematic Theology II (in Theologian of the Boundaries)*, 193.
24. Marsh, *A Cultural Theology of Salvation*, 217.
25. "Exit Interview—We Have to Interrogate How We Feel about Our Heros."
26. Tillich, *The New Being,* 12.
27. "Charles Bukowski Quotes."
28. "Meghan Markle Said She Was 'Complete with or without a Partner' in an Open Letter to Herself from 2014."
29. "The 10 Deepest Thoughts John Lennon Shared about Love, Life, and Happiness."
30. "The Last of Us Podcast, Episode 9."
31. Tillich, *The Protestant Era*, 80.
32. "What 'The Last of Us,' 'Snowpiercer' and 'Climate Fiction' Get Wrong."
33. "Climate Anxiety: How to Turn Your Worries into Action."
34. Tillich, *Systematic Theology III*, 107.

BIBLIOGRAPHY

"The 10 Deepest Thoughts John Lennon Shared about Love, Life, and Happiness." Goalcast.com, https://www.goalcast.com/john-lennon-thoughts-sayings-love-life-happiness/.

"Charles Bukowski Quotes." GoodReads.com, https://www.goodreads.com/quotes/6946540-if-you-have-the-ability-to-love-love-yourself-first.

"Climate Anxiety: How to Turn Your Worries into Action." BBC Bitesize, https://www.bbc.co.uk/bitesize/articles/zhd94xs.

"Exit Interview—We Have to Interrogate How We Feel about Our Heroes." Vulture.com, https://www.vulture.com/article/last-of-us-craig-mazin-season-finale-ending-interview.html.

"The Last of Us Podcast, Episode 1. When You're Lost in the Darkness." HBO, https://podcasts.apple.com/us/podcast/episode-1-when-youre-lost-in-the-darkness/id1660320068?i=1000594548838.

"The Last of Us Podcast, Episode 2. Infected." HBO, https://podcasts.apple.com/us/podcast/episode-2-infected/id1660320068?i=1000595989756.

"The Last of Us Podcast, Episode 9. Look for the Light." HBO, https://podcasts.apple.com/us/podcast/episode-9-look-for-the-light/id1660320068?i=1000603849713.

Marsh, Clive. *A Cultural Theology of Salvation*. Oxford, UK: Oxford University Press, 2018.

"Meghan Markle Said She Was 'Complete with or without a Partner' in an Open Letter to Herself from 2014." Insider.com, https://www.insider.com/meghan-markle-birthday-letter-happy-without-partner-feminism-2018-8.

Thompson, Mel. *Through Mud and Barbed Wire*. Amazon Digital Services 2017. [Ebook.]

Tillich, Paul. *Systematic Theology I*. London: Nisbet, 1953.

———. *The New Being*. New York. Charles Scribner & Sons, 1955, https://www.holybooks.com/wp-content/uploads/The-New-Being-by-Paul-Tillich.pdf.

———. *The Eternal Now*. New York: Scribner, 1963.

———. *On the Boundary*. London: Collins, 1967.

———. "The Protestant Era." In *The Essential Tillich: An Anthology of the Writings of Paul Tillich*, edited by F. Forrestor Church (pp. 69–86, 112–119). New York: Collier Books, 1987.

———. "Systematic Theology II," in *Paul Tillich, Theologian of the Boundaries*, edited by Mark Kline Taylor (pp. 190–198). London: Collins, 1987.

———. *The Courage to Be*. New Haven and London: Yale University Press, 2000. [Kindle Edition].

———. *Systematic Theology III*. Chicago: University of Chicago Press, 2011.

———. *The Shaking of the Foundations*. Eugene, OR: Wipf and Stock, 2012.

———. *Systematic Theology II*. Chicago, University of Chicago Press, 2013.

"What 'The Last of Us,' 'Snowpiercer' and 'Climate Fiction' Get Wrong." BBC Culture, https://www.bbc.com/culture/article/20230418-what-snowpiercer-and-climate-fiction-get-wrong.

"You Are Accepted (Paul Tillich's Famous Sermon)." *Cave and the Cross* blog, http://www.areopagus.co.uk/2012/05/you-are-accepted-paul-tillichs-famous.html.

Chapter 14

Conclusion: "Too Much Faith in Humanity?"

Peter Admirand

THE LAST OF US WITHIN US

In the famous "Grand Inquisitor" section in *The Brothers Karamazov*,[1] Jesus appears in sixteenth-century Spain only to be arrested by Church authorities for being too dangerous. The various inquisitions, especially in Spain, Malta, and Portugal, were not only about Church power but also occluded by latent anti-Jewish and anti-Muslim sentiments.[2] In Dostoevsky's novel, though, the charge against Jesus is that he has too much faith in human beings, who the Grand Inquisitor claims, cannot handle the freedom and high expectation of living morally (which also sounds like something David of Silver Lake would say). "Better that you enslave us, but feed us."[3] The Grand Inquisitor thought demanding more from people does them an injustice.[4] Jesus' revolutionary talk, therefore, had to be suppressed. While the context of a Russian Orthodox writer imagining the Catholic Church arresting Jesus is not the most ecumenical of stories, it still highlights our glaring moral failure and misuse of responsibility.

While we often are ready to fight and even die for our freedom (think of the Fireflies or the WLF), once gained or born into freedom, we often squander and adulterate it. Moral freedom especially can seem onerous as the desire to try to do the right thing is not only complicated by competing interests and contexts but can also be very confusing to adjudicate. We can argue until the next outbreak day,[5] for example, on whether Joel should have saved Ellie or let her be operated on, let alone how to alleviate poverty, the most compassionate policy to help refugees, or how best to respond to another country's descent into civil war or genocide. Too often, it can seem easier to do nothing or just obey what someone tells us to do, as Erich Fromm famously wrote in *Escape from Freedom*.[6]

In *The Last of Us* (*TLOU*), any evaluation of a character's ethical compass should consider the post-apocalyptic context. We must not forget, though, that many memoirs and testimony during the Shoah, the Rwandan genocide, the state-orchestrated famine in China, or the Russian-induced famine in Ukraine in the 1930s[7] still decried examples of those who betrayed or injured others and praised and celebrated those who maintained their moral dignity and worked to help others no matter the risk.[8] Of course, systemic attempts to destroy people's bodies and souls through food and sleep deprivation, forced migration, torture, concentration camps, and all the other evils that humans have devised can destroy the will of most people. And true accountability and moral blame rest with the perpetrators and especially those who devise and implement the systemic violations.[9] Those left to survive such degradation are mired in what Lawrence Langer termed "choiceless choices." Others, pushed to the limit of near-death, have been described famously by Primo Levi, Agamben, and others as death-in-life or similar terms.[10] Some of those enduring the hellish famine in Leningrad, for example, especially in the winter of 1941–1942, were called "dystrophics . . . emaciated in the extreme, on the verge of physical and spiritual disintegration, and ceasing to appear fully human."[11] Only thinking and dreaming about food, mothers could snatch moldy bread from their own children while brothers hoped their sister would die so there was one less person to share bits and crumbs.

While real, such description also seems to describe zombies and the walking dead, or in our contexts, stalkers and runners—but it is too easy to turn these into caricatures and those other than us.[12] If clicker obsession for flesh is substituted for lust for power, then the Rattlers (let alone a Putin or Pol Pot) could be called a type of clicker. Or even more problematically, what if it's not power, sex, or money that are our clicker-like cravings? What if in the name of love of our family or group, we do almost anything, no matter the consequences to others or to the world around us?[13] Can we also here become another kind of clicker? Sadly, what people, religions,[14] and nations have not succumbed to this creed?

In *TLOU* such a moral failure describes Joel as a Hunter or the actions of FEDRA or the Fireflies. Was the Grand Inquisitor right in wanting to imprison Jesus for believing in human beings too much and thinking they can handle freedom responsibly? Or should we take no responsibility like David by saying everything happens for a reason?

Perhaps, and yet, this book is part of a series pairing pop culture with theology. Theology, as the study of God, is ultimately concerned with godtalk, about what is the highest and ultimate good, the *summum bonum*, according to Thomas Aquinas. At its best, godtalk seeks to find, spread, and praise a

Creator who loves and serves all and deploys that love of God toward all living beings and all of creation. *TLOU*, though, is an acutely violent game. We see the breakdown of society, the imprisonment and murder of many innocent people, and a world where the divine is non-existent, or at best hidden and buried. We play as a character who has done unspeakable evils in the name of surviving. We rescue a girl who revels in the thrill of the kill. We murder and have ready replies after doing so. *The Last of Us Part II* (*TLOU2*) is so unrelentingly dark and cruel, it can veer toward the nihilistic, that point where goodness, innocence, and morality have no real anchor—and everyone seems shaded and defamed by shame, vengeance, and selfishness.[15]

And yet, many of the authors here, expressing if not seeking some belief in God or a higher power, scour these very violent games and even claim to see some glint of the presence of God, goodness, light, and those looking for the light.[16] In both games, though, there are few moral exemplars. Main exceptions are Lev and Dina, two characters who have been surrounded by suffering but have still maintained a moral core and essence—and interestingly both have some kind of religious or spiritual identity—Judaism for Dina and Seraphitism for Lev.[17] Dina's faith gives her connection beyond herself linked to her sister and Jewish people; Lev views the world through his Prophet's call for peace and simplicity. Abby and Ellie come to believe in nothing but vengeance yet have (or had) companions that could help them in their journey toward some kind of renewal and repentance. Whether either can achieve any stable peace and redemption remains tenuous and fragile.

And then there is Ish. We never meet him except in notes that Joel can find in the sewers and abandoned houses.[18] Like Joel, Ish also witnessed many atrocities and deprivations. Despite this, he even forms a community and school for the children and families he encountered. Unlike Frank and Bill, who seemed happy with a community of just themselves,[19] Ish sought to save as many as he could. He wanted to give the children some semblance of a normal life—even water guns!—despite life in the sewers where one unlocked door could mean annihilation; which, of course, happened. Their commune and school are "overrun by monsters," with so many devoured—more horrors upon horrors—a father (Kyle) who then had to kill children (and himself) to save them from a worse fate. In his last note, Ish wrote that every "part of my being just wants to give up. It'd be so easy to surrender to this world."

In this book, and in our world, there are also attempts to find or trace some hope, some purpose and meaning. For many, it's rooted in those we love or a life that seeks to make the world better, healthier, more enriching, happier, or safer for others—especially the marginalized. For theists, this search is often enmeshed in or with belief in some higher power and notions of the transcendent. And faith is so essential even if only focused on saving someone or something.[20]

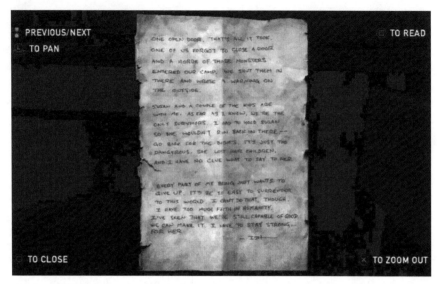

Figure 14.1. Ish Notes, Number 5, from *The Last of Us. In-game screenshot*

Despite the call to renounce everything, Ish continues: "I can't do that, though. I have too much faith in humanity. I've seen that we're still capable of good. We can make it. I have to stay strong for her"[21] (see Figure 14.1). Here Ish signals a hope and call beyond the self; a sign and example that Christ in the Grand Inquisitor story was not amiss and negligent to place his trust in human beings—and that those like David are wrong. Ish still hopes and abides in a higher way.

Again, what about Ellie and Abby, and other characters still alive like Lev, Tommy, and Dina? Will they find meaning and purpose, the possibility for healing and redemption? Or will they be further battered and morally compromised by *TLOU*'s unrelenting, broken world? Whose word will be final: David's or Ish's?

Such, of course, is a vital question, not only for the next *TLOU* game or season, but during our own struggles and searches, not only to look for the light, but to be that light.

NOTES

1. For more on Dostoevsky in this volume, see Goodin's chapter (chapter 3).
2. Schama, *The Story of the Jews*, 403–406.
3. Dostoevsky, *The Brothers Karamazov*, 253.
4. Dostoevsky, *The Brothers Karamazov*, 256.

5. *TLOU* Outbreak Day is September 25. See O'Connor's and Clancy's evaluation of the science behind cordyceps and the likelihood of a *TLOU*-type outbreak in chapter 1.

6. Fromm, *Escape from Freedom*, 139.

7. Systemic U.S. racism against African Americans and Indigenous people should also be added here. See Banks's contribution in chapter 8.

8. See Admirand, *Humbling Faith*, chapter 7.

9. See, especially, Gretton, *I You We Them*.

10. In Shoah memoirs, you come across the (offensive) term *der Muselmann* for those who were deemed to have submitted to their fate and given up living. Levi writes of them as the "drowned . . . non-men who march and labour in silence, the divine spark dead within them, already too empty to really suffer" (Levi, *Survival in Auschwitz*, 90). See also Agamben, *Remnants of Auschwitz*, 41–86. For a call to decenter this trope by looking at female inmates, see Oster, "The Female Muselmann." Also note that camp slang then is obviously offensive, especially to those who profess Islam as their religion and way of life.

11. See Yarov, *Morality Under Siege*, 241.

12. See especially Price's contribution in this volume (chapter 6).

13. The ravages of climate change from our poor choices are discussed, for example, by Tang in chapter 11, while nature's ability to regenerate (after humanity's fall) is noted by Chapman in chapter 13.

14. See Cameron's chapter for his account of Religious Trauma Syndrome as exemplified by "Pastor" David in the HBO version (chapter 4).

15. See especially Green's analysis of Abby's and Ellie's paralleled hospital missions (chapter 2).

16. See Bargár's chapter (10) and Millsap's and Spellman's (12).

17. See Rupčić's chapter on the Seraphites for context and background (5).

18. I discuss Ish a bit in my chapter on fathers in *TLOU* (9).

19. Discussed by Banfi in chapter 7, among others in this volume.

20. See MacFarquhar, *Strangers Drowning*.

21. The "her" is Susan whose only children were killed in the sewers.

BIBLIOGRAPHY

Admirand, Peter. *Humbling Faith: Brokenness, Doubt, Dialogue—What Unites Atheists, Theists, and Nontheists*. Eugene, OR: Cascade Books, 2019.

Agamben, Giorgio. *Remnants of Auschwitz: The Witness and the Archive*. Translated by Daniel Heller-Roazen. London: Zone Books, 2008.

Dostoevsky, Fyodor. *The Brothers Karamazov*. Translated by Richard Pevear and Larissa Volokhonsky. London: Vintage, 2004.

Fromm, Erich H. *Escape from Freedom*. New York: Owl Book, 1969.

Gretton, Dan. *I You We Them. Journeys beyond Evil: The Desk Killers in History and Today*. London: William Heinemann, 2019.

Levi, Primo. *Survival in Auschwitz*. CreateSpace, 2013.

MacFarquhar, Larissa. *Strangers Drowning: Voyages to the Brink of Moral Extremity*. London: Allen Lane, 2015.
Oster, Sharon B. "The Female Muselmann in Nazi Concentration Camp Discourse." *Journal of Holocaust Research* 34.3 (2020): 198–219, https://doi.org/10.1080/25785648.2020.1779502.
Schama, Simon. *The Story of the Jews: Finding the Words 1000 BCE–1492CE*. London: Vintage Books, 2014.
Yarov, Sergey. *Leningrad, 1941–1942: Morality under Siege*. Translated by Arch Tait. London: Polity Press, 2017.

Index

Page references for figures are italicized. Characters from TLOU have been sorted under their first names, e.g., Joel Miller.

1 Corinthians, 160
2 Corinthians, 166
1 John, 156, 186, 195
1 Peter, 186
1 Samuel, 104

Abby Anderson: dreams, 42; and Ellie, 29, 36–37, 39, 43–44, 145; Lakehill Seattle Hospital visit, 17–18, 19, 20–22, 28–29; murder of Joel, 18, 25, 27, 35–36; and Nora, 17, 18, 21, 24, 25–26, 27; player embodying, 17–18, 28, 36, 65–66; and Rat King, 22–23, 26; redemption of personality, 17, 18, 20–21, 23, 28, 33, 36, 75; vengefulness, 17, 18, 20, 23, 25, 35–36, 141; and WLF, 18, 21, 23; and Yara/Lev, 18, 20–21, 23, 29, 33, 36–37, 42, 68–69, 75
Abby–Jerry relationship: Abby's name for Jerry, 143; Abby's response to Jerry's death, 17, 18, 20, 25; Jerry appearing in Abby's dream, 42; Jerry's love for Abby, 145, 146n24. *See also* Abby Anderson; "Jerry" (Gerald) Anderson
abjection, 75
Adam and Eve, 97, 99–100, 101, 104, 108n32. *See also* Eden; the Fall; original sin
afterlife, 186–87
Agamben, Giorgio, 208
agápē, 33, 35, 40, 44
agency, players,' xiv, 26–27, 142, 191n12
agriculture, 100. *See also* crops
airborne fungal spores, 5–6, 7, 10–11, 12–13
Alec (murdered Silver Lake father), 49, 58, 152–153
Althaus-Reid, Marcella, 104, 162n31
altruism, 42, 44, 45
Ambrose (Saint), 104
anarcho-primitivism, 69
"angel of history" (Boym), 19
animals: ants, 6–7, 8; Dostoevsky on, 39–40; ethical responsibility toward, 41; giraffes, xiii, 158, 191n12, 202; zebras, 39, 41, 141–142
Anna Williams (Ellie's mother), 199
annihilation, 121–122, 128n51
ants, 6–7, 8

anxiety: Bill, 91, 194, 196; and finitude, 195, 202–203; Joel, 203; Tillich on, 195, 196, 198
apocalyptic genre, 65, 66–67, 74, 167. *See also* dystopia; eschatology; pandemics; post-apocalyptic genre; zombies
Aquarium, Seattle Waterfront, 18
Aquinas. *See* Thomas Aquinas
Arbery, Ahmaud, 111, 126
arcade games, 183, 190n7
Aspergillus fumigatus, 9
Atwood, Margaret, *Oryx and Crake*, 67
authoritarianism, 56
authority, charismatic, 73, 76

Bainbridge, William, 66, 70–71
beauty, 189, 191n12, 202
Bernauer, James, 104, 108n32
Bible: David's misuse of, 49–50, 51, 58; gay relationships in, 97, 104, 106n1; inspiring characters' names, 102; on marriage, 103–105; racist use of, 111. *See also specific Bible books, e.g., Matthew*
Bill: compared to Adam, 100, 101, 103; home, 91, 188; isolation, 90–93, 195–196; and Joel, 91, 98, 101, 102; purpose, 198, 200; sexuality, 101, 107n12, 201; suicide, 92–93, 102–103, 159–160; vulnerability, 91, 194, 196; as "white self-sufficient man," 159. *See also* Bill–Frank relationship
Bill–Frank relationship: character arcs, 105–106; community of two, 92, 93–94, 209; game vs. series versions, 97–99, 101, 105–106; interdependence, 159–160; marriage, 103, 105; mirroring creation story, 97, 99–103, 105–106; relationship, as productive union, 97, 100; saving each other, 92, 94, 200, 201, 203. *See also* Bill; Frank
BlackLivesMatter, 111–12
Blackness, 113, 115–116, 118–119, 123

Black Panther Party for Self Defense, 120, 126, 128n51
Black people: education, 116; protests, 111–112, 123; violence against, 111, 112, 113, 114–120, 123–127
Bonhoeffer, Dietrich, 89–92
Booker, Keith, 53
Bosch, Hieronymus, *Hell*, 132, *136*
Boym, Svetlana, 19
Brenner, Marie, 19
Brettler, Marc, 100
Brock, Rita Nakashima, 157, 160
The Brothers Karamazov (Dostoevsky), 37, 45–46n1, 46n10, 207, 208, 210
Buber, Martin, 84
Bukowski, Charles, 201

Cahill, Lisa Sowle, 121–122
Candida auris, 4, 9
cannibalism, 90, 140, 152
capitalism, 69, 116, 157, 173
Carden, Michael, 100
Carmichael, Stokely, 117–118, 119, 120, 127
Catholic priests, 106n1
charismatic authority, 73, 76
charity, 38–39
Cheng, Patrick S., 104
cherubim, 101, 107n14
children: Black, education of, 116; in *The Dream of a Ridiculous Man*, 42–43; killing of, 40–41; mercy killing of, 139, 141, 209; and religious trauma syndrome (RTS), 56, 57; saving of, 142–143, 199; suffering, 132–134, *133*, *134*
Christensen, Kit R., 27
Christianity: abuse in, 58–59; church-state separation, 52, 103; and community, 89–90, 92; Hollywood bias against, perceived, 50, 51; and racism, 124; on relations, 89; relevance of, in post-apocalyptic world, 33, 44–45; rhetoric, misuse of, 50, 57–59; and same-sex marriage,

103; temporal finality, 169. *See also* the Bible; churches; Jesus Christ; religious trauma syndrome (RTS); salvation

churches, 154–155, 187–188, 191nn12–13, 200–201

cinema, 197

civilization: and anarcho-primitivism, 69; of Bill and Frank, 92, 93–94, 209; vs. brutality, 44; crises in, 34, 40. *See also* community; Jackson, Wyoming; relations; Silver Lake (community)

civil rights movement, 111–112. *See also* BlackLivesMatter; protests

Claeys, Gregory, 52

clickers. *See* zombies

climate change, 4, 9–10, 71–72, 172, 202

Colombo, Agustín, 104

coloniality, 153, 167, 169

comic books, 114, 144, 190n8

communication, 88–89, 99, 182

community: Bill and Frank's, 92, 93–94, 209; Bonhoeffer on, 89–90; Christian, 89–90, 92; forming of, 90; Ish's, 141, 209; loss of, in *TLOU*, 18–19, 35; and solitude, 90–91; vs. tribalism, 157. *See also* relations; Silver Lake (community)

compassion: Abby, 20, 33; Ellie, 33; and Jesus, 137, 154; Joel, 33; Schweitzer on, 41; and soullessness, 115–116; Yara and Lev, xvii

confessions, 107n12

Constitution, U.S., 103

conversion, 58, 153

cordyceps fungi: communication by, 88–89; David on, 54, 153, 157, 201; evilness of, 54; game vs. series versions, 3–6, 8, 10, 11–12; inspiration for, real-life, 6–7; mind-control characteristic, 6–7; mutations, 7; real-life uses of, 7; Seraphites on, 69, 71, 74–75; spores, airborne fungal, 5–6, 7, 10–11, 12–13. *See also* Rat King; zombies

Counterintelligence Program (COINTELPRO), 117

courage, 198

Court, Joseph-Désiré, *Scene from the Great Flood*, 134–135, *134*

COVID-19 pandemic, 7, 67

creation: and Bill and Frank, 97, 99–103, 105–106; and gay marriage, 103–104, 105, 106n1; and gender, 104–105; and salvation, 121, 169; Thomas Aquinas on, 172. *See also* Adam and Eve

Crimean War (1853–1856), 37

critical dystopia, 53. *See also* dystopia

crops, 3, 7–8, 102, 107n15

cults, 66, 70–71, 77n6. *See also* Seraphites

cultural memory: arcade games, 183, 190n7; comic books, 144, 190n8; in Jackson, Wyoming, 197; in *The Road*, 182–84; in *TLOU*, 182–184

darkness, 100, 188. *See also* light

David (biblical figure), 104, 126

David (pastor of Silver Lake community): on cordyceps, 54, 153, 157, 201; and Ellie, 49, 51, 53–54, 152, 153, 157, 200; identifying as God, 49, 152–153; on love, 157; misuse of Bible, 49–50, 51, 58; religious abuse by, 56–57, 90; series vs. video game version, 51–52

Dawn of the Dead, 87–88

Day, Dorothy, 137

death, 121, 133, 160, 173, 194. *See also* afterlife; executions; suicide

deconversion, 58

defamiliarization, 53

Deloria, Vine, Jr., 169, 172, 176n8

demons, 135–136, *135*, *136*

destinations, 167, 180–181

Deuteronomy, 103

Devecka, Martin, 19

Dina: and Ellie, 27–28, 29, 144; as moral exemplar, 209; religious affiliation, 145n8, 191n13, 209
diphtheria, 40
Doctors Without Borders (MSF), 34
domination and subjugation, 153–54, 157, 165
doppelgängers, 46n10
Dostoevsky, Fyodor, 34, 37–38, 39–40, 45; *The Brothers Karamazov*, 37, 45–46n1, 46n10, 207, 208, 210; *The Double*, 46n10; *The Dream of a Ridiculous Man*, 42–43; *The Idiot*, 39
The Double (Dostoevsky), 46n10
Downie, Alison, 55, 57
The Dream of a Ridiculous Man (Dostoevsky), 42–43
dreams and nightmares, 42, 43
Druckmann, Neil, 137, 199, 202
dystopia, 50, 52–53, 54, 58–59, 71. *See also* apocalyptic genre; post-apocalyptic genre

Ecclesiastes, 100, 194
E. coli outbreaks, 11
ecological concerns, 71. *See also* climate change
Eden, 99, 101
education, 116, 157
Einstein, Albert, 34
Ellie Williams: and Abby, 29, 36–37, 39, 43–44, 145; bite, 5; compassion, 33; cultural artifacts, interest in, 144, 182–184, 190n8; and David, 49, 51, 53–54, 152, 153, 157, 200; and Dina, 27–28, 29, 144; immunity, 138, 181, 197; and Jesus, 138; Lakehill Seattle Hospital visit, 17–18, 20, 23, 24–29; and light, 138; and Nora, 17, 18, 21, 24–28; and rat metaphor, 23; and religion, 186–187; and salvation, 197; and Sam and Henry, 115, 197; sexuality, 65, 99; trauma, 28; vengefulness, 18, 24, 27, 28, 36, 141; wanting a life of meaning, 37, 38. *See also* Joel Miller, and Ellie
Ephesians, 103
epistemic harm, 54, 57–58
Erb, Valerie, 28
ergot fungi, 8
eros/erotic power, 157, 160
eschatology: decolonial critique of, 169–170; etymology, 166, 169; and failure, 172–176; and futures, 165–166, 169, 170, 171; and hope, 165–166, 168, 170–171, 172; and salvation, 168–170, 172, 196; temporal vs. spatial view of, 169–171, 172–175; triumph, 167–171, 172, 175. *See also* apocalyptic genre; death; dystopia; post-apocalyptic genre
estrangement, 195, 196
eternal damnation, 55
eternal life, 173
ethics: ethical failures of *TLOU* characters, 208; Jesus' ethic of love, 33–34, 40, 44, 45–46n1; of killing other people, 85–86; of killing zombies, 85–86; and relationality, 84, 85, 93; Reverence for Life (Schweitzer), 40–42. *See also* morality
eugenics, 40
executions: of Black people, 123, 124, 126; in Miropol, Ukraine, 133, *133*; by Seraphites, 70; of Seraphites, 73, 74
Exodus, 102, 103
"eye for an eye" mentality, 35, 120–121, 122
eyesight, 89

faith, 44, 121, 198, 209, 210
Faith and Order study on Theological Anthropology, 158
the Fall, 45–46n1, 101, 105, 108n32, 155, 170
fanaticism, 75

Farca, Gerald, 53
Farley, Margaret, 103
fathers and fatherhood: "failed fathers," 141, 142–143, 144–145; murder of, 141; parental love, 33, 35, 86–87, 94, 102, 131, 197, 200; in *The Road*, 137–38, 139, 143, 145, 146n14; and sacrifice, 142; in *TLOU*, 140–143. *See also* children; *specific fathers and father figures, e.g., Joel Miller*
fear. *See* anxiety
Federal Disaster Response Agency (FEDRA), 72, 115, 118–119
femininity, 65
Fernández, Samuel, 56
finitude, 160, 195, 202–203
Fireflies: attempting to restore government, 186; and Ellie, 180; and freedom, 207; Joel killing, 87; moral failure of, 208; motto ("look for the light"), 28; and Tommy, 166, 181, 186; as trigger-happy, xiv; vaccine, creation of, 38, 40, 87, 102, 138, 170, 199
First World War, 34, 40, 193–194
Fleming, David, 198
Fletcher, George P., 25
floods, 134–135, *134*
Florence (woman living in isolation with husband), 171
flour, 4, 7–8, 107n15
Floyd, George, 111, 126
forgiveness, 18, 37, 39
Foucault, Michel, 104–105, 107n12
Francis of Assisi (Saint), 72, 137
Frank: and community, 90–93; compared to Eve, 100, 101; suicide, 91, 92–93, 98, 102–103, 159–160. *See also* Bill–Frank relationship
freedom, 112, 207–208
Fricker, Miranda, 57
friendships, 21, 25–26. *See also* community; loyalty; relations
Friesem, Elizaveta, 99
Fromm, Erich, 208

fungi: *Aspergillus fumigatus*, 9; *Candida auris*, 4, 9; carriers of disease, 11–12; categorization, 7; crops, infecting, 3, 7–8, 107n15; ergot fungi, 8; infecting mammals, 7; mind-control characteristic, 8; outbreak, hypothetical, 11–13; recreational use, 8; treatment of infections, 9; WHO's Critical Priority fungal pathogen list, 9–10. *See also* cordyceps fungi
futures, 165–166, 169, 170, 171, 197

Game of Thrones (television series), 46n26
gay people: homosexuality, 65, 99, 101, 103, 107n12, 201; marriage, 103–105; popularity of gay and queer characters, 65, 99; same-sex marriage, 103–104; Torah on gay relationships, 97
gender. *See* gay people; queerness; transgender people
Genesis, 84, 100–105, 138. *See also* Adam and Eve; creation; the Fall; original sin
genocide, 121–122
Gerald ("Jerry") Anderson. *See* "Jerry" (Gerald) Anderson
Giotto, 137; *The Last Judgment*, 132, *135*
giraffes, xiii, 158, 191n12, 202
global average temperature, 4, 9
God: David identifying as, 49, 152–153; image of, 104–105, 155, 157, 158; kin-dom of, 122, 138, 160, 162n33; relationality of triune, 89, 93, 158, 174; in *The Road*, 138, 140, 184; separation from, as death, 173
God, absence of: in *The Brothers Karamazov*, 37; in *The Road*, 184; in *TLOU*, 138, 151–152, 155, 160–161
godtalk, 184–188, 189, 190n11, 208–209
Goliath (biblical figure), 126
goop (lifestyle brand), 7

Gowdy, Trey, 111, 112, 125
Graham, Jennifer, 51
Grande, Rutilio, 175
Grand Inquisitor, parable of, 45–46n1, 207, 208, 210. *See also The Brothers Karamazov* (Dostoevsky)
Greenberg, Irving, 131, 136–137, 141, 144
Gregory of Nyssa (Saint), 104
Gruber, Judith, 156
guitars, 29, 37, 145
guns and gun ownership, 73, 91, 101, 119–20

Hall, John R., 74
Han, Byung Chul, 88–89
han and *jeong*, 154, 155, 161n5
Hannah (Silver Lake girl), 49, 54, 58, 152–153, 157
Hannah-Jones, Nikole, 112
Hart-Brinson, Peter, 103
haunting, 156
hay fever, 10
Heaney, Robert, 153
Hebrews, 104
Hell: demons, 135–136, *135*, *136*; Dostoevsky on, 38–39; eternal damnation, 55; Jesus' descent into, 168; paintings depicting, 132–133, *135*, *136*
Hell (Bosch), 132, *136*
Henry. *See* Sam and Henry
hermeneutical injustice, 57–58
heroism, 100, 154, 195
Hicks, Heather, 67
Hinton, Elizabeth, 115–116
Hitler, Adolf, 34, 44
Hobbesian human nature, 33, 35, 37, 44, 68
Hoff, Gregor, 156
Holy Saturday, 168
homosexuality, 65, 99, 101, 103, 107n12, 201. *See also* gay people
hope: Bill and Frank's hopeful union, 106; in critical dystopia, 53; David's manipulation of, 56; in dystopian literature, 54, 58; and eschatology, 165–166, 168, 170–171, 172; in image of God, 151, 158; Joel's lies as act of hope, 87; in *The Road*, 137, 145, 180, 181, 189, 190n4; in *TLOU*, 87, 106, 161, 181, 189, 197, 202, 210
hospital scene. *See* Lakehill Seattle Hospital
humanitarianism, 34, 44
humanity: created in God's likeness, 104–105, 155, 157, 158; Dostoevsky on, 37–38, 39–40; failure, human, 172; the Fall, 45–46n1, 101, 105, 108n32, 155, 170; "higher," 34, 40; Hobbesian human nature, 33, 35, 37, 44, 68; vs. natural world, 202–203; objectification of, 89, 94; original sin, 55; queer theology on, 160; relationality of human beings, 83–85, 87, 89; and self-sufficiency, 157, 158, 159, 161; subjecthood, 84, 85–86, 87, 93; in *TLOU*'s title, 35; zombies, human relations with, 88, 93; zombies compared to humans, 155–156, 208
humiliation, 122, 125

I Am Legend (Matheson), 67
The Idiot (Dostoevsky), 39
incarceration, 116
Indigenous peoples, 167, 169–170, 171
individualism, 43
infected. *See* zombies
injustice, 57–58
innocence, 138, 200
interdependence, 154, 155, 158–161
Irenaeus of Lyons (Saint), 155
Isaac Dixon, 36, 73, 74
Isaiah (biblical book), 128n52
Isaiah (biblical prophet), 126–127
Isasi-Díaz, Ada María, 162n33
Ish, 44, 47n27, 141, 209–210, *210*
isolation, 71–72, 91, 171, 195–196

Jackson, Wyoming, 52, 102, 154–155, 162n13, 186, 197, 203
Jael (biblical figure), 126
Jakarta, 4, 10
Jakobsen, Janet, 103
James, Joy, 117, 121
Jeffries, Hasan Kwame, 120
Jennings, Willie, 154, 157
jeong and *han*, 154, 155, 161n5
Jerome (Saint), 104
"Jerry" (Gerald) Anderson: murder of, 17, 18, 20, 23, 25, 35, 36, 140, 141; player forced to kill, 142; rescuing zebra, 39, 41, 141–142; sacrificing Ellie for vaccine, 40, 138; and whether a "false father," 142. *See also* Abby–Jerry relationship
Jesse (Jackson patrol leader), 140
Jesus Christ: *agápē*, 33, 35, 40, 44; in *The Brothers Karamazov*, 45–46n1, 207, 208; cross, 154, 156; descent into hell, 168; and Ellie, 138; on end times, 131–132; ethic of love, 33–34, 40, 44, 45–46n1; as failed Messiah, 131, 136–137, 144; humanity's material needs, awareness of, 197; rhetorical misuse of, 57; salvation through, 121, 195, 198, 200–201; spectral theology on, 156; on turning the other cheek, 35, 111, 112, 113, 120–122, 123, 124, 125–126; The Word, 57, 59, 138
Job, 190n10
Joel (Bible book), 102, 107n15
Joel Miller: and Abby, 35; and Bill, 91, 98, 101, 102; compassion, 33; estrangement, 195–196; as "failed"/"false" father, 142–143, 144–145; grave, 145n8, 190n11; knowledge, 102; murder of, 18, 25, 27, 35–36, 143; purpose, 197–199, 200, 203; racism, 116; religious affiliation, 145n8, 185–186, 190n11; responsibility to others, 86–87; and Sam and Henry, 114, 115, 116; as

serpent in fall of humanity, 101, 102; and Tess, 35, 91, 98, 101, 105, 106, 118, 142, 156, 159, 181, 193, 195; vulnerability, 195, 196. *See also* Joel Miller, and Ellie; Joel Miller, murders committed by; Joel Miller, and Sarah
Joel Miller, and Ellie: collecting comic books for, 190n8; death's influence on Ellie, 24, 29, 36, 141; educating Ellie, 102; as "false father," 143; forgiveness, 37; guitars, 29, 37, 145; initial reluctance of escorting Ellie, 86, 196; lies, 87, 93–94, 142, 167, 199–200; life of meaning, fight over, 37, 38; love for Ellie, 144, 145, 157–158, 196, 199; nicknames, 143–144, 146n22; parental love, 33, 35, 86–87, 94, 102, 197, 200; player empathizing with, xiii–xiv; preventing Ellie's sacrifice, 142, 143, 195, 199, 202; rupture, 143, 167, 175; saving each other, 195, 196, 197–198, 199, 201, 203; spatial-relational hope, 174
Joel Miller, murders committed by: Alec, 49; Fireflies, 87; Jerry, 17, 18, 23, 25, 35, 36
Joel Miller, and Sarah: good father, 142–43; moving on after Sarah's death, 35, 94, 102, 118, 158, 197–198, 199; nicknames for Sarah, 86–87, 142, 143; pleading to God after Sarah's death, 185–186; trauma after Sarah's death, 86, 138, 195; wanting to sacrifice everything for Sarah, 139
Joh, Wonhee Anne, 154, 161n5
Johnson, Stephen Michael, 20, 28, 29
Jonathan (biblical figure), 104
Judaism, 103, 209
Juergensmeyer, Mark, 74
justice: climate justice, 202; and communion, 175; and forgiveness, 18; in a fractured world, xviii; and

God, 122; and injustice, 50, 57–59, 136, 144, 168, 175, 207; Jesus and, xviii; and love, 166, 175; and racial system of United States, 27; retributive, 27, 120; social justice, 137–138, 145n2, 175; structural, 168; for victims, 168; vindictive, 35; violence, as form of, 27

Kathleen Coghlan, 114–115, 116
Keller, Simon, 21, 25
kerusso (the preached word), 50
Kim, Grace Ji-Sun, 154
kin-dom of God, 122, 138, 160, 162n33
King, Martin Luther, Jr., 123–124
knowledge, 57–58, 101, 102, 157
Ku Klux Klan (KKK), 114, 120, 124
Kunsa, Ashley, 182
Kyle, 141, 209

Ladevèze, Charlotte, 53
Lakehill Seattle Hospital: Abby's visit, 17–18, 19, 20–22, 28–29; Ellie's visit, 17–18, 20, 23, 24–29
Lamarque, Peter, 28
Langer, Lawrence, 208
The Last Judgment (Giotto), 132, *135*
The Last Man (Shelley), 67
The Last of Us (*TLOU*, franchise): cultural memory in, 182–184; destinations, 167, 180–181; fanbase, 33, 34, 35, 45; fatherhood portrayed in, 140–143; flashbacks, 141, 143, 190n11; hope in, 87, 106, 161, 181, 189, 197, 202, 210; narrative developments, hypothetical, 33, 34, 35; and *The Road*, 138, 140, 189; salvation in, 171, 193, 197, 198, 204; theological discourse in, 179, 185–189, 191n13; title, 35. *See also specific characters, places, and themes*
The Last of Us (*TLOU*, HBO series): Bill and Frank in, 98, 99, 101, 105–106; character arcs, 44, 46–47n26, 98, 105–106; David in, 51, 52; Druckmann on, 137, 199, 202; Joel's life before meeting Ellie, 86; Kathleen in, 114–115, 116; Mazin on, 97, 98, 99, 102, 106, 137, 195, 199; outbreak in, 4, 10; queerness in, 99; soundtrack, 198
The Last of Us (*TLOU*, video game): artifacts complementing narrative, 98–99, 141; Bill and Frank in, 97–99, 101; David in, 51; Joel's life before meeting Ellie, 86, 95n14; outbreak, 3–4; player agency, xiv, 26–27, 142, 191n12
The Last of Us: Left Behind (DLC), 5, 190n7
The Last of Us Part II (*TLOU2*, video game): darkness, 209; Joel's religious affiliation, 190n11; maturing of Ellie, 138; queerness, 99; synagogue scene, 191n13; violence, 65–66, 68, 76
Left Behind (DLC), 5, 190n7
Leningrad, 208
Lennon, John, 201
Lev: and Abby, 20–21, 23, 29, 33, 36–37, 42, 68–69, 75; as moral exemplar, 209; mother of, 75, 141; pacifism, 75, 76; transgender, 23, 75
Levi, Primo, 208, 211n10
Levinas, Emmanuel, 84–85, 88
Levine, Amy-Jill, 122–123, 123–124, 125
Leviticus, 104
LGBTQ+ community. *See* gay people
life: and community, 89; eternal, 173; persistence of, amidst death, 168; Reverence for Life (Schweitzer), 40–42; spectral theology on, 156. *See also* death; sacrifice; survival and survivalism
light, 28, 100, 138. *See also* darkness
Lincoln, Massachusetts, 99, 101–102
listeria, 11
logos (The Word), 57, 59, 138
London, Jack, *The Scarlet Fever*, 67

"Long, Long Time" (Ronstadt), 101, 159, 200
love: *agápē*, 33, 35, 40, 44; as antidote for revenge, 38, 45; of Bill and Frank, 99, 103, 159, 196; Bonhoeffer on, 90; David on, 157; of Dina and Ellie, 27; Dostoevsky on, 39–40; Ellie's love for Joel, 87; emotional vs. spiritual, 90; ethic of, 33–34, 40, 44, 45–46n1; and failure, 75; and forgiveness, 39; of God, 39, 131, 137; *jeong*, 154, 155, 161n5; Jerry's love for Abby, 141–142, 145, 146n24; and Jesus, 34, 40, 44–45, 121; Joel's love for Ellie, 33, 85, 144, 145, 157–158, 196, 199, 203; Joel's love for Sarah, 142; of others, 89; parental love, 33, 35, 39, 86–87, 94, 102, 131, 141, 197, 199, 200; in *The Road*, 139; and salvation, 199–200, 203–204; self-love, 201–202; and violence, 139, 157; and vulnerability, 194. *See also* community; friendships; relations
Lowndes County, Alabama, 113, 114, 116–118, 119, 125
Lowndes County Freedom Organization (LCFO), 120, 126, 128n51
loyalty, 21, 24, 25–26, 36

malaria, 7
Manifest Destiny, 165, 167–168, 170–171, 174
Manny Alvarez, 141, 146n17
Margenau, Kurt, 22
Maria Miller, 162n13
Mark, 132
Markle, Meghan, 201
Marlene: as "false mother," 146n19; murder of, xiv, 87, 118; player forced to kill, 142; willingness to sacrifice Ellie, 138, 199, 202
Marlon, 171
marriage, 103–105

Marsh, Clive, 194, 195, 196–197, 200–201
martyrdom, 76, 121
Maspero, Giulio, 89
Matheson, Richard, *I Am Legend*, 67
Matthew, 33, 35, 44, 111, 112, 113, 121, 125, 128n38
Mazin, Craig, 97, 98, 99, 102, 106, 137, 195, 199
Mbembe, Achille, 156
McCarthy, Cormac. *See The Road* (McCarthy)
McDonald, Leon, 114
McDonald, Pattie, 114
the media, 117–118, 123, 202
medicine, 40–41. *See also* the vaccine
Meghan, Duchess of Sussex, 201
Mel, 18, 20
mental health issues: RTS, 50, 54–59, 59n9; of Seraphites' Prophet, perceived, 71
Miles, Frank, Jr., 119
Miropol, Ukraine, 133, *133*
Moltmann, Jürgen, 174
monkeys, 11
morality: in *The Brothers Karamazov*, 37; freedom, moral, 207–208; and realism, 33–34; in *TLOU*, 28, 93, 209. *See also* ethics
Morrison, James, 101
mortality, 102
Moses (biblical figure), 126
Moynihan, Daniel Patrick, 116

Naomi (biblical figure), 104
nation-states: anti-Blackness, 114–115, 116; epidermalization, 114–115; violence by (police force), 111, 112
nature, 71–72, 202. *See also* animals; climate change; fungi
Nazism, 34, 44, 89, 133, *133*
the New Being, 198
New Religious Movements (NRMs), 77n6
nicknames, 143, 145, 146n22

Nietzsche, Friedrich, 37–38
nightmares and dreams, 42, 43
nihilism, 44, 47n28
Noble, Alan, 190n4
nonviolent resistance/defense: futility of, 112–113, 125; by King, 123; and righteousness, 121–122; by Sam and Henry, 114, 119, 126; self-defense as, 124–127, 128n51; suicide, equating, 118, 119–120, 123–124; turning the other cheek, 111, 112, 113, 120–122, 123, 124, 125–126. *See also* self-defense
Nora Harris: and Abby, 17, 18, 21, 24, 25–26, 27; beating of, 17, 18, 26–28; and Ellie, 17, 18, 21, 24–28
nuclear weapons, 34
Nwigwe, Tobe, 112

Oppenheimer, J. Robert, 34
organ transplants, 7
original sin, 55. *See also* the Fall
Ortiz, Dianna, 137
Oryx and Crake (Atwood), 67
Osgood, Jeffrey M., 18
otherness, 52, 74–75, 84, 88, 89, 92, 93
Owen, 28

pacifism, 75, 76, 112, 118–119, 121. *See also* nonviolent resistance/defense; violence
Paltrow, Gwyneth, 7
pandemics, 67, 69, 76. *See also* cordyceps fungi; COVID-19 pandemic; zombies
parents, 132–136, 199. *See also* children; fathers and fatherhood
Pastoureau, Michel, 23
Paul: Ephesians, 103; Hebrews, 104
Pellegrini, Ann, 103
Pinnacle Theater (Seattle), 18–19
plagues, 102
Planet Earth (BBC series), 6
Podvalny, Maxim, 75
police force, 89, 111, 112, 117–118

pollen, 10. *See also* spores, airborne fungal
pollutants, 10–11
popular culture, 44, 45, 65
post-apocalyptic genre: in general, 66–67; absence of God in, 152–153, 184; and cultural memory, 182; false prophets, 153; and morality, 208; and redemption, 168; and survival, 65, 68, 72, 156, 168; and violence, 68. *See also* apocalyptic genre; dystopia; eschatology
potato blight, 7–8
prayer, 73, 90, 140, 186, 191n13
preachers, 50, 56, 57, 153. *See also* David (pastor of Silver Lake community)
priests, 106n1
prisons, 116
procreation, 100, 103–104
Prophet, Seraphites,' 69–70, 71, 73–74, 209
protests, 111–12, 123, 175
Purnell, Derecka, 117

Qohelet. *See* Ecclesiastes
Quarantine Zones (QZs), 89
queerness, 99
queer theology, 97, 100, 160

racism: anti-Black violence, 111, 112, 113, 114–120, 123–127; by churches, 124; epidermalization, 114–115; ignored by media, 117–118, 123; incarceration, 116; institutionalized, 116–117, 124; in Lowndes County, Alabama, 113, 114, 116–118, 119, 125; and protests, 111–112; systematized, 116–117; in *TLOU*, 114
Rambo, Shelly, 168–169
Ramler, Mari, 57–58
rape, 90
Rat King, 22–23, 26
realism, 33–34

red color, 23, 26
redemption: and Abby, 22, 69, 75; critiques of, 168–169; and Ellie, 39, 145; false, 54; in God, 58; and Jesus as failed Messiah, 136–137; and Joel, 146n21; and religious abuse, 54; in *The Road*, 168; Schweitzer on, 41–42; of sin and evil, 170; in *TLOU*, xv; through the vaccine, 170. *See also* salvation; triumph
Reilly, Lucas, 22
relations: Christianity on, 89; differences, 83–84, 88, 89, 93, 94; and eschatological space, 169, 173–176; and ethics, 84, 85, 93; and face-to-face encounters, 84–85, 93; friendships, 21, 25–26; human beings, relationality of, 83–85, 87, 89; between humans and zombies, 88, 93; and image of God, 158; interdependence, 154, 155, 158–161; loyalty, 21, 24, 25–26, 36; and objectification, 89, 94; in post-apocalyptic world, 171; reciprocal, 85, 87–89, 93, 94; sameness, 88, 89, 93, 157; and subjecthood, 84, 85–86, 87, 93; triune God, relationality of, 89, 93, 158, 174. *See also* community; estrangement; isolation; love; *specific relationships, e.g., Joel–Ellie relationship*
religion. *See* Christianity; faith; Judaism; sacred spaces
religious trauma syndrome (RTS), 50, 54–59, 59n9
reproductive sexuality, 100, 103–104
resistance: and power dynamics, 154; violent, 111–112, 114, 121, 124–127, 128n51. *See also* nonviolent resistance/defense; pacifism; protests; self-defense; violence
restoration. *See* salvation
Restoration Counseling, 56
Revelation, 49, 51, 152, 166

revenge: Abby, 17, 18, 20, 23, 25, 35–36, 141; Ellie, 18, 24, 27, 28, 36, 141; endlessness of, 38; and justice, 18, 27; love as antidote for, 38, 45. *See also* pacifism; violence
Reverence for Life (Schweitzer), 40–42
revitalization movements, 71
rhetoric, religious, 50, 57–59
righteousness, 121–122
Riley Abel, 194
The Road (McCarthy): cultural memory, loss of, 182–184; destination, 180; fatherhood portrayed in, 131, 137–138, 139, 143, 145, 146n13; hope in, 137, 145, 180, 181, 189, 190n4; narration, 139–140, 146n14; redemption in, 168; sacrifice in, 139; story, 137–138; theological discourse in, 179, 184–185, 189; and *TLOU*, 138, 140, 189
Robbins, Thomas, 73
Romero, Oscar, 137, 175
Ronstadt, Linda, 101, 159, 200
Ruback, R. Barry, 22
ruins, 19, 28–29
Ruth (biblical figure), 104

sacred spaces: churches, 154–155, 187–188, 191nn12–13, 200–201; synagogues, 191n13
sacrifice: as cost for salvation, 198–200, 203–204; Ellie, for vaccine, 38, 40, 87, 102, 138, 199; in *The Road*, 139; Sam and Henry, 115; of self, vs. others, 142; Seraphites' ritualistic sacrifice, 70; Tess, 35, 83, 118, 193, 197, 198
Saint Petersburg, 208
Salem witch trials, 8
saliva, 4–5
Sally, 71
salvation: and apocalypse, 66; Bill–Frank, 92, 94, 200, 201, 203; children, saving of, 142–143, 199; and destruction of evil, 58; effects

of, 198, 201–202; Ellie, 197; and eschatology, 168–170, 172, 196; etymology, 193; through Jesus, 121, 195, 198, 200–201; Joel–Ellie, 195, 196, 197–198, 199, 201, 203; and love, 199–200, 203–204; Marsh on, 194, 195, 196–197, 200–201; through relationships, 200–203; sacrifice as cost for, 198–200, 203–204; in *TLOU*, 171, 193, 197, 198, 204. *See also* redemption

Sam and Henry: alternative eschatology of, 171; deaths, 118–119; and Ellie, 115, 197; God's likeness, loss of, 126; racism experienced by, 113, 114–115, 116–117, 120; on religion, 186–187; survivalism, 113–114, 115, 117, 118, 119, 126; sameness, 88, 89, 93, 157; same-sex marriage, 103–4

Santaolalla, Gustavo, 198

Sarah Miller: biblical inspiration for, 102; compared to boy in *The Road*, 138; and Ellie, 86–87, 94; murder of, 35, 86, 118, 185–186; Tommy's monument for, 162n14. *See also* Joel Miller, and Sarah

The Scarlet Fever (London), 67

Scene from the Great Flood (Court), 134–135, *134*

Schubert, Stefan, 26–27

Schuyler, Philip Daniel, 74

Schweitzer, Albert, 34, 40–42, 44, 45

science fiction, 65

Scruton, Roger, 87

Seattle, 18–19, 20. *See also* Lakehill Seattle Hospital

Second World War, 133, *133*, 208, 211n10

seeds, 100, 101

self-defense: in Bible, 126; in Lowndes County, Alabama, 119–120, 126; violent resistance as, 112–114, 124–127, 128n51. *See also* nonviolent resistance/defense

self-determination, 111, 112

self-sufficiency, 157, 158, 159, 161

Seraphites: about, 66, 68–70; antitechnology atittude, 69, 70, 71–72, 74–75; on cordyceps infection, 69, 71, 74–75; cult formation, 71; Elders, council of, 70, 73, 74; Lev quoting scripture from, 20; Prophet, 69–70, 71, 73–74, 209; radicalization, 74–75, 76–77; Scars, 69; self-sustainability, 72; violence used by, 70, 73–75; and WLF, 21, 72–73, 74

Sermon on the Mount, 33, 44, 111, 112, 113, 120–122, 123, 124, 125–126

sermons, 50, 51, 69

the serpent (Genesis), 101

sexual abuse, 53, 90

sexuality: homosexuality, 65, 99, 101, 103, 107n12, 201; reproductive, 100, 103–104

Shaw, Adrienne, 99

Shelley, Mary, *The Last Man*, 67

Silver Lake (community): David's leadership of, 49, 56–57, 152; as "emotional community," 90; vs. Jackson, Wyoming, 52, 154–155

sin: Bill and Frank, 103; Dostoevsky on, 39; and estrangement, 195; and finitude, 160; original sin, 55; and sacrifice, 70. *See also* the Fall

sincerity, 41–42

Sisera (biblical figure), 126

sky bridge scene, 20

Slade, Darren M., 55

Smith, Christian, 185

solitude, 90–92, 101

Sommerville, Margaret, 88

soteriology. *See* salvation

soullessness, 115–116, 123, 125

spectral theology, 156, 159

spiritualism, 71–72

spores, airborne fungal, 5–6, 7, 10–11, 12–13

Stark, Rodney, 66, 70–71

stealth, 24

Steiner, Rudolf, 71–72
Stone, Alyson M., 55, 56, 57
strawberries, 101, 159
Student Nonviolent Coordinating Committee (SNCC), 113, 114, 119–120
subjecthood, 84, 85–86, 87, 93
subjugation and domination, 153–154, 157, 165
suicide: of Bill, 92–93, 102–103, 159–160; in *The Dream of a Ridiculous Man*, 42–43; of Frank, 91, 92–93, 98, 102–103, 159–160; of Henry, 118; Joel contemplating, 142, 146n20, 158; nonviolence equating, 118, 119–120, 123–124; of Tess, 35, 118, 193, 197, 198
superpowers, 114
survival and survivalism: and Blackness, 113–120; Hobbesian human nature, 33, 37; in post-apocalyptic context, 65, 68, 72, 156, 168; Sam and Henry, 113–114, 115, 117, 118, 119, 126. *See also* self-defense; violence
Susan, 141, 210, 211n21
synagogue scene, 191n13

Tabb, David, 104
Tanner, Kathryn, 172–173, 175
Tatum, Beverly Daniel, 116
Taylor, Breonna, 111, 126
Taylor, Bron, 66
Teilhard de Chardin, Pierre, 72
temperature, global average, 4, 9
temporality, 169–171, 172–175, 182
"Tess" (Theresa) Servopoulos: and Joel, 35, 91, 98, 101, 105, 106, 118, 142, 156, 159, 181, 193, 195; sacrificial suicide, 35, 83, 118, 193, 197, 198; smuggling of Ellie, 35, 181, 197; visiting Bill and Frank, 159; zombie kissing, 83, 198
theaters, 18–19, 197
theocracies, 52
theodicy, xviii, 168

theology: and godtalk, 184–188, 189, 190n11, 208–209; queer theology, 97, 100, 160; and RTS, 54, 55, 58; spectral theology, 156, 159; T-Theology, 160, 162n31
Thomas Aquinas, 172, 208
Tillich, Paul, 193–194, 195, 196, 197, 198, 200, 201–202, 203, 204
Tinker, George E., 176n8
Tisby, Jemar, 124
Tolstoy, Leo, 121, 122, 125
Tommy Miller: allowed to live by Abby, 36; as a Firefly, 166, 181; as hunter with Joel and Tess, 156; and Joel, 186; killer of Manny Alvarado, 141; living in Jackson, 154, 162n13; monuments for Sarah and Kevin, 162n14; and Nora, 18; saving Joel, 86
Tonstad, Linn Marie, 160
Torah, 97, 191n13
Torrance, T. F., 61n56
transgender people, 23, 75
trauma: Ellie, 28; in landscapes, 29; religious trauma syndrome (RTS), 50, 54–59, 59n9; spiritual, 56; survival after, 168
Tree of Knowledge, 101
triumph, 167–171, 172, 175. *See also* redemption
T-Theology, 160, 162n31
turning the other cheek, 35, 111, 112, 113, 120–122, 123, 124, 125–126

union, ideal, 103, 104–105, 106n1
United States (U.S.): Constitution, 103; Manifest Destiny, 165, 167–168, 170–171, 174
utilitarianism, 40–41, 199
utopia, 53, 101. *See also* dystopia

the vaccine: sacrifice necessary for creation, 38, 40, 87, 102, 138, 199; as salvation, 170
Vargas, João Helion Costa, 114

vengeance. *See* revenge
vermin, 22
video games, 99. *See also The Last of Us* (video game)
violence: anti-Black, 111, 112, 113, 114–120, 123–127; extreme, by religious groups, 73, 74; gun traded for seeds symbolism, 101; Hobbesian human nature, 33, 35, 37, 44, 68; perpetrated by player, xiv, 26–27, 142; and post-apocalyptic genre, 68; resistance, violent, 111–112, 114, 121, 124–127, 128n51; self-defense, violent, 112–114, 124–127, 128n51; Seraphites, used by, 70, 73–75; in *TLOU2*, 24, 65–66, 68, 76; Tolstoy on, 121, 122, 125; turning the other cheek, 35, 111, 112, 113, 120–122, 123, 124, 125–26. *See also* executions; nonviolent resistance/defense; pacifism; resistance; self-defense; weapons

Wallace, Anthony, 71
Washington Liberation Front (WLF): and Abby, 18, 21, 23; rat metaphor, 22; and Seraphites, 21, 72–73, 74
water, 29
weapons: guns and gun ownership, 73, 91, 101, 119–120; nuclear weapons, 34
Weber, Max, 73
Westhelle, Victor, 169, 173

whiteness, 157, 158, 159, 161, 167. *See also* Blackness
Wilderson, Frank B., III, 116
Wilson, Rainn, 50, 51
Winell, Marlene, 55, 56, 57, 59n9
Wink, Walter, 122, 125
witches, 8
The Word, 57, 59, 138
World Health Organization (WHO), 9–10
World War I, 34, 40, 193–194
World War II, 133, *133*, 208, 211n10. *See also* Nazism
Wundram, Jane, 22

X, Malcolm, 111–112, 124

Yara: and Abby, 20, 23, 33, 36, 42, 68–69; pacifism, 76; surgery, 17, 18, 20; violence used against, 75

zebras, 39, 41, 141–142
zombies: communication, lack of, 88; ethics of killing, 85–86; and God's likeness, 155–156; humans compared to, 155–156, 208; isolating of infected, 8; kissing Tess, 83, 198; nonrelationality, 83–84, 85, 87–88, 93, 94; objectification of, 85, 87; relations with humans, 88, 93; stages of infection, 4, *5*; and survivalism, 72; symptoms, 4, *5*, *6*, 89; trope, 67; x-ray of infected, *6*. *See also* cordyceps fungi

About the Contributors

Peter Admirand is associate professor of theology, a deputy head of school, and director of the Centre for Interreligious Dialogue at Dublin City University. His most recent book is *Destruction, Ethics, and Intergalactic Love: Exploring* Y: The Last Man *and* Saga.

Ryan Banfi is a PhD candidate in Martin Scorsese Cinema Studies at New York University (NYU) Tisch School of the Arts. He is a Corrigan Fellow at NYU and a Hispanic Scholarship Fund Scholar. Banfi has been published in *New Review of Film and Television Studies, International Journal of James Bond Studies, Games and Culture, Game Studies, Mediapolis, Flow Online Journal, Studies in European Cinema,* and *In Media Res*. He is on the editorial board of *Games and Culture*.

Adam B. Banks is a PhD student in the Department of Comparative Studies at Ohio State University. His research brings critical theory to bear on the intersection of hip-hop consumption and the project of humanism. Going beyond previous research that focused on hip-hop artists, Banks's research critically explores how dynamics of culture, class, race, and history place constraints upon and/or create possibilities for enactments agency for Black consumers of hip-hop in the United States. While engaging in doctoral studies, he serves as pastor of First Baptist Church in Springfield, Ohio.

Pavol Bargár is associate professor at the Protestant Theological Faculty of Charles University in Prague, Czech Republic. His research interests lie in theology and culture, theological anthropology, mission studies, and interreligious relations. Bargár is a vice president of the Central and Eastern European Association for Mission Studies. He also serves on the executive board of the International Council of Christians and Jews. In addition to numerous articles and book chapters, Bargár is the author of *Narrative, Myth, Transformation: Reflecting Theologically on Contemporary Culture* (2016) and *Embodied Existence: Our Common Life in God* (2023). He edited the volume *The Bible, Christianity, and Culture: Essays in Honor of Prof. Petr Pokorný* (2023).

Daniel J. Cameron (PhD, University of Aberdeen) holds an MA from Trinity Evangelical Divinity School and a PhD in divinity from the University of Aberdeen. He is a co-editor of *Theology and the Office* and the author of *Flesh and Blood*. He serves as the Bible Department head and director of spiritual life at Chicago Hope Academy in Illinois, where he teaches twelfth-grade systematic theology and the elective course "Finding God in Film."

Rebecca Chapman holds a BA in theology from Durham University and is a freelance journalist who writes about culture, in particular streaming services, as well as the state of the Anglican church. She is a trustee of Christians in Media and a lay member of the Church of England's General Synod. Chapman has three young sons who frequently like to try to fight her for the remote. Sometimes they even win.

Jerry Hourihane Clancy is a researcher at Dublin City University, Ireland, where he also completed his PhD, which investigated how such biological aerosols as fungal spores and pollen grains can be detected, identified, and forecasted. Some parts of this work are what allowed him to further understand the pathogenic cordyceps fungus that ravaged the entire planet in *The Last of Us*.

David K. Goodin earned a PhD in religious studies from McGill University in the philosophy of religion, with a concentration in patristic theology. He is a *professeur associé* at the Université Laval, Institut de Théologie Orthodoxe de Montréal, and formerly a lecturer for the McGill School of Religious Studies and instructor for the Pappas Patristic Institute at the Holy Cross Greek Orthodox School of Theology. Goodin's research interests include theodicy and eco-theology, with a specialization in the sacred forests of the Ethiopian *Täwaḥədo* tradition. Originally from Miami, Florida, he resides and teaches in Montreal, Quebec, Canada.

Amy M. Green is an associate professor of English at the University of Nevada, Las Vegas. Her focus is on video game study, specifically the narrative analysis of video games and how gameplay mechanics intersect with story. Green is the author of numerous books and articles, including *Storytelling in Video Games: The Art of the Digital Narrative*; *Posttraumatic Stress Disorder, Trauma, and History in Metal Gear Solid V*; *A Cure for Toxic Masculinity: Male Bonding and Friendship in Final Fantasy XV*; and

Longing, Ruin, and Connection in Hideo Kojima's Death Stranding. She is editor in chief of the academic journal *Popular Culture Review*.

Matthew C. Millsap is dean of Library Services and associate professor of Christian studies at Midwestern Baptist Theological Seminary in Kansas City, Missouri. His research interests lie at the intersection of theology and popular culture and the intersection of theology and the arts. Millsap's PhD dissertation, *Playing with God: A Theoludological Framework for Dialogue with Video Games*, proposes a framework informed by both systematic theology and game studies by which theologians or other Christians might analyze video games and dialogue with them. When not traversing post-apocalyptic worlds, he runs an academic library and teaches his favorite undergraduate course, "Christianity and the Arts."

David O'Connor is an assistant professor in the School of Chemical Sciences at Dublin City University. He formerly worked at Technological University Dublin (2015–2021), and previously he held post-doctoral positions at the University of Denver (Marie Curie Fellowship) and the University College Cork, which involved numerous field and laboratory studies on atmospherically relevant species and processes. O'Connor's current research interests are focused on the primary biological aerosol particles, which encompass things like pollen, bacteria, and particularly fungal spores, and their impact on the world around us. In essence, his work looks to make sure *The Last of Us* never happens.

Robert Grant Price lectures at the University of Toronto Mississauga. His recent contributions to studies in pop culture, philosophy, and religion include essays in *Theology and H. P. Lovecraft* (2022), *Indiana Jones and Philosophy* (2023), and the forthcoming *Theology and The Office*.

Tijana Rupčić is a PhD candidate at Central European University, Department of History, Austria. After finishing a BA in history at the University of Belgrade, Serbia (2011), she completed her MA in ancient Greek and Roman history and philosophy at the University of Novi Sad, Serbia (2014) and her MA in comparative history at Central European University, Budapest, Hungary (2020), focusing on the history of technology and science and history of Yugoslavia.

Ched Spellman is an associate professor at Cedarville University. He is also the author of *Toward a Canon-Conscious Reading of the Bible: Exploring the History and Hermeneutics of the Canon* and *One Holy Book: A Primer on How the Bible Came to Be and Why It Matters*. Spellman teaches biblical and theological studies, researches the biblical canon, and is usually looking for dank memes.

Flora x. Tang (MTS, Harvard Divinity School) is a PhD candidate in peace studies and theology at the University of Notre Dame. Her current research brings together eschatology and decolonial theory to consider the ethical responsibility of Christians toward co-creating decolonial futures alongside indigenous, diasporic, and other marginalized populations. In Tang's public writings she also writes about queer Catholic theologies and liturgies. Her published writings can be found in *Theological Studies*, *Political Theology Network*, and the *National Catholic Reporter*.